Calcutta

Also in the series

Calcutta

A CULTURAL HISTORY

Krishna Dutta
foreword by Anita Desai

Interlink Books

An imprint of Interlink Publishing Group, Inc.
Northampton, Massachusetts

This edition first published 2008 by

INTERLINK BOOKS
An imprint of Interlink Publishing Group, Inc.
46 Crosby Street, Northampton, Massachusetts 01060
www.interlinkbooks.com

Copyright © Krishna Dutta, 2003, 2008
Foreword © Anita Desai, 2002, 2008

Library of Congress Cataloging-in-Publication Data

Dutta, Krishna.
Calcutta ; a cultural history / by Krishna Dutta.
p. cm.
Includes bibliographical references and index.
ISBN 978-1-56656-721-3 (pbk.)
1. Calcutta (India)—Description and travel. 2. Calcutta (India)—History—Miscellanea.
3. Calcutta (India)—social life and customs. 4. Calcutta (India)—Intellectual life.
5. Popular culture—India—Calcutta. I. Title. II. Series.
DS486.C2D885 2003
954'.147—dc21
2002156603

Drawings by Wendy Skinner Smith
Typesetting: Devdan Sen
Cover images: Courtesy Andrew Robinson; Chandra Prasad/Link; Mark Henley/Panos

Printed and bound in the United States of America

Contents

Foreword

When one asks oneself if Calcutta can be called "a great city", is one merely asking if it is historic, important, wealthy, grand and imposing? I think another, less definable quality is called for, the quality of myth, and that "a great city" is one that possesses a reality that verges on the mythical. A book that portrayed the city would be insufficient if it presented only details of its history, climate, architecture and civic life; it would need to go beyond and convey the indefinable and non-substantial that make the city even greater in the mind than it is on the ground.

I do believe that Calcutta possesses such a quality because I have seen how profoundly it has affected anyone who has lived in it (and I say lived with reason, not merely visited). I did not set eyes on it myself till I was twenty years old when my father died, our house in Old Delhi was given up and the family moved to Bengal where my brother and sisters had all found employment. Yet it had been present in my life in the form of my father, a Bengali albeit not from Calcutta, for whom the city had always been a destination. He grew up in the countryside of East Bengal, spoke to us of the luminescent green of the rice fields, the riverine life of the people, and the fish and coconuts and rice of his cuisine, the finest in the world, he gave us to understand. I would see his eyes come to life and glow if he heard a snatch of *baul* music from his land, and I remember the expression on his face as of one who had seen a vision, when we went together to a matinee show of Satyajit Ray's first film, *Pather Panchali*. Sometimes a tangible piece of that world came our way in the form of an earthen pot of date palm syrup, or a box of Bengali sweets, the soft milky *sandesh*, each shaped like a conch shell and packed in rice for freshness. These spoke to us of another culture, a more subtle one. A visitor from Calcutta, on opening a suitcase to unpack, would release a particular odour into the air— damp, mouldy, deltaic, even swampy—that was totally alien to our own arid surroundings. It was as if a large, dark moth had blundered into the crackling dry air of the north. This Calcutta has been most elegantly evoked in Nirad C. Chaudhuri's chapter on the city in his *Autobiography of an Unknown Indian.* In it he exactly replicated my father's experience of going as a country boy from East Bengal to study in the great "second city of the British empire". It is a piece of prose I can read and reread with unfailing pleasure: that line about "the feathery and shot effect of the Calcutta sky" and what lay beneath it as "a crowd of misbehaved and naughty children showing their tongues and behinds to a mother with the face of Michelangelo's Night"!

Trying now to retrieve my impressions on first seeing Calcutta as that newly graduated twenty-year old with a vague sense of launching upon a literary career, I remember that my first reaction was that although I came from the capital of India, Calcutta was the first true metropolis I had seen. Delhi in the 1950s, even New Delhi, was really nothing more than a handful of villages clustering together on the sand and dust of the northern plain. Calcutta, by contrast, seemed to pulse with a sense of purpose, a confidence in its *raison d'être*. The reason may have been taken away when the capital moved to Delhi but a tradition had been established and habits formed. One saw it in the confident flow of traffic up Chowringhee, in the orderly variety of the markets. Here was no compromise between city and suburb; here was city. How wonderful, I thought, to have piped gas supplied by the city, so a flame leapt up at the turn of a knob! In Delhi we might as well have been camping in the desert, the way we had to construct our lives, but here the city constructed our life for us, making us city-dwellers, not *junglees*. What was more, in Delhi my attempt at breaking into journalism or publishing had been dismissed with scorn whereas in Calcutta I quickly became a member of a Writers' Workshop held regularly on Sunday mornings where everything I wrote was considered with flattering seriousness. The city had a sophistication about it, I thought, to be found in the delicious *sandesh* from Ganguly's as well as the pastries from Flury's, and the immaculately starched muslins worn by Bengalis. Not to speak of the night-long concerts of classical music that only broke up at dawn, and the film club where I first saw the films of Eisenstein and Bergman.

To counterbalance all this urbanity and sophistication, there were the fervent rites and rituals of worship of the goddess Kali, at times in her ferocious and at other times her benign aspect as the mother goddess, Durga. Also the elaborate rituals of lesser ceremonies like those associated with marriage—all in the heat and humidity, to the lowing of conch shells and wreathed in the heady fragrance of tuberoses. In fact, there was a certain murkiness about the city, too. I thought it had to do with the gas lamps along the shadowy streets, the tides that rose and fell on the inland river, the reflection of tall houses in the still, dark ponds that took the place of city parks and squares. But it was much more than that: a covert danger and implicit violence that warned one that the various currents of city life swirled around in it, restless and unresolved—the past and the present, the rich and the poor, the literate and artistic and the illiterate and hungry. They contradicted each other at every turn: the smog that smothered the city could be of winter mist or of factory smoke, the monsoon rains could be cooling and refreshing or intemperate and disease-ridden, the colour red could be festive and celebratory or a signal of danger and violence... In his reminiscences of his childhood in the city, Rabindranath Tagore wrote: "Something undreamt of was lurking everywhere, and every day the uppermost question was: where, oh where would I come across it?"

When I left Calcutta in 1962, I carried with me a sense that I had not discovered its secret, it had eluded me, and this led me to start reading its literature. The very best of writing gives voice to the essential spirit of a place; think of the writers of the deep South of the United States, those from the coasts and forests of Latin America, or from the vastness of the Russian steppe. Bengal, too, has its voice—and one hears it in the poetry of Tagore, the prose of Bibhuti Bhushan Banerjee, as well as the music produced by the wandering minstrel, the *baul* singer, and encounters it in the films of Satyajit Ray—all possessed by the mystery, the mystique of Bengal, with Calcutta at his heart.

I too wrote my book about Calcutta, calling it *Voices in the City* and portraying it as a vast temple of Kali, its citizens her devotees who worshipped in a thick smog of smoke from kitchen fires instead of incense, to the clamor of traffic instead of temple bells. A book so callow I would not allow it to be reprinted now—but I find this is a metaphor Krishna Dutta too has employed, so perhaps it is not without validity. I returned to Calcutta only on visits in the 1970s. By then it had been written off by the rest of India, and the world at large, as a pariah, a terrorist state in the grip of anarchy. The government had proved totally incapable of dealing with its monumental problems, the best and brightest of its youth drawn to revolution instead, in the form of the communist-inspired Naxalite movement. Nothing had come of it, only violence, and the streets were littered with its casualties, the city itself almost perpetually in darkness. If it had once been "the graveyard of the British Empire", it was now the graveyard of the ideals and dreams of an independent and renewed India. This was no city of dreams: it was a city where one came up against the face of reality at its most physical and ferocious. Eventually, the Calcuttans adjusted to it, as people do, and learned to accept it as the truth. Out of that, today's Calcutta has emerged.

Krishna Dutta's book is a record of the city's many adjustments—from its humble beginnings as a group of fishing villages in the Gangetic delta where Job Charnock, an agent of the East India Company, chose to situate its chintz and muslin, jute and indigo business, to the "city of palaces" where adventurers and entrepreneurs, generals and satraps fought duels and dined by candlelight on "goat curry and Madeira", and entertained themselves by watching "nautch" in the "zenana"; from the scholarship of early Orientalists like Sir William "Asiatic" Jones to the flaunting of wealth by "nabobs" and the somewhat ludicrous struggles of the Bengali "babu" to ape such western ways. She follows the course of a violent history that includes the sensational "Black Hole of Calcutta" affair, the great famine of 1943-44, the riots during partition and the huge influx of refugees during the birth of Bangladesh, and points out how such events as these led to ground-breaking work by Nobel prize winners like the scientist Sir Ronald Ross, economists like Amartya Sen, missionaries like Mother Teresa and, not least, the stupendous output of Bengal's "Renaissance Man", Rabindranath Tagore. It is as dramatic a history as one can find in the annals of the building and breaking of empire. Almost too dramatic. It could prove a bludgeon that leaves one dazed. A guide is essential.

This guide cannot be a foreigner who does not know the city intimately from within, yet it cannot be a local citizen who knows no other and has no standards of comparison or breadth of vision. Krishna Dutta was born in the city and spent her childhood and was educated in it, but has lived for many years now in England although she returns regularly to Calcutta where she still has a home and family. This allows her to balance subjectivity with objectivity and arrive at a remarkable fairness.

The history of Calcutta provides her with rich material of course but she brings her particular familiarity to it—an intimate, almost tender one as when she recalls the lullabies she heard as a child or revisits the cafés and bookshops around the university where she studied. Yet she remains capable of standing aside and observing the follies and foibles of the Calcuttans with a wry and at times satirical vision. She will surely be taken to task for pointing out that the uniform worn by that favourite son of Bengal, Subhas Chandra Bose, was designed and made by Harman's, a firm of British tailors, and that Gandhi compared Bose's volunteer corps to the Bertram Mills Circus, while her sallies about Mother Teresa will amuse some, scandalize others: she comments on the juxtaposition of the Albanian nun's famous home for the dying and the Kalighat temple "where the supply of moribund poor Hindus is ample... Like Mother Kali's garland of human heads who are sinners-turned-devotees, Mother Teresa too acquired a reputable head count of dying souls saved for her faith by conversion in her home's small gloomy hall lined with washable green mattresses." Her description of the famine of 1943-44, on the other hand, is unremittingly horrific; she spares no details of eye and ear-witness accounts. She is, in fact, as likely to depict the harshness of lives lived in Calcutta as voice the romanticism that comes so easily to the Bengali. Coming upon Rose Aylmer's grave with Walter Savage Landor's famous ode carved on the headstone, she cannot resist quoting from a contemporary account of her death in 1800 from "a most severe bowel complaint brought on entirely by indulging too much with that mischievous and dangerous fruit, the pineapple." Her mind frequently makes such nimble leaps: she compares the Black Hole affair of 1756 with the fictional Marabar Caves affair in E. M. Forster's *A Passage to India*, and walking through the British cemetery in Park Street leads her to comment that "Perhaps Karl Marx should have a memorial here where people still profess faith in him rather than in Highgate." The images she employs are vivid and apt—Calcutta's trams look, she writes, like "battered and burnt cooking pans", and she points out a telling detail in a portrait of an aging diva who has "a flower garland lying on the sagging flesh of her arm." With such gifts she proves herself the ideal guide—knowledgeable, entertaining and stimulating—to this complex, confusing and contradictory city.

Anita Desai

For Andrew

Preface and Acknowledgments

"I don't feel very creative when I'm abroad somehow. I need to be in my chair in Calcutta!"

Satyajit Ray

In one of Woody Allen's films, Mia Farrow threatens to leave New York and do charity work in Calcutta, and Woody is aghast: the place has "a hundred unlisted diseases!" he cries. Sitting in a London cinema, I catch myself suppressing a solitary sigh. To Calcuttans, the depiction of Calcutta in the international media as a packed and pestilential metropolis crawling with destitutes is as irritating as the old stereotype of New York as the world's number-one murder capital must no doubt be to New Yorkers.

Hence, yet another book on Calcutta. Written by a former Calcuttan who now lives in London, this book tells the story of a city with admittedly fading physical charms but with remarkable cultural richness. Since the early nineteenth century, Calcutta has nourished a wide range of writers, painters, musicians, actors and filmmakers, not to mention thinkers and scientists. Its exterior may have been grimy, but its inner life was always the most exciting in India. It was also a great city of commerce, politics and religion, expressed through its many temples and festivals. After all, Calcutta, once the City of Palaces, is where the British empire in India became wealthy and powerful in the eighteenth century and where today, in a post-communist world, Marxism still clings precariously to government. In spite of its many contradictions and some terrible disasters during the twentieth century, the city somehow manages to regenerate itself. Anyone who wants to understand modern India has to visit Calcutta.

The river Hugli (Hooghly) gave birth to the city. Its broad curve running from north to south, flowing towards the Bay of Bengal, slices the city in two unequal halves. On the west is the main railway station at Haora (Howrah), Belur Math (the international headquarters of the Ramakrishna Order), and the Botanical Garden founded in 1787 by the East India Company, containing a huge 250-year-old banyan tree. On the east is the main part of the city: north, central and south.

Chowringhee (Chourangi), described in Chapters 3 and 5, is the central area of Calcutta where the Europeans settled. As the colonizers pushed the original inhabitants out of the center in the early eighteenth century, north Calcutta flourished, as we shall see in Chapters 2 and 4. During the second half of the nineteenth century, south Calcutta slowly evolved from the southern end of Chowringhee Road, although there were earlier settlements in Alipur (Alipore) and Khidirpur (Kidderpore). But Calcutta was never a planned city. It grew haphazardly around the port, the old fort and the ancient Barabazar market by the river.

There are three bridges linking the halves of the city, and about twenty ghats (landing stages) on the riverbanks. Ferry services operate from some of these ghats. The most northerly bridge is the Haora Bridge, now called Rabindra Setu after the city's most famous citizen Rabindranath Tagore. It was originally a pontoon bridge, built in 1874; the present 27,000-ton steel structure, built for the war effort in 1943, is a cantilever bridge. Fifteen hundred feet long, it feels like the busiest bridge in the world, carrying approximately two million people daily and a myriad types of transport (although trams no longer ply its tracks). Further south, the second bridge, Vidyasagar Setu, opened in 1992, is a cable-stayed toll bridge and comparatively less crowded; it is a road link from Calcutta to Bombay, Delhi and Madras. Vivekananda Bridge, also known as Bally Bridge, furthest to the north outside the city, is both a road and rail bridge. It was built in 1931 and was originally known as Willingdon Bridge.

Apart from the railway station at Haora, the other major railway station, Sealdah, founded in 1862 in north Calcutta, is also connected to major cities all over the country. Right up to the 1950s, Sealdah station used to have a special loading platform to transport Calcutta's refuse to a garbage disposal area at Dhapa in the southeast of the city.

The colonial heritage —discussed throughout this book—makes it almost impossible to standardize the English spellings of Calcutta's people and places. For instance, Bose and Basu are equivalent spellings of the same name, as are Mitter and Mitra, Tagore and Thakur; ditto Datta/Dutta/Dutt, Roy/Ray and Chowdhury/Chaudhuri, and the situation is still more complicated for names like Banerjee, Chatterjee and Gangully. So far as possible, I have retained the spellings for famous individuals that are widely accepted, for example Subhas Chandra Bose, Rabindranath Tagore and Michael Madhusudan Dutt, and standardized the rest, which vary widely in common use. With place-names I have generally retained the period spelling but given the modern spelling in parentheses, for instance Kidderpore (Khidirpur), but in a few cases, where the two names differ radically, I have used the modern spelling with the older spelling in parentheses, for example Sutanuti (Chuttanuty/Soota Loota). As for street names, many were changed in the period after independence in 1947; to avoid confusion, a list of equivalents appears on page 245, which can be used in conjunction with the map opposite.

I thank my publisher James Ferguson for inviting me to write this book. I am grateful to my daughter Ronita for salvaging the major part of the manuscript from a crashed computer. My nephew Nilayan Dutta took some photographs for my reference and accompanied me in trips round the city. Special thanks to Sunil Janah for letting me use one of his Bengal Famine photos.

Krishna Dutta

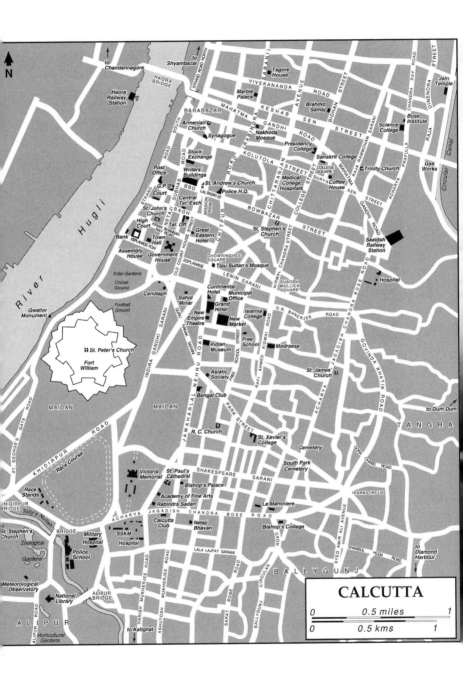

N

to Chandannagore
to Shyambazar

HAORA
BRIDGE

Haora
Railway
Station

Tagore
House

Marble
Palace

VIVEKANANDA ROAD

BARABAZAR

Brahmo Samaj

Armenian
Church

Synagogue

Nakhoda
Mosque

Presidency
College

Bose
Institute

Science
College

Jain
Temple

Stock
Exchange

KOLUTOLA

Sanskrit College

Gas
Works

Post
Office

Writers'
Buildings

Medical
College
Hospitals

Trinity Church

G.P.O.

St. Andrew's Church

Surya

Coffee
House

BBD

Court

LALBAZAR

Police H.Q.

Central
Tel. Exch.

BOWBAZAR

STREET

St. John's
Church

Tel. Off.

Great
Eastern
Hotel

St. Stephen's
Church

Sealdah
Railway
Station

High
Court

Bank

Town
Hall

Assembly
House

Government
House

CHOWRINGHEE
SQUARE

Tipu Sultan's Mosque

Hospital

Eden Gardens
Cricket
Ground

Football
Ground

Cenotaph

LENIN SARANI

SUBODH
MULLICK
SQUARE

Gwalior
Monument

Sahid
Minar

Continental
Hotel

Grand
Hotel

Municipal
Office

S.N. BANERJEE ROAD

River
Hugli

New
Empire
Theatre

New
Market

Islamia
College

St. Peter's Church

Fort
William

Indian
Museum

Free
School

Madrassa

MAIDAN

MAIDAN

Asiatic
Society

St. James'
Church

to Dum Dum

Bengal Club

PARK STREET

TANGRA

R. C. Church

St. Xavier's
College

Cemetery

SHAKESPEARE
SARANI

South Park
Cemetery

PARK CIRCUS

Victoria
Memorial

St. Paul's
Cathedral

Bishop's Palace

Race Course

Academy of Fine Arts

Rabindra Sadan

Le Martiniere

ACHARYA JAGADISH CHANDRA BOSE ROAD

Race
Stands

Calcutta
Club

Netaji
Bhavan

Bishop's College

KHIDIRPUR
BRIDGE

Tolly's Nullah

St. Stephen's
Church

BRIDGE

Military
Hospital

SSKM
Hospital

LALA LAJPAT SARANI

to
Diamond
Harbour

Zoological
Gardens

Police
School

BALLYGUNJ

Meteorological
Observatory

National
Library

ALIPUR
BRIDGE

ALIPUR

to Kalighat

Horticultural
Gardens

CALCUTTA

| 0 | 0.5 miles | 1 |
| 0 | 0.5 kms | 1 |

INTRODUCTION

Kolikata, Calcutta, Kolkata

In 1990, Calcuttans celebrated Calcutta's tercentenary. With a cultural zeal characteristic of Bengal, they published books, organized seminars and exhibitions, wrote poems, composed songs, and held parties. Yet only ten years later, many of them began lobbying to change the name of the city. Soon the West Bengal Government passed a constitutional amendment. From January 1, 2001, the beginning of the new millennium, Calcutta was officially renamed Kolkata.

The demand for renaming came from scores of writers, poets and other Bengali-speaking cultural figures. They argued that the new name would reflect the pronunciation of the city's name in Bengali and would protect the state's linguistic identity. (In general, Bengalis say *Kolkata*—with a fairly long o—among themselves and Calcutta to the rest of the world.) But other influential Calcuttans, no less Bengali in background, were less convinced. The novelist and activist Mahasweta Devi remarked: "We wanted a change, but what will happen to the names of our venerable institutions? Will Calcutta University be renamed Kolkata University or Calcutta High Court be Kolkata High Court from now?" The film-maker Mrinal Sen commented: "We can see an assertive cultural movement here, which speaks about making it mandatory to paint signboards in Bengali. Will it help us to integrate with the world? I am not sure." Annada Shankar Roy, an octogenarian littérateur said: "I'm vehemently opposed to the decision which will make a mockery of the history behind Calcutta's name. You can pronounce the name of the city differently, but how can you change the spelling that has evolved over a period of time? Besides, phonetically and linguistically Kolkata and Calcutta go hand in hand."

There were yet other possibilities for the name change, given the cosmopolitan nature of the city, in whose labyrinthine lanes jostle turbaned Sikh taxi drivers from the Punjab, tobacco-chewing Bihari and Oriya laborers from neighboring Bihar and Orissa and dark-faced accounts clerks from southern India—not to mention Marwari businessmen from Rajasthan, Sindhis and Gujaratis from western India, Bangladeshis and Assamese from the east, the Chinese community which has adopted Indian citizenship, and many other groups. Most inhabitants of the city are partially bilingual, constantly switching between Bengali and English, Bengali and Hindi, and combinations of these languages with other regional tongues such as Urdu, Telegu and Malayalam, in cacophonous conversation. Meanwhile, the shop signs and film advertisements on Calcutta's roof tops may be among the earliest examples of multilingual posters anywhere in the world, with Bengali script cosying up to English and Hindi lettering without somehow appearing incongruous. Hence, for Bengali villagers the city is pronounced *Koliketa*, for many Bangladeshis it is *Koilkata*, for the Oriyas it is often called *Kalikata*, and the Punjabis, Gujaratis and others from the rest of India nearly always call it *Kolkatta*. Perhaps it is not surprising that in an opinion poll published in the Calcutta *Telegraph* in mid-2000, 52 percent of Calcuttans thought renaming the city was unnecessary and only 38 percent were in favor, while the rest were undecided.

For the majority Bengali community, the new name, Kolkata, suggests a compromise between acknowledging the city's colonial past and the need to restore its threatened identity as a Bengali city. They want to avoid the British-given name Calcutta but they also do not like the original Bengali name of the place, Kolikata, that of a swampy fishing village. "Kolkata sounds natural but Kolikata sounds comical," said a young person speaking in English, when I was chatting in Bengali to a group of students and teachers at my old college in Calcutta. Bengalis have always been acutely aware of how they relate to the rest of the world, particularly the English-speaking world. Thus for them the new name serves as a natural, if unconscious, metaphor for the cultural fusion in the city's architecture, art, literature and other artistic manifestations. After all, Bengal, and especially its capital city, is where the East first came face to face with the West—its intellect as well as its colonial brutality—and responded creatively to the encounter through Bengali culture. Rather than taking a strongly nationalist stance, like Bombay, which changed its name to Mumbai, or Madras, which has become the unrecognizable Chennai, Calcutta has preferred a comparatively minor name change, which frankly is a bit of a multicultural mishmash.

But how did the name—whether Kolikata or Kolkata—originate? What does it mean, if anything? Although reams have been written on the subject, the name remains a mystery.

There is a story that when one of the first British arrivals inquired about the place, a bewildered grass-cutter took the question to be: when was the grass cut? Not knowing any English, he replied in Bengali "kal kata"—"cut yesterday". This was duly noted down as the place-name.

A bizarre and more lugubrious explanation comes from early missionary sources that liken the name to Golgotha, the place of the skulls where Jesus was crucified. Calcutta was of course a very unhealthy spot for its early European inhabitants and large numbers died there. (We shall visit their graves in the Park Street cemetery in due course.)

An authority on Bengal, Jogendranath Bhattacharya, suggested that the name had a rural Bengali origin. The Bengali word *kol* means literally "lap" and also the alluvial indentations in river banks formed by water currents in the Ganges (known as the Hugli, or Hooghly, at Calcutta). These formations have been used as natural harbors since time immemorial. When after some years the river cut a new channel and abandoned the *kol*, its new course might then be described as *kol kata*—"lap cut"—and perhaps Kolikata evolved from this. Geographically and culturally, such an explanation rings true.

Yet the most popular hypothesis links the name with the city's presiding deity, the goddess Kali. There are the two arguments in its favor, one linguistic, the other historical, though neither is by any means conclusive. Linguistically, Kolikata may be a derivative of the Sanskrit compound *Kalikshetra*, meaning "the domain of Kali". But according to reputable Sanskritists, no Hindu would distort *Kali* to *Koli* and the usual corruption of *kshetra* is *khet*, not *khata* or *kata*. Moreover, the ancient Sanskritic place-names of India have tended to survive, sometimes alongside their anglicized forms; yet the name Kalikshetra was never used alongside Kolikata.

The historical argument is perhaps somewhat stronger. Put simply, it goes as follows. In the south of the city in an area called Kalighat named after a landing stage (or ghat) on the banks of the Hugli, there is a temple to Kali. This temple and its site have been of overriding importance, the religious focus for all Hindus in the region. Therefore, so the argument goes, the Bengali name of the city must in some way be intertwined with Kali, even though no one suggests that the name Kalighat could have been transformed into Kolikata.

Kalighat

If you take the Calcutta Metro, the city's underground, to Kalighat, you get off at a station with a huge mosaic depiction of a haloed Mother Teresa. An Albanian by birth, she came to the city as a Catholic nun in 1931, learned to speak Bengali, wore a sari, took Indian citizenship, and established her famous home for the dying right next door to the Kalighat temple—where the supply of moribund poor Hindus is ample. The juxtaposition is strangely appropriate. Like Mother Kali's garland of human heads who are sinners-turned-devotees, Mother Teresa too acquired a respectable head count of dying souls saved for her faith by conversion in her home's small gloomy hall lined with washable plastic mattresses. There the destitute lie awaiting their final deliverance, served by nuns in white, blue-bordered saris and by a few sincere young westerners mostly in their "gap year" between school and university, their work supported by donations from guilt-stricken visitors. Sadly, as with all faiths, most of the money collected seems to go into religious and missionary activity, instead of into the building of the modern hospitals, hospices and children's homes that would have made Mother Teresa a true saint of Calcutta rather than a Catholic icon.

But Mother Kali, unlike Mother Teresa, is a black-skinned, fierce-looking, four-armed, naked goddess with a blood-red protruding tongue and a piercingly hypnotic third eye in her forehead. Her black marble image on a red granite slab at Kalighat may appear hideous to unaccustomed eyes, but according to Hindu mythology she is the destroyer of all evil and the female principle at the root of all creation. Indeed, she embodies the ideal empowerment of woman: *shakti*, the positive energy, the primal force that ever renews the world and prevents its stagnation. (I was not surprised to spot a painting of Kali on a wall in a television documentary about Germaine Greer!)

There could hardly be a more suitable deity for Calcutta, with its extreme mixture of decaying and redeeming features. The annual adoration of Kali in October/November is one of the city's major festivals, with public and private worship of more than two thousand Kali images and spectacular fireworks displays. Luminous darting streaks and deafening bangs and booms enliven the evenings, and most homes celebrate the Diwali festival of light, with a wondrous display of candles along roof tops, verandas and window sills; during the afternoon, thousands of beautifully decorated hot-air balloons fill the sky. In its festive display of skulls, skeletal figures, ghoulish masks and candles, Kali Puja looks similar to the famous Mexican festival in November, the Day of the Dead, without having any element of remembrance of the deceased.

Over several centuries numerous devotional songs have been composed to portray Kali's dual powers of destruction and creation. When Ramprasad Sen, a lowly Bengali clerk in eighteenth-century Calcutta, was caught writing such verses in the office account ledger, they were so much appreciated that he was given not the sack but rather a monthly allowance to write more of them. *Shyamasangit*—"songs in adoration of Shyama, the Dark One" (i.e. Kali)—are widely sung in today's city, and CD recordings of these fervent songs are tremendously popular. They form a key part of the film *Devi* (*The Goddess*) by Satyajit Ray, the great Bengali film director, in which they convey the passion of orthodox Bengal for Kali worship. Anyone who wants to understand Kali in Bengal should see the film. It will help to explain why Kali was the patron deity of the nineteenth-century Thug assassins, and also of the twentieth-century fighters of the Indian nationalist movement and the Maoist Naxalite rebels who followed them in the 1960s and 70s. Kali provokes terror in her enemies, but to her devotees she is a provider.

In Calcutta, she is often called, endearingly, Kali Kalkattawali, meaning "Kali the owner of the city", the deity who watches over its fate. The more one knows Calcutta, the more meaningful Kali becomes as a metaphor for the place. It can be a hard, and even frightening city, but it is also stimulating for those who take trouble to know it. To be sure, there are pitfalls for the outsider. Most foreigners assume that Kali is sticking out her tongue with blood lust. The novelist Günter Grass, on the other hand, who spent some months in Calcutta and was haunted by the lolling red tongue of the goddess (he called his book about the city *Show Your Tongue*), settled for a facetious and meaningless comparison between Kali and the famous photograph of Einstein sticking out his tongue. Perhaps Grass was hunting for an image to convey his own bafflement. At any rate, the widely accepted Bengali explanation is that Kali is showing her tongue as a sign of speechless embarrassment: a gesture very common among Bengalis. She is embarrassed because in her frenzy of destruction she has accidentally trodden on her sleeping consort, the god Shiva. Thus to most Bengalis the tongue does not symbolize a love of gore, but rather represents the humanity in divinity—a hallmark of everyday Hinduism.

Kalighat itself is full of contradictory images. Within the temple precincts, you can hear the agonized bleat of a vermilion-smeared goat being dragged to the sacrificial altar, but you can also catch the tender exchange of looks between two lovers who have just got married in secret. In British terms, the Kalighat temple is a bit like Gretna Green used to be: couples can lawfully wed there, without the consent of their families, for a few rupees to the priest and a meager offering of flowers and sweetmeats to the deity. (There is a romantic fictional version of this in Chitra Banerjee Divakaruni's recent *Sister of My Heart*.) And Kalighat is also a place to abandon a fond possession, for instance a head of lovely hair—even perhaps one's past existence: numerous men and women go there to become *sannyasis*, ascetics in saffron robes. Whatever an individual's purpose in visiting Kalighat, the place rejoices in perpetual festivity amidst heaps and bunches of bright-orange marigolds and scarlet hibiscus blossoms, piles of vermilion powder (*sindur*) symbolizing holiness and matrimony, and stacks of utensils in stone and shiny copper and brass. It is also a place to indulge in sex; there is a thriving red-light district nearby.

The origin of Kalighat as a site of worship is, perhaps unsurprisingly, shrouded in legend. The Hindu deities Shiva and Devi (another name for Kali) were husband and wife. King Daksha, Devi's father, did not approve of Shiva's wayward manners and ash-smeared face. Therefore when Daksha hosted a meeting of the gods, he did not invite Shiva. When his daughter, as a virtuous wife, asked her father why Shiva was not invited, Daksha made some disparaging remarks about him. This upset her so much that she immolated herself. An enraged Shiva then lifted his wife's burning body on his shoulder and began a frenzied dance to quell the fire. This made the world tremble and the other gods became concerned about impending doom. Vishnu, the third member of the supreme Hindu trinity (along with Shiva and Brahma), decided to unleash his sacred flying circular saw, which chopped the body of Shiva's wife into 52 pieces. The place where each piece landed became a pilgrimage spot. The toes of her right foot are supposed to have fallen beside the old course of the Hugli river near the present site of Calcutta. Naturally, a temple was built to mark the spot.

Legend has it that the temple was built further north at Posta, but there is no evidence for this. In the sixteenth century, the temple is said to have stood at Bhabanipur (Bhabani is yet another name for the goddess) about a mile northeast of Kalighat. The present temple—quite small by Indian standards—dates only from 1809 and was built by Santosh Roy Chowdhuri, a descendant of the family who sold the fishing village of Kolikata to the East India Company, with the financial assistance of another rich Hindu, Kaliprasad Datta, who had been ostracized from society and hoped to regain his lost status. Many devotees, including one from the orthodox branch of the Tagores, Calcutta's most celebrated family, also contributed, both to the building of the temple and to the construction of its precincts, while yet more benefactors provided Kali's gold accoutrements and other valuable ritual objects and funded the building of the adjoining landing stage. The architecture is typical of Bengali *ath-chala* temples with a main roof like a large squashed loaf supporting a similar smaller roof carrying a decorative pinnacle 90 feet high (now marred by TV antennae), a long aisle on the south side and a raised platform all around—the whole being built of brick, part tiled and part painted. Within the temple compound are also two later small temples devoted to Shiva and Krishna, making Kalighat a pilgrimage place for the Shaivas (worshippers of Shiva) and the Vaishnavas (worshippers of Vishnu and Krishna).

On the parapet of the adjoining hall, local boys throng to fly kites or just to sit and dangle their feet while watching the fervid scene below. The atmosphere is metropolitan: a melange of plastic festoons and tinsel decorations, shops selling fridge magnets and key rings with images of Kali, taxis ferrying devotees and priests clutching mobile phones. In 2000, an engineer from Bangalore donated a mechanical ensemble of gongs, bells and drums, which can be switched on during the daily service. But the temple committee, concerned that the musicians who have been playing sacred music in the inner sanctum for decades should not be made redundant, decided to install the machine in the temple's outer courtyard, not near the image of Kali.

There are regular *pujas* (prayers) on Tuesdays and Saturdays and in addition on the dark-moon nights traditionally dedicated to Kali. At the Bengali New Year (mid-April) businessmen ceremoniously bring new red cloth-bound account books to procure blessings from the goddess, and at the end of the year, during the Charak Puja, devotees pierce their bodies, walk on beds of nails, hang themselves from hooks on high poles and perform other similar acts of ritual excess. If you cannot be there in person to worship and you are a technologically savvy member of the Bengali diaspora, you can still send *puja* offerings by credit card and receive a casket containing blessed dried fruit and flowers by post, simply by clicking on a website proclaiming the following mission statement: "In the name of God, it is our commitment that we maintain honesty."

Yet for all its modern trappings, Kalighat can still exude its original old swampy air, triggered by the muddy smell from the nearby canal, Tolly's Nullah, dug between 1775 and 1776 by an East India Company man, Major William Tolly, whose name also appears in the neighboring Tollygunj, where he set up a *ganj* (market). His plan was to shorten the Company's ships' river journey into Bengal by opening up an old dried-up channel of the Hugli. Tolly dug it at his own cost and collected a toll. Hence, but for the demands of commerce, Kalighat would have lacked its all-important ghat.

Let us now go back to the foundation of Calcutta in 1690 by the East India Company near the fishing village of Kolikata and follow how it grew into the second city of the British Empire.

CHAPTER ONE

Company Calcutta

Early European navigational maps of the Bay of Bengal, such as Thomas Bowrey's of 1687 and George Herron's of 1690, do not show Calcutta or the fishing village of Kolikata, but they do show neighboring Sutanuti (Chuttanuty/Soota Loota), a weavers' village, on the eastern bank of the Hugli, and Gobindapur (Govindpore). Both places were then trading centers for muslin, chintz and other wares. The first mention of "Calcutta" comes in 1688 in a letter written from Dacca (Dhaka) by two East India Company servants of the chief agent of the Company in Bengal, Job Charnock—the man who has become known as the founder of Calcutta. In 1689, Charnock began using "Calcutta" in official communications, while negotiating with the Mughal emperor Aurangzeb for a trading license.

The Portuguese had started a trading post in Bengal as long ago as 1535; the Dutch had done the same a hundred years later, in 1636; and in 1673 the French had followed, establishing a settlement upriver at Chandernagore (Chandannagar). The British came last, although they had already secured a foothold in India in 1650 (at Surat in the far west). Charnock arrived in the subcontinent soon after this, became a junior member of the Council of Bay of Bengal at an annual salary of £20 in 1657, and by 1686 was governor of the Bay of Bengal, answerable to a council of Company directors based in Madras. But he became embroiled in a serious dispute over the trading rights of the Company with the Muslim rulers of Bengal, who at one point had him flogged and the Company's factories burned down. Nevertheless, by mid-1690, through tenacious diplomacy, Charnock succeeded in obtaining the emperor's *firman* or trading license. Rowing in the monsoon rain towards Sutanuti with some loyal followers and an escort of thirty soldiers from his ship anchored in the Hugli, he pitched his tents on the site of the charred ruins of the Company's old factory and made a lavish offering at the old temple of Kali. The exact location of his landing place is not known, but it may have been between today's Beniatola and Shovabazar ghats in the north of the city.

The date, however, is certain: August 24, 1690. On that day, Charnock noted in his logbook: "In consideration that all the former buildings here are destroyed, it is resolved that such places be built as necessity requires and as cheap as possible... these to be done with mudd walls and thatched till we get ground whereon to build a factory." And so Calcutta, unusually among the major cities of the world, can claim to have a precise founding day.

When Rudyard Kipling visited the city briefly as a newspaper correspondent a couple of centuries after Job Charnock, he wrote:

Thus the midday halt of Charnock—more's the pity!—
Grew a city
As the fungus sprouts chaotic from its bed
So it spread
Chance-directed, chance-erected, laid and built
On the silt
Palace, byre, hovel—poverty and pride—
Side by side...

Calcutta is still a chaotic place with "poverty and pride—side by side". But from the window of an aircraft landing at Dum Dum airport (close to the small arms factory where a lead-nosed bullet, the so-called dumdum bullet, was invented by Captain Bertie Clay in 1898), Calcutta seems verdurous. You see the land below colored many shades of green, dotted with pools, ponds, lakes, canals and rivers. The city is surrounded by marshes, tidal creeks and mangrove swamps. Indeed, fertile Bengal inspired many Bengali poets and writers to lyricism; in the nineteenth century, the novelist Bankim Chandra Chatterjee called Bengal "shujala shufala shasya shyamala"— "abundant in water, fruit, grain, and green".

As you come out of the airport and drive along the Eastern Bypass you will see the contrasting lifestyles of a modern metropolis and rural Bengal. There are wicker and bamboo-built tea stalls beside high-rise modern housing, and poor villagers bringing fresh fruit and vegetables to market by push-carts as they have always done move cheek by jowl with smart, dark-windowed air-conditioned cars transporting jet-setting executives to modern offices. Bullock carts lumber through side alleys carrying the latest model of refrigerator while cows stroll along the bald grass verges looking for greener patches.

Driving from the claustrophobic north towards the more spacious south, along Chowringhee or the faster-moving Red Road, the sky-scraping American Centre building, the imposing Victoria Memorial across the Maidan and the colonnaded arcade of the Grand Hotel will seem like visions from a different, western world. But as soon as you spot a once-magnificent colonial building with wrought-iron balconies and trees sprouting through its windows, you will know you are in Calcutta. Like all major Indian cities, Calcutta is congested and polluted, although recently efforts have been made to improve the environment through stricter traffic regulations and tree planting projects. The pollution count is very high but falls dramatically during the monsoon months from July to October. Over 11,000 factories in and around the city, some 750,000 automobiles, and coal burning cookers constantly spew fumes into the atmosphere. More and more people can now be seen wearing protective masks as they take to the city roads which cover a mere 6.5 percent of the city's total surface area.

It is a noisy city. There is a medley of babble consisting of—for example—peddlers' street cries, slogan-shouting processions, children chanting their multiplication tables, the metallic clamor of trams, the harsh cawing of crows, and the gentle but insistent tinkle of rickshaws—all contributing to the city's daylight cacophony. Only after dark does it quieten down.

Besides his poem, Kipling also gave Calcutta its most disparaging epithet, "The City of Dreadful Night", a title he borrowed from an earlier Victorian poet James Thomson and reused in a rambling poem on Lahore. Yet if Calcutta's backstreets in Kipling's time, the 1880s, were indeed sites of Dickensian squalor, other parts of the city were as grand as the wealthiest parts of Victorian London.

Job Charnock and the Early Settlement
Calcutta's founder Job Charnock definitely had a larger ambition than suggested by the above entry in his logbook. He took note of the

potential of the area as a port for trading vessels sailing up the Hugli from the Bay of Bengal; it seemed to offer a safe and spacious harbor. On this basis, he decided to establish a British settlement. Although none of his fellows shared his vision—and his superior in Madras advised against it—Charnock was determined. The story goes that he bargained for the purchase of the land while sitting in the courtyard of the ancestral house of the local landowners, the Sabarno Roy Chaudhuri family of Barisha-Behala (now a southern suburb of Calcutta), of which the pillars still stand. What is definite is that some eight years later, Charnock's successor and son-in law Charles Eyre bought the rights to the three fishing villages of Sutanuti, Govindpore, and Dihi Kolikata from their Bengali landlords, for the paltry sum of only 1,300 rupees. Eyre's deed of purchase is dated November 10,

1698, a time when Aurangzeb's grandson Azim-us-San was the ruler of Bengal. This second date, rather than August 24, 1690, should really be regarded as the beginning of Calcutta.

Regrettably little is recorded about Charnock, apart for some anecdotes told by his contemporaries. Though he kept his logbook systematically, he never wrote about himself. Sometime in 1663 he is supposed to have taken as his wife a young Hindu woman, a suttee (*sati*) who was about to jump on her husband's funeral pyre when Charnock was smitten by her grace and rescued her. They lived together for twenty years and had four children, before she died in 1683. But if she was a Hindu, why did her husband sacrifice a cock on her tomb on her death anniversary? (And where is her tomb?) Did they marry but keep their own religions? We know Charnock adapted to Indian life with some contentment: he

Sale of deed of Calcutta, dated November 10, 1698

wore loose and floppy Indian attire, smoked a hookah, and drank arak punch. We also know that he died on January 10, 1693, though his tombstone says 1692, and is said to have been buried in the churchyard of St. John's Church, where an octagonal Islamic-style mausoleum was later erected later by Eyre. Whether it marks the original grave is uncertain, but it is undoubtedly the oldest piece of British masonry in the city. Charnock's epitaph reads: "He was a wanderer, who

Job Charnock's mausoleum

after sojourning for a long time in a land not his own, returned to his Eternal Home." One of the pioneering British adventurers who laid the foundation of a great empire, he also respected the local culture and realized the value of cooperation between the British and the local people in developing a prosperous interracial community.

Those who followed Charnock during the early and mid-eighteenth century cared less about India and her inhabitants. While working as employees of the Company, the more influential traded for themselves on the side, and it did not take them long to discover how relatively easy it was to amass a personal fortune through corrupt practices uncontrolled by English law. Soon boatloads of young Englishmen with few scruples were being lured to the heat and humidity of the Bay of Bengal. On arrival they became "writers" on the payroll of the East India Company with the duty of keeping commercial accounts. They had lodgings in rooms along a corridor in old Fort William, which had been built in 1712, until 1777, when the impressive, three-story Writers' Building came into existence. The bureaucratic tradition continues there today, as the Writers' Building is now the powerhouse of the West Bengal Government, famous for its ceiling-high piles of moldering files stirred by gently circulating fans, though attempts are being made to accelerate its operations with email, the internet and video conferencing.

Trading rights having been secured, Company officials, backed up by Company soldiers, plundered local villages for spices, rice, sugar, saltpeter, opium and other profitable goods. Boatloads of tobacco, chintz, ginger, bamboo, gunnies and many other products were dispatched to England. The Company was quickly doing a roaring trade.

To expand its domain, it sent a deputation to the Mughal emperor in Delhi, in 1715. The deputation offered gifts valued at £30,000 and personal medical attention in the shape of a British physician, William Hamilton, who was able to ease the emperor's swollen groin just before his marriage. In return, the Company was granted the rights to 37 more villages including Haora across the Hugli, with a "degree of freedom and security unknown to the other subjects of the Mogul Empire." According to Charles Stewart in his *History of Bengal* (1813), as a result Calcutta "increased yearly in wealth, beauty, and riches". The Mughal rulers were every bit as corrupt as the Company, and predictably mutual self-interest prevailed in their dealings.

But Mughal power had begun to wane with the death of Aurangzeb in 1707. Thomas Babington Macaulay summed up the period inimitably in his *Historical Essays*: "A succession of nominal sovereigns, sunk in indolence and debauchery, sauntered away life in secluded places, chewing bhang, fondling concubines and listening to buffoons. A succession of ferocious invaders descended through the western passes to prey on the defenceless wealth of Hindostan." In Calcutta, fear of the Maratha power in western India alerted the Company to protect its property. In 1742, 25,000 rupees were raised towards the digging of a ditch around the southeast of the city, though it was never completed because the possibility of invasion receded after a deal between the Marathas and the emperor. Years later, in 1799, the half-dug ditch was filled to build a circular thoroughfare known as Lower Circular Road (now Acharya Jagadish Chandra Bose Road) and Upper Circular Road (now Acharya Prafulla Chandra Ray Road). However, the memory of the aborted moat lives on in an old street name in nearby Baghbazar, Mahratta Ditch Lane, and in a Bengali folk lullaby: "Chelay ghomolo para jurolo borgi elo deshe!" ("Now Baby sleeps, peace reigns in the neighborhood, when suddenly the Maratha marauders invade!")

Gradually, Calcutta was developing into a home from home for its founders. The first church, St. Anne's, went up as early as 1709. By the middle of the century, the land occupied by the British in Calcutta was about three miles in length and about a mile in breadth. They called it the White Town, in contrast with the native Black Town beyond. The total population of both towns was about 400,000, conducting trade worth one million pounds annually. Some fifty vessels were now calling at the East India docks and warehouses on the Hugli each year. Protection came from Fort William, an enclosure 650 feet long by 360 feet wide with four bastions in an eighteen-foot-high surrounding wall, but with only a few cannon.

The Company's rich treasury, combined with its air of confidence, attracted the attention of the young and haughty nawab of Bengal, Siraj-ud-Daula, successor to Mughal power. On June 19, 1756, his army approached Dum Dum, now the site of Calcutta's airport, and he saw that the bazaars had been set on fire by the British. This infuriated him and soon his army swarmed into the fort on ladders and captured its European inhabitants. But Siraj did not kill them, instead he ordered that they be imprisoned until the morning when he would interrogate them about the treasury. Since the only available prison was the fort's tiny punishment cell, the Europeans were herded into it on the night of June 20. This was the place that during the British Raj became synonymous with infamy as the Black Hole of Calcutta.

The Black Hole

Perhaps few other English phrases more chillingly evoke menace, even half a century after the passing of the British Raj. Much serious historical research on the event has been done, but still the dominant perception is that of a blatant atrocity by the Indians against the British. Generations of British schoolchildren once grew up reading of the heroic sacrifice of British lives at the hands of a barbaric race. Even in a recent BBC radio series on the history of Britain, *This Sceptred Isle*, the Black Hole was deemed important enough to warrant a mention:

"The Indian leader had marched on Calcutta and imprisoned those who had not previously escaped in the Black Hole, a room measuring 14 feet by 18 feet. There were too many in too small a space and most of them died of suffocation in the hot Indian night. The British wanted revenge." During the closing decades of the twentieth century, as a result of the world attention focused on dying destitutes by the work of Mother Teresa, the Black Hole became almost a transferred epithet for Calcutta as a whole.

The standard version of the event—a tale told with the flourish of a fine story-teller—came originally from the pen of one of the survivors, John Zephaniah Holwell, who sailed to India as a surgeon's mate in 1732 and eventually rose to be temporary governor of Bengal in the 1760s. The grandson of the astronomer royal and surveyor of crown lands John Holwell and the son of a London merchant, he had some literary ambition and was known for his narrative skill; even Voltaire paid tribute to him. As well as books on the history of Bengal, Holwell wrote on Indian mythology, cosmogony and festivals and put forward the view that Hindu scripture was indispensable to the full interpretation of the biblical canon—notably the Hindu belief in the transmigration of souls. Thus Holwell was an early Orientalist with a zeal to interpret the East in western terms.

What happened on the night of June 20, 1756, according to him, is that 146 English people and other Europeans were crammed into the eighteen-by-fourteen-foot cell with only one barred window. It was the hottest part of the year and the prisoners rapidly began to collapse and die. Holwell himself survived because he stayed close to the window and sucked perspiration from his shirtsleeves to relieve his thirst. He remembered:

> *Whilst I was at the second window, I was observed by one of my miserable companions on the right of me in the expedient of allaying my thirst by sucking my shirt-sleeve. He took the hint, and robbed me from time to time of a considerable part of my store; though, after I had detected him, I had ever the address to begin on that sleeve first, when I thought my reservoirs were sufficiently replenished, and our mouths and noses often met in contest. This plunderer, I found afterwards, was a worthy young gentleman in the service, Mr Lushington, one of the few who*

escaped from death, and since then paid me the compliment of assuring
me he believed he owed his life to the many comfortable draughts he had
from my sleeve.

Holwell also applied his medical knowledge to others, which brought some solace in the inferno. Nevertheless, when the cell was opened in the morning, the majority of prisoners were said to have died.

Holwell's account, entitled *A genuine narrative of the deplorable deaths of the English Gentlemen and Others, who were suffocated in the Black-Hole in Fort William, at Calcutta, in the Kingdom of Bengal; in the night succeeding the 20th Day of June, 1756,* was written as a part of a letter to a friend while its author was recovering on a ship bound for England, and published in England in 1758. In Calcutta, Holwell put up a brick-built and plastered obelisk memorial at his own expense in 1760, near the northwest corner of old Tank Square (now named Benoy-Badal-Dinesh Bag—BBD Bag—after three martyrs of the independence movement). The monument was struck by lightning, and the damage was immediately repaired. Yet in 1821 it was demolished on the orders of the governor-general because it had become an unsightly venue for local barbers.

Exactly how many went into the Black Hole and how many survived has been hotly disputed ever since Holwell's time. When in 1901 the viceroy, Lord Curzon, built a new monument to the Black Hole victims (also an obelisk, standing on a hexagonal base with steps all round), the marble inscription recorded that "146 British inhabitants of Calcutta were confined on the night of 20th June 1756, and from which only 23 came out alive." But Curzon added the names of several Europeans who are known to have died during the siege of Calcutta, though not in the Black Hole, to the 27 names originally provided by Holwell. Curzon's inscription reads:

The names of those who perished in the Black Hole prison, inscribed upon the reverse side of this monument are in excess of the list recorded by Governor Holwell upon the original monument. The additional names, and the Christian names of the remainder, have been recovered from oblivion by reference to contemporary documents.

Curzon's memorial still exists, though it was transferred from its original site in 1946 as a result of road works and is now in the grounds of Calcutta's earliest surviving church, St. John's. The keeper of the church archive told me that some years before the move, the firebrand Bengali patriot Subhas Chandra Bose was given a tiny ceremonial hammer as mayor of Calcutta. This he tapped gently on the monument as a symbolic warning of the forthcoming demise of colonial rule.

The Black Hole monument erected by Lord Curzon

According to modern scholars, the reality of the Black Hole was far less brutal than Holwell described. (Compare the Amritsar massacre in 1919, when troops under British command killed some 350 Indians by firing on an unarmed crowd.) There are, in any case, many inconsistencies in Holwell's account. For a start, it would have been physically impossible to squeeze 146 thin Bengalis into a cell of the size he describes, let alone 146 well-built Europeans. Holwell gives the impression that he was able to move about in the cell comforting others. How could he, if it was so packed? Apparently he kept count of time by glancing at his watch. How was this possible in an unlit cell on a pitch-dark night? And how could he recognize most of the captives and describe their agonized faces without light? It has long been accepted that Holwell exaggerated to a great degree and that his "genuine narrative" is nothing of the sort. Karl Marx, in his notes on Indian history, commented on British hypocrisy over the incident: "[they] have been making so much sham scandal to this day!" Iris Macfarlane, in her 1975 book on the Black Hole, comments perceptively that: "The non-event of the Black Hole of Calcutta has assumed, historically, the indefinable importance of the Marabar Caves" (the notorious setting for the assault on Miss Quested in *A Passage to India*). It is highly significant that after the eventual British victory over Siraj-ud-Daula, the East India Company never claimed any compensation for the lives lost in the Black Hole, despite presenting the defeated nawab with a long and detailed list of other damages suffered during his siege of Calcutta.

To understand what really happened, one must recall that at the time of the incident the British in Calcutta were traders. According to the Mughal *firman*, they were only *talukdars* or rent-collectors, and not zamindars or landlords, and had no sovereign rights. So when the Company sought to expand its trading domain by shoring up Fort William, Siraj-ud-Daula naturally became suspicious and decided to march on Calcutta. With 30,000 foot soldiers, 20,000 mounted soldiers, 400 trained elephants and 80 pieces of cannon, there was clearly no contest. But the Company panicked, and instead of adopting a diplomatic approach, it rashly embarked upon confrontation, backed only by its tiny and under-prepared army. The British threw up terraces for guns, dug ditches, stockpiled gunpowder, and evacuated women and children to neighboring European settlements. Inevitably they lost. Having captured the fort, the nawab hoped that the defenders would lead him to the Company's treasury. He was unaware of the fort's lack of serious provision for holding prisoners. Giving orders that they be held, he went to bed at 8 p.m., telling his commanders not to disturb him. The prisoners' overnight confinement in the only cell available on what happened to be the hottest and sultriest night of the year was more the result of a bungle by the commanders than a cold-blooded conspiracy to murder by the nawab.

For a long time, the exact location of the Black Hole was uncertain because of the dismantling of most of the old Fort William around 1818. But in the 1890s, the scholar C. R. Wilson determined its position conclusively and published the details in the *Asiatic Society Journal*. Nothing of the original site exists today, and it requires some effort even to find the place near an arch next to the General Post Office hidden by street vendors selling religious images, men's briefs and mobile phones.

Robert Clive

Whatever may have been the truth of the Black Hole, it was the first blow to national pride suffered by the British in India and they were indeed determined to exact revenge. When news of the defeat in Bengal reached Madras in August 1756, a punitive expedition was organized. Its commander, Robert Clive (1725-74), had originally come to Madras as a young Company writer. He did not like the job and missed England. At first he had been disgusted by the malpractice accepted by his fellow Company servants in India, but in due course, after a highly successful military career in southern India, he came to wallow in corruption with the worst of them, while remaining prone to fits of manic depression (he eventually took his own life).

Clive arrived at Fulta (Falta), about forty miles downstream from Calcutta, on December 15, 1756. Governor Roger Drake and other British refugees from the capture of the city by Siraj-ud-Daula were living on ships anchored there, dependent on food smuggled to them by their Indian ally Nabkissen (later known as Raja Nabakrishna Deb, an influential intermediary between Bengalis and British, as we shall see). Clive managed to recapture Calcutta overnight with one onslaught launched under cover of dense mist. He immediately compelled the nawab to pay heavy compensation for the damage inflicted six months before. The city was re-fortified and a mint was set up, marking the beginning of British rule in India. Clive then consolidated his victory by defeating the French and capturing their colony at Chandernagore.

Soon Siraj-ud-Daula was losing his grip on Bengal. His character was undoubtedly despicable; notorious as a tyrant who indulged freely in various vices including sexual debauchery, he liked to disguise himself as a woman and gain entry into the women's quarter of respectable Hindu households. Among his victims was the daughter of the well-off Calcutta merchant Jagat Seth. Predictably, he had many enemies.

Clive took advantage of this. He struck a deal with Mir Jafar, Siraj's uncle and also an ally of Jagat Seth. If Mir Jafar would agree to help the Company, financially and in other ways, to defeat his nephew Siraj, Clive promised him the throne of Bengal, Bihar and Orissa. Together with Jagat Seth and Umichand, another rich and influential merchant, a plot was hatched against Siraj. On June 23, 1757, at the battle of Plassey (Polashi), a place north of Calcutta some twenty miles from Siraj's capital Murshidabad, the Company defeated the nawab's much larger army. The nawab had believed false intelligence that Clive's ammunition was wet and he would not go through with the battle, and so had ordered a truce for the day. As the nawab's army laid their weapons down, Clive suddenly attacked. Siraj suffered heavy casualties. Clive entered Murshidabad in ceremonial state, loaded one hundred boats with 7,500,000 silver rupees, and sent them down river to Calcutta where they were received with great fanfare. He also annexed nearly nine hundred square miles of land to the south of Calcutta known as the 24 Parganas. And he demanded, and procured, a one-off personal payment of £234,000 from the East India Company in compensation for his toil and trouble in Bengal, before he left for England in 1760. From then until his death, he enjoyed an annual income of £30,000.

In the words of Bengal's greatest poet, Rabindranath Tagore, referring to Plassey, "Boniker mandondo pohale sharbari dekha dilo rajdondo rupay"—"at night's end the trader's scales became a ruler's scepter." Clive initiated the "financial bleeding of Bengal", noted the historian Percival Spear. After Siraj fell, puppet nawabs of Bengal were obliged to pay huge sums of money to the East India Company's Calcutta Council. Company servants were permitted to conduct free trade as independent merchants, in effect as freebooters. The avarice and abuse of power by these men crippled the livelihoods of ordinary Bengalis. From the most senior to the most junior, Company servants made huge personal profits from trading in textiles, salt and opium. The remains of warehouses built on the site of the original Company buildings along the banks of the Hugli are a haunting reminder of those days.

But very soon the court of directors of the Company in London were becoming increasingly concerned that they were no longer receiving the lion's share of revenue from Bengal; and there was also military trouble from the Mughal emperor. In 1765 the Company dispatched Clive, now Baron Clive of Plassey, to Calcutta as both governor of Bengal and commander-in-chief. In less than two years he made the Company effective ruler of Bengal and Bihar, and also reformed its inner workings by imposing strict rules on Company employees, such as the regulation of private trade. Then, in 1767, he returned to England for good.

Calcutta's reputation as a "city of palaces" dates from this time, the 1760s, when the Company "nabobs" began to enjoy a lavish way of life in huge mansions attended by fleets of servants. A few of these extraordinary old houses still exist in reasonable condition around Russell Street (now Anadilal Podder Sarani) and Sudder Street. But Clive's residence, built in a mixture of Dutch and Indian style on a hillock near what is now Dum Dum airport is seriously dilapidated, though it is being restored after many years of neglect through a British initiative. For those with imagination, the ruin may still evoke the halcyon days of candle-lit dinner parties with menus of goat curry and Madeira—with bread pellet flicking by the gentlemen as accompanying amusement.

The White Town and the Black Town
Although Bengal as a whole suffered from the depredations of the Company, certain Bengalis did very well out of the new regime. In Calcutta, while the White Town became a place of neoclassical

grandeur, the Black Town also expanded rapidly as a separate locality. The White Town grew around the nucleus of the original Fort William, the Black Town around the village of Sutanuti.

Old Bengali manuscripts and archaeological evidence reveal that from ancient times trading communities had operated from a small cluster of islands, Agradwip, Chakradwip, Nabadwip, Sukhsayar and others, in the Gangetic delta, formed by tidal and alluvial action. Saptagram (Satgaon), now an insignificant village northwest of Chunchura (Chinsura, the Dutch settlement in Bengal) was a busy port during the late sixteenth century, the time of the emperor Akbar. Bengali families such as the Basaks (Bysacks) and the Seths (Setts) exported chintz to Europe from Saptagram. But as the river meandered away, trading vessels could no longer moor at Saptagram. Govindpore and Sutanuti, further south on the Hugli, began to develop as harbors during the sixteenth century.

During the nawabi period, before the rule of the Company, there were many Bengali Hindus serving the Muslim rulers. Most of the wealthy Bengalis of this time were well educated, literate in both Sanskrit and Persian. Nawab Murshid Quli Khan, who reigned from 1717 to 1727, appointed several of them as *diwans* (administrative supervisors); prior to this, *diwans* in Bengal had come from Agra and Punjab. This particular nawab, though a faithful Muslim, was appreciative of Hindu talents. In his land settlement of 1722, Bengal was divided into 25 *zamindaris*, out of which only one, Birbhum, had a non-Hindu zamindar. During his rule, Hindus and Muslims co-existed peacefully in Bengal while maintaining separate ways of living without inter-marriage.

When the Company began to trade in the region, some of these already-prosperous Hindus became moneylenders to the Company, along with the Armenians who were already in Bengal. Less prosperous but equally enterprising Bengalis, *baniyas* (tradesmen) such as the Basaks and the Seths, became contract suppliers of goods. The adventurous Ratan Sarkar, a laundry man, reincarnated himself as an interpreter, learning English on the job. Others became *gomosths* (brokers). The rest served as laborers, messengers, and servants in the White Town.

It was these newly wealthy Bengalis who developed the Black Town. They invested in land, set up bazaars, brought in artisan communities such as potters, tailors, blacksmiths, tanners and oil pressers. The names of certain parts of Calcutta reflect their artisan origins: Kumortuli (potters' neighborhood), Darjipara (tailors' neighborhood), Muchipara (tanners' and cobblers' neighborhood) and Kolutola (oil presser's neighborhood). Soon, substantial brick-built, flat-roofed houses with verandahs and inner courtyards stood amidst mud-and-thatch dwellings in narrow, unpaved, dirty alleys. Rich and poor lived next to each other in mutual dependence, unlike in the White Town. It is the same today in north Calcutta: for example, the family home of the Tagores in Jorasanko, built in 1784, is right next door to a thriving market place, and Raja Rajendralal Mullick's Marble Palace, built in 1834, is close to Kumortuli. The servants and other employees of these great houses all lived locally, not in other parts of the city or in the nearby villages. A British resident, Mrs. Kindersley, described the Black Town as follows in her *Letter from the East Indies*, in an entry dated June 1768:

> ...*it looks as if all the houses had been thrown up in the air, and fallen down again by accident as they now stand. People keep constantly building; and everyone who can produce a piece of ground to build a house upon, consults his own taste and convenience without any regard to the*

The house of the Tagores at Jorasanko

beauty or regularity of the town. Besides, the appearance of the best house is spoiled by the little straw huts, and such sort of incumbrances, which are built up by the servants for themselves to sleep in...

One can see this urban chaos in the engravings and paintings of the Calcutta gallery and a life-sized Calcutta model in the Victoria Memorial. In the White Town, the impression is of European-style mansions set among clean, wide, tree-lined streets and avenues, with no poor natives dwelling on the pavements and indeed few Indians other than servants in evidence—in stark contrast to the Black Town. Even today the feeling of a divided city lingers. In general, the inhabitants of crowded north Calcutta cherish old ways; the population of the central city exudes a cosmopolitan atmosphere; while those who live in the south follow a comparatively modern, westernized lifestyle.

Orientalism
In spite of the segregation, the White Town had a far-reaching impact on the Black Town that was both economic and cultural, and even philosophical. This was because, in broad terms, the British, once secure in their position, no longer viewed their existence in Bengal merely as a commercial enterprise. Some, at least, began to develop an interest in the culture and heritage of their new acquisition. Orientalism was at the time fast gaining ground in Europe. Warren Hastings (1732-1818), the next significant British ruler of Bengal after Clive, who was appointed the first governor-general in 1774 following the British government's decision to control the East India Company, was a keen Orientalist. He could speak Bengali and Urdu and knew some Persian. He visualized the creation of a generation of Company servants with an appreciation of local languages and culture. This, he foresaw, would encourage humane administration of the colony and promote affection between ruler and subject.

Under Hastings' patronage, Charles Wilkins, the first Briton to master Sanskrit, translated the *Bhagavad Gita* in 1776; Nathaniel Brassey Halhed published *A Grammar of the Bengali Language* in 1778; and Sir William Jones, known as "Asiatic" Jones, was invited to Bengal. His ostensible profession was law—he sat as a judge in Calcutta—but his real fame is as a remarkable polyglot who knew thirteen languages well and had a working knowledge of twenty-eight others. It was this ability that enabled Jones to propose that Sanskrit, the ancient language of north India which he learned while in India, together with Greek and Latin, the languages of classical antiquity, shared a common "Indo-European" origin—the most celebrated of his many scholarly achievements.

Jones arrived in the city in 1783 and soon gathered together thirty or so enthusiasts for the study of the cultures of Asia. On January 15, 1784, the Asiatic Society of Bengal, with Jones as president, held its first meeting in the grand jury room of Calcutta's Supreme Court. From 1808, the society acquired its own premises at the western end of Park Street, then known as Burial Ground Road (since it led to the cemetery). The first Indian members were admitted in 1829; they included Dwarkanath Tagore, the grandfather of Rabindranath Tagore. There was also an important journal, *Asiatick Researches*, initially edited by Jones, which was sought after in Europe and translated into German and French. The society was the world's first scholarly organization devoted to the study of the Orient, and was soon followed by similar societies in various European countries.

Much of the society's early activity was scientific. It also looked after a collection of Indian antiquities, which became the core collection of the Indian Museum when it opened to the public in Chowringhee in 1878. The society's building at 1 Park Street, occupied in 1965, still houses 40,000 valuable old manuscripts, a library of some 100,000 volumes, and coins, paintings and archaeological finds. Sadly the conservation of these objects and the promotion of new scholarship by the society have been in decline for some years in spite of efforts to rejuvenate it. But the building is still worth a visit for its significance in bringing together some remarkable scholars from two civilizations, who aspired to a mutually rewarding intellectual experience.

Of course, there was more to Orientalism than intellectual curiosity. Individual Englishmen such as Jones and Halhed were also keen to ensure the continuity of British rule in India. Hastings believed that Indians would be more loyal if they were regulated by their own laws rather than by alien European legislation. He therefore requested Jones to prepare a digest of Hindu and Muslim laws from Sanskrit and Persian sources. Halhed's grammar of Bengali was prompted by the notion that mastery of the language would enhance the competence of Company servants posted in Bengal. Yet in the process of fulfilling these official objectives, Jones, Halhed and others extended the boundaries of knowledge and revealed the wisdom of the East to the West. At the same time, unwittingly, they planted the seeds that would eventually germinate into Indian nationalism.

Two other events important to the development of education and scholarship were the arrival of printing in Calcutta in 1777 and the founding of Fort William College in 1800. The Company brought over a press from Britain mainly in order to publish administrative material, including the books prepared by Jones and Halhed. But soon other presses, printing in both English and Bengali, started to operate, with the Bengali typefaces designed by devoted local craftsmen; the craft of engraving followed. Halhed's Bengali grammar contained literary excerpts in a Bengali typeface, for example, and Balthazar Solvyns' famous album, *A Collection of Two Hundred and Fifty Coloured Etchings Descriptive of the Manners, Customs and Dresses of the Hindoos*, was printed as early as 1779. At this time, book publishing in Calcutta ranked above "Vienna, Copenhagen, Petersburg, Madrid, Venice, Turin, Naples or Rome", said William Dune, a contemporary publisher. Besides English and Bengali, there were books published in many other regional Indian languages—Urdu, Oriya, Tamil, Telugu, and Marathi—as well as Sanskrit and Persian. Many were published by the Mission Press at Serampore (Srirampur), the Danish mission north of Calcutta founded in 1800 by a Baptist missionary, William Carey. Like "Asiatic" Jones, Carey was a talented linguist who did much to promote the Bengali language. The first vernacular book to come off his press was a Bengali translation of the Gospel of St. Matthew, translated by Ramram Basu and John Thomas.

Newspapers were also quick to get going. The most famous was William Hickey's colorful weekly, the *Bengal Gazette*, started in January 1780, which thrived on social gossip. Its sensational success prompted the governor-general, Lord Wellesley, to issue the first regulations curbing press freedom in Calcutta in 1799.

It was Wellesley who founded Fort William College. The aim was to educate a generation of civil servants who would be well versed in local languages and customs. In spite of prejudice against Baptists,

Wellesley enlisted Carey's publishing expertise, and as a result western engravers and local type-makers worked together to produce quality books for the college. Printed words and pictures became a genuine bridge between East and West at this time. There was a sensitizing of western minds to things Oriental, as intended by Hastings and Wellesley—and a less calculated movement among Indians towards things western.

Literary activities mushroomed. Apart from the production of works of scholarship and textbooks, English ladies with ample time on their hands in India became avid diarists and gossip writers, while their husbands felt inspired to chronicle their exotic existence—partly in the hope of literary immortality in case they did not survive to retirement in Britain. Both men and women began to paint dozens of pen pictures of India and of their Anglo-Indian society. The genre of Raj literature had been born.

As for the Bengalis, there had long been a tradition of composing oral ballads and satires on contemporary life and narrating these to audiences, while itinerant performers with picture scrolls and masks provided popular entertainment. Now, many Bengalis realized they could have books in their homes like the British. The first Indian-owned press, a tiny set-up, was started by one Baburam in 1818 in Kidderpore (Khidirpur) in the south; it published in Hindi as well as Bengali. In the same year Biswanath Deb began printing popular books in Bengali in the north of the city, and soon a neighborhood of printers and illustrator-cum-authors, who had served apprenticeships with European printers in the White Town, grew up. In the area of Bat-tala in north Calcutta, they published the Hindu epics, *The Ramayana* and *Mahabharata,* and the Koran, folk stories with illustrations and stories for women and children, lives of the saints and popular heroes, almanacs and horoscopes, and traditional arithmetic as well as jokes and smut. The typefaces were usually worn out, having been bought second hand, and the compositors were poorly paid; but if Bat-tala books showed shoddy workmanship and lack of originality in content, they did bring cheap reading material to the masses and promote literacy. Today they provide much insight into the lives of people in north Calcutta in the nineteenth century. For today's Bengali book collectors, anything from Bat-tala commands a premium. Although it is no longer the place for printing in Calcutta, hundreds of hand presses in the dingy alleys of College Street and Sealdah carry on the Bat-tala tradition, in tandem with electronic typesetting.

Most of those who bought books from Bat-tala belonged to the community of orthodox religious believers, both Hindu and Muslim, educated in religious schools. For the Hindus, Bat-tala books might have been used to teach boys in a *pathsala*, funded by a rich and influential family living in the area, in order to dispense primary education. Among the Muslims, the books were used by boys from well-off families in *madrassas*, where teaching was based on the Koran. Warren Hastings himself promoted the founding of the Calcutta Madrassa in 1781 to promote the study of Arabic, Persian and Islamic law. Perhaps he was trying to ameliorate the mistrust between Muslims and British that followed Clive's deposition of Siraj-ud-Daula. "You may lay it down as a maxim that the Musalmans will never be influenced by kind treatment to do us justice," Clive had remarked.

Cultural Mixing

There can be no doubt that such interaction and social mixing as there was between the colonizers and the colonized occurred between the British and the Hindus, not the British and the Muslims. During the time of Hastings, English society opened up for some exotic exposure to the social and cultural lives of the natives. Civil servants and officers attended musical soirées in the great Bengali houses and watched the dancing of glittering nautch girls (*nach* means dance in Bengali). They lent their presence to the major festivals and attended Bengali wedding feasts and Bengali New Year celebrations. The most zealous, such as Sir John Macpherson, the governor-general who succeeded Hastings, could even sing in Gaelic and Hindustani with equal ardor. Here is William Hickey reporting one such occasion in his *Bengal Gazette*:

> On Monday night, Rajah Nobkissen gave a nautch and magnificent entertainment to several persons of distinction in commemoration of Miss Wrangham's birthday. As the ladies arrived, they were conducted by the Rajah through a grand suite of apartments into the zenana, where they were amused until the singing began, which was so mellifluous as to give every face a smile of approbation. The surprising agility of one of

the male dancers occasioned loud acclamations of applause. The princi-
pal female singers called the nymphs and swains to celebrate the festiv-
ity of the day and spoke a few complimentary lines suitable to the
occasion. After supper there was a ball. Which was opened by Mr Livius
and Miss Wrangham, who were dressed in the character of Apollo and
Daphne. When the minuets were ended, country dances struck up and
continued till past three in the morning, when the company departed
highly pleased with the elegant festival. And when the Rajah was attend-
ing Miss Wrangham to her carriage, he thanked her in very polite terms
for having illuminated his house with her bright appearance.

Although such meetings may have been mutually entertaining, one
wonders if they made any deep impression on either side—especially in
the field of music and dance, where East and West were at their most
unintelligible without proper training, and of course in literature,
where the language barrier would always hinder genuine appreciation.
Almost a century later, during his first visit to England in 1879-80,
Rabindranath Tagore frequently encountered such incomprehension
when he was asked to sing an Indian song for a British audience. He
recalled in *My Reminiscences*:

I happened to get acquainted with the widow of some Anglo-Indian offi-
cial. She was good enough to call me by the pet name Ruby. An Indian
friend of hers had composed in English a doleful poem in memory of her
husband. I need say nothing of its merit as poetry or of its felicity of
diction. The composer, as ill-luck would have it, indicated that the dirge
was to be chanted in the raga Behag. One day the widow entreated me
to sing it to her thus. Silly innocent that I was, I weakly acceded… I met
the lady frequently at different social gatherings, and after dinner when
we joined in the ladies in the drawing-room, she would ask me to sing
that Behag. Everyone clearly anticipated some extraordinary specimen of
native music and added their entreaties to hers. From her pocket would
emerge printed copies of the fateful composition, and my ears would
begin to redden and tingle. At last, with head bowed and quavering
voice I would have to make a stab at it—while only too keenly conscious
that no one but me in the room would find the performance heartrend-

ing. Afterwards, amidst much suppressed tittering, would come a chorus of "Thank you very much!" "How interesting!" And in spite of its being winter I would perspire all over.

But if they were not always culturally enriching, such encounters were certainly materially profitable. During the last decades of the eighteenth century, Bengali compradors—in other words business agents for the East India Company—developed a prominent lifestyle that was a strange hybrid of nawabi, Hindu and western living. They built ostentatious mansions, patronized Indian classical music and the European arts, held lavish feasts, and paid court to the British.

Raja Nabakrishna Deb, i.e. Rajah Nobkissen mentioned above, was one such figure. His family mansion, Sovabazar Rajbati, now much truncated, stands in Raja Nabakrishna Deb Street in north Calcutta with a huge lion gate opening up to a courtyard. In 1750, Nabakrishna taught Persian to young Warren Hastings as his *munshi* or tutor. He worked for Clive in 1756-57 as his unofficial intelligence agent, supplying him with vital information on Siraj-ud-Daula, and was suitably rewarded for this invaluable service to the Company. He was appointed to an influential position: that of political intermediary between the Indian princes and the Company. Soon he was fabulously rich. Loving pomp, he would hold lavish nautch parties with court dancers from Murshidabad and Lucknow, and invite his Company friends and contacts. In 1784, he obliged the Christian community in Calcutta by shrewdly donating the land on which to build St. John's Church. Yet he cultivated his image as an orthodox Hindu beholden to the rigid dictates of caste (the land he had gifted to the Christians was in fact used earlier for Christian burials and was therefore polluted ground for an orthodox Hindu). For the funeral ceremony of his mother, the word went round that anyone attending the event would receive a sumptuous charitable donation. The common people are said to have traveled for days from far afield carrying their infants, some of whom died on the way. Yet, exceptionally for his time, each of the raja's six wives was literate in Bengali.

With all his contradictions, men like Nabakrishna shaped the elite culture of Bengal for a century and a half, even up to independence in 1947. They and their descendants introduced a new word into English:

babu. The Bengali babu was the Indian counterpart, in a way, of the British "nabobs" such as Clive who flaunted their Indian-made wealth back in England. Babus were the product of western influence upon the fertile mind of Bengal, which was open to making the most out of an imported civilization, while remaining steeped in tradition. We shall delve into the babus' unique world in the next chapter.

The Permanent Settlement

But before leaving Company Calcutta and entering the nineteenth century proper, we cannot omit the Permanent Settlement of Bengal, which established the fortunes of many Calcutta babus as absentee zamindars. Promulgated by Lord Cornwallis in 1793, it was a colonial interpretation of the Whig ideology of justice and contractual agreement. By the terms of the settlement, peasants were secure on their land so long as they paid a fixed annual due to the zamindar, who in turn had to pay a similar fixed due to the British government. Failure to pay the zamindar would result in forfeiture of the peasant's land, which could then be transferred or sold. Although the new system broke the hold of a few extortionist zamindars, it undermined the loyalty of the good zamindar to his tenants. For under the settlement, there was no provision for years with good and bad harvests—the fixed due had to be paid to the zamindar regardless of the crop. Here was an opportunity for a new breed of native investor, the *nouveau riche* comprador of Calcutta, to buy agricultural land with sitting peasants. These men coveted the social status of calling themselves zamindars, but without subscribing to the zamindar's traditional obligations.

As a consequence, after the Permanent Settlement, the peasants became more insecure and impoverished. They could no longer find a dependable refuge in the zamindar's generosity in times of famine and flood, or seek a generous loan to pay the dowry for their daughter's marriage or the expenses involved in a parent's funeral rite. The old support network between landlord and peasant was eroded; no longer would the zamindar provide meals when a cultivator's wife was confined by childbirth. Often the only hope for the peasant was to leave the village and go the town. And this helped to create yet another famous feature of Calcutta—its slums.

CHAPTER TWO

City of the Babus

Most of the traditional Bengali families, such as my own, who first prospered in the sprawling family houses among the narrow lanes and winding alleys of the Black Town in what is now north Calcutta, are the descendants of one of the renowned babus of colonial Calcutta. Notable names include the Debs of Sovabazar, the Duttas of Hatkhola and Rambagan, the Mitras of Kumortuli, the Nandys of Cossimbazar, the Sinhas of Paikpara, and the Thakurs (Tagores) of Pathuriaghat and Jorasanko. These houses were generally built after 1800, though there are older buildings such as the house of Nabakrishna Deb and the Tagore house at Jorasanko that go back to the last quarter of the eighteenth century.

The mansions that survive are generally crumbling, but you can still get a good idea of what they looked like in their heyday: similar to an old Spanish hacienda with high ceilings, shaded inner courtyards, wrought-iron wall brackets, ceiling hooks for lamps and chandeliers and punkahs, heavy furniture, and European (or at least imitation-European) paintings. The best preserved is the house of Rajendra Mullick (1819–87), who began its construction at the age of sixteen, completed it five years later, and cunningly inserted a binding clause in the trust deed to prevent any alteration of the original design. Having been orphaned at the age of three and brought up by an English guardian, Sir James Weir Hogg, Mullick had tastes that were mainly European. His Marble Palace (named by Lord Minto after a visit)—which is located off the otherwise-ordinary Muktaram Babu Street in an area known as Chorbagan (Thieves' Garden)—is an imposing, bone-gray Palladian edifice stuffed with an eclectic assortment of *objets d'art*, ranging from the genuinely precious to the frankly tawdry. In the view of Geoffrey Moorhouse in his book on Calcutta:

There is marble everywhere, in ninety different varieties it is said, transported across the seas by the ton to provide floors, wall panels and table tops. There are great swathes of satin hanging round windows and enormous follies of crystal glass hanging in chandeliers from ceilings. There are mirrors from Venice and vases from Sèvres and golden goblets from Bohemia and stags' heads from the Trossachs and figures from Dresden and swords from Toledo and ormolu clocks from Paris and carvings from Bavaria and vast quantities of Victorian bric-a-brac that look as if they were scavenged in job lots from the Portobello Road on a series of damp Saturday afternoons in October.

Although a visit to the Marble Palace is a "must" for a first-timer in Calcutta (with a free entry pass to be obtained from the West Bengal tourist office), a peep into other great houses of the Bengali babus, less written about and less westernized, is equally if not more rewarding. To name a few, there is the dilapidated Sovabazar Rajbati; the well-preserved house of the sons of the merchant Ramdulal Dey—Chhatu Babu and Latu Babu—on Beadon Street; and the Victorian building, Dhurjathidham, near Belgachhia tram depot. These houses, and many others, embody a free mixture of architectural influences: Hindu, Islamic and neoclassical. Usually the front of the house boasts large Corinthian or Ionic pillars with a baroque architrave. Entering the courtyard, you see the traditional Hindu *thakur dalan* (hall of worship) and the *nat mandir* (temple of dramatics). Then you encounter the *baithakkhana* (formal reception room) and the *jalsaghar* (the music and dance hall). Look upwards from the courtyard and there are arabesque grilles on the verandah leading to the zenana or the women's wing—an Islamic adaptation. Some of the rooms have Dutch tiles set half way up the wall or oak paneling; many of the windows are of colored glass for decorative effect and to reduce the glare of the tropical sun; the floor is either of marble or a mosaic. In the larger houses there may be an Italianate fountain or a Victorian nude statue decorating the terrace.

Babu (also spelt "baboo") was originally said to be a Persian honorific, conferred by the Mughal rulers of Bengal. During the early colonial period, the title continued to be used, as with Babu Nabakrishna Deb, the supporter of Clive. But from the later part of the

Babu's great house interior

eighteenth century, when the British consolidated their hold on empire, "babu" gradually acquired a pejorative generic meaning. For the British in Bengal, it came to signify a jumped-up Bengali attempting unsuccessfully to imitate his western superiors—rather as "nabobs" like Clive had attempted to imitate their social superiors in Britain.

Thus in England during the 1840s, where Baboo Dwarkanath Tagore (grandfather of the poet Rabindranath) was well known, Dickens joked to his friend Count D'Orsay that he feared to write "baboo" in case his pen made a slip and added an extra "n". Meanwhile in Bengal, Bhabani Charan Bandopadhyay's 1825 Bengali farce *Nabababubilas* (Follies of the Nouveaux Babus) depicted a budding babu who could write only a few elementary words in Bengali but liked to sprinkle his Bengali conversation liberally with English "goddamit" and "rascal" and expressions like "go to hell"—"babu" English picked up from a Eurasian teacher. The young babu's rich father provides him with palanquins and expensive clothes and he spends his days foppishly smoking the hookah in the company of sycophants and supplicants and his nights with dancing girls and prostitutes. And Bankim Chandra Chattopadhyay (Chatterjee), the most influential figure in nineteenth-century Bengali literature and himself an outstanding product of education in English, poked fun at the babus for their aping of western fashion in a brilliant essay:

> *We have exchanged the cumbrous forms of Bengali epistolary correspon-dence for those of Cook's* Universal Letter-writer, *and the tight-fitting jackets and loose-flowing* chapkans *of our grandfathers for shirts* à l'anglaise *and* chapkans *that are everyday steadily approaching towards the shape and size of English coats...*
>
> *In the houses built by English-educated Bengalis, the* poojah dalan *[hall of worship] is conspicuous only by its absence... Chairs, tables, punkahs—seldom meant to be pulled, American clocks, glassware of variegated hues, pictures for which the* Illustrated London News *is liberally laid under contribution, kerosene lamps, book shelves filled with Reynolds'* Mysteries, Tom Paine's Age of Reason *and the* Complete Poetical Works *of Lord Byron, English musical-boxes, compose the fash-ionable furniture of the Young Bengal.*

The Marble Palace shows how accurate Bankim Chandra's description was. Most of the babus were indeed superficial followers of fashion. The worst of them squandered their money on lavish pursuits such as washing their mansions daily with rose water, holding grand ceremonies for the wedding of their pet cats with fanfares, feasts and fireworks, and distributing expensive gold and silver-brocade saris woven in Varanasi (Benares) to the prostitutes of the neighborhood; Bengalis still relish these stories and tell them with gusto. But some of the babus were trendsetters who left a lasting impression on the life of Bengal. The best were discriminating patrons of the arts, who set up philanthropic societies, started serious, even polemical, newspapers and journals on contemporary issues, and campaigned for educational and social reforms. Their responsiveness to new thinking sharpened the natural agility of the Bengali mind.

Hence the word babu has ambiguous connotations, even today. It can mean a dandy and a poseur, or an intellectual and man of culture, depending on the context. It is the term by which servants address their employer. Calcutta taxi-drivers and prostitutes refer to their clients as babus. It is also a common and polite form of address; for example, the long-serving former chief minister of West Bengal, Jyoti Basu, was referred to as "Jyoti Babu"— both by admirers and detractors. Now the distinctive clothes of the nineteenth-century babu, long shunned by aspiring professionals, are again fashionable among Bengali men.

Kalighat Paintings

Not surprisingly, babu culture was a rich field for writers and artists. Western-educated Bengalis may have bristled at British contempt for babus, but they enjoyed lampooning them, particularly their humiliation by women. Rabindranath Tagore wrote some remarkable satirical short stories with babu characters, and his nephew, the painter Gaganendranath Tagore, Bengal's most talented cartoonist, painted a series of scathing cartoons depicting degenerate babus in the second decade of the last century (see Chapter 9). But the most famous caricatures of babus are from Kalighat.

As Calcutta became a stylish metropolis, it attracted fortune-seeking migrants from all over India, many of whom settled in the bazaars around the Kalighat temple. Folk painters or *patuas*—itinerant narrators of mythological stories—had long roamed rural Bengal with rolled-up canvas scrolls carrying "strip cartoons" painted on hand-made paper with vegetable and mineral dyes—to be gradually unrolled before the assembled village as the story was narrated. But such rustic entertainment did not work for visitors to the Kalighat temple and the more sophisticated urban population. To survive in the city, the *patuas*, like other craftsmen such as potters and wood carvers, took to painting and selling small icons and images, mainly from the Hindu pantheon. In the days before photography and cheap color printing, these *pat* paintings became popular souvenirs.

With growing demand, the chief *patua* would often sketch an outline in swift calligraphic brush strokes on a plain background, and leave members of his family to color it in. The paper changed from hand-made sheets to standard-sized paper milled at the Baptist Mission Press in Serampore, and imported water-based paints were employed. The *patuas* discovered how water-based colors blended through the capillary process, provided the surface was damp. This magical way of representing volumes on a flat surface endowed their paintings with vigor, sensuality and charm. Kalighat paintings are intriguingly modern. They may even have influenced twentieth–century European painters like Léger, Matisse and Modigliani through examples brought to Europe from Bengal by missionaries as examples of heathen icons.

During the nineteenth century, influenced by contemporary dramatic performances, the content of the Kalighat paintings branched out. Hindu gods and goddesses were still staple images, but the babus were fair game as well. Their dandyism is strongly satirized: the babu is seen as a spendthrift and fake gentleman. His oiled hair is nattily parted in Prince Albert style and his mustache glued symmetrically to his cheeks. The lower part of his body is draped in a decoratively bordered *dhoti* with fanned pleats, while on top he wears a fine Islamic *kameez*

Kalighat painting of a babu

or a European shirt. A pair of shiny pumps adorns his feet. In his hand he holds a hookah or a fragrant flower such as a rose, or a fancy walking stick.

Since Kali embodied female power, Kalighat painters often empowered their painted women by turning their suitors into charlatans and lap dogs. Women—both wives and mistresses—are often shown thrashing and trampling on worthless, vain men. In one famously witty Kalighat painting, there are no women but the preening babu poses outside his home immaculately attired with a hovering butterfly lured by the aroma of his Persian or European perfume. Behind him is an open window through which a band of Disney-esque muskrats can be seen playing drums in his empty room, signifying the babu's inner hollowness. When a scandal in babu society developed, the *patuas* might well depict it. The Tarakeshwar incident of 1873, in which a young wife was debauched by the head priest of a local temple and the wife was eventually murdered by her enraged husband, was a subject ideally suited for a moral Kalighat tableau. Most people bought one or two of these *pat* paintings, if not the entire series.

Kalighat painting is a unique documentation of aspects of ordinary life in Calcutta between 1800 and about 1930, when it finally faded away, swamped by printed reproductions. Among collectors, it was already admired as far back as the 1850s, the date of the first European and Russian collections, but it was not generally regarded as fine art. However, in recent decades it has often featured in the sale catalogues of auction houses, both in the West and in India, and there is a strong market for it now. Today there are no painters living around the Kali temple—but there is certainly a thriving cottage industry in Calcutta producing "original" Kalighat paintings!

Babu Dwarkanath Tagore

There may have been Kalighat *pat* paintings showing the extravagance of Babu Dwarkanath Tagore, at least judging by the existence of a contemporary (1830s) Bengali doggerel about the dinner parties thrown by Dwarkanath at his pleasure mansion in Belgachhia:

> *The garden villa at Belgachhia rattles a lot of cutlery.*
> *How can we ever know of such fun in feasting*
> *Enjoyed only by the Tagore Company?*

The villa was once the country house of Governor-General Lord Auckland. Dwarkanath had it redesigned and decorated by an English architect in European style, after he was refused entry to the recently established Bengal Club in the White Town. If the English did not want him, he would start his own club where he could freely associate with the whites and exclude those who did not interest him. It soon turned out that the most influential people in Calcutta society were happy to attend "Prince" Dwarkanath Tagore's parties, which became the talk of the town on account of their lavishness. Emily Eden, the lively sister of Lord Auckland, visited the Belgachhia villa more than once in 1836 and wrote:

all Calcutta got greatly excited, because the Governor-General was going to dine with a native. The fact of a native dining with a Governor-General is much more remarkable, and Dwarkanath is one of the very few that would even sit by while we were eating... Dwarkanath talks excellent English, and had got Mr Parker, one of the cleverest people here, to do the honours; and there were elephants on the lawn, and boats on the tank and ices in the summer house, and quantities of beautiful pictures and books, and rather a less burning evening than usual, and so it answered very well... we hear he gives remarkably good dinners to everybody else.

As a Brahmin, Dwarkanath is said not to have dined with his guests but waited until after they had departed, in deference to his mother's wishes, at least until her death in 1838.

The Belgachhia villa was sold to repay Dwarkanath's debts after his death. When it was auctioned in 1856, a wealthy Bengali family bought it, who still live there at 64B Belgachhia Road. The surrounding garden is much reduced, and the building has been greatly altered, but a special atmosphere somehow clings to the place.

What makes Dwarkanath (1794-1846) much more interesting than almost any of his babu contemporaries is not his wealth and extravagance, but his achievements and intelligence. Well educated in Persian and English, Dwarkanath was a successful zamindar who became an extraordinary entrepreneur willing to invest in new ventures as soon as he sensed a prospect, despite the stranglehold of the East India Company and British-run commerce. In 1828, while serving as a revenue agent for the Company, he launched into independent banking with some wealthy Bengalis and appointed William Carr as the bank's secretary. With Carr as his business partner he gave up his Company job and founded Carr, Tagore and Company in 1834. He monopolized coal mining in 1836 and compelled the East India Company to pay a higher price for his superior-quality coal; he pioneered tea-growing in Assam and sent his first shipment of tea to London in 1838; he supported India's first enterprise to build a railway; he owned several ocean-going ships which traded as far afield as China; and he promoted the Calcutta Steam Tug Association to help vessels navigate the perilous mouth of the Hugli up to Calcutta. (His old tug

Interior of the house of the Tagores at Jorasanko

equipment can be seen at the entrance of the Birla Industrial Museum in Gurusaday Dutt Road.) He also had the major share in a life insurance company, and owned two English-language newspapers.

As a patron of culture and major philanthropist, Dwarkanath supported a substantial number of charitable and cultural institutions, including the Asiatic Society, the Calcutta Medical College and the Sans Souci Theatre. By the time of his first voyage to Europe in 1842, traveling via Suez in his own steamship, he was a celebrity. He became friendly with Queen Victoria and King Louis-Philippe of France, met Sir Robert Peel, the British prime minister, had memorable dinners with writers such as Dickens and Thackeray, and became the first Indian to receive the freedom of the city of Edinburgh.

But in the end he was a prisoner of both the ostentatious babu culture of Calcutta and the imperial ruthlessness of a growing empire. Dwarkanath had a vision of bettering India's material prospects through collaboration with Europeans, including scientists and engineers, but he did not have the immense stamina required to see it through—perhaps no Indian could have done so in the mid-nineteenth century. Certainly none of his family shared his vision. When he died in London on his second visit, in 1846, his business empire collapsed, along with his reputation—so much so that even his progressive grandson Rabindranath, in spite of inheriting some of his grandfather's remarkable characteristics and pre-occupations, paid Dwarkanath no tribute in writing; indeed Rabindranath seems to have regarded his grandfather chiefly as a businessman who did well out of empire. Only very lately have Bengalis begun to appreciate Dwarkanath's true qualities. As Blair Kling, an American economic historian, perceptively observed:

> *In Calcutta he was the bold and uncringing political leader trying to whip up support for political action. In England he was the urbane diplomat, emissary from the people of India, playing the 'Grand Mogul', surrounded by his retainers, and exchanging gifts, courtesies, and hospitality as an equal... At the bottom, however, he believed [that]... the East India Company had exploited and robbed his people. On the other [hand he knew that] in the contemporary world the British alone could provide the best possible government for India.*

Young Bengal

Despite its predominant hedonism, there was an intellectual side to babu culture. Hindu College was founded in 1817 by a group of wealthy Bengalis, including Dwarkanath Tagore. It was the first institution of higher education in India dedicated purely to the study of European thought. Here, Indian young men were exposed, in English, to the works of Enlightenment philosophers and western literary figures, and were encouraged to cultivate critical thinking and individualism. In 1855, the college became Presidency College, near College Street in north Calcutta; it is still the best-known university institution in Calcutta, despite periods of turmoil and stagnation.

Hindu College created the nucleus of what would become a Bengali intelligentsia, known as Young Bengal, in the middle part of the century. By 1830, some 1,200 students had been educated there. These were the youth who supported the controversial minute written in 1835 by Macaulay, then a member of the governor-general's council. Macaulay advocated purely English education for India and the total rejection of the Oriental learning that had been supported by Hastings, Jones and others in the last decades of the preceding century, which Macaulay believed to be worthless nonsense. Like Macaulay, if for somewhat different reasons, the Hindu College graduates believed passionately in the beneficial effect on Indians of western education, despite the fact of British colonial exploitation. They actively aspired after the western liberal and democratic values they had studied at the college and the emotional freedoms discussed in western literature.

Two teachers exerted a particular influence. David Lester Richardson (1801–65) compiled a selection of British poetry, and the Hindu College students immediately began to read and discuss Shakespeare, Milton and Byron. Henry Louis Vivian Derozio (1809-31), a gifted Eurasian poet and teacher, was only 17 when he began teaching English literature in 1826. Born in Calcutta of part-Portuguese extraction, he had attended a school run by an eccentric Scottish dominie, David Drummond, and been inspired by his dialectical methods. Derozio infused his own pupils with liberal and skeptical ideas. Charismatic and of the same age as his pupils, Derozio's unconventional methods provoked a strong rebellion against orthodoxy. To the alarm of the older generation, Young Bengal became haughty and iconoclastic, speaking and writing only in English, wearing only European clothes, drinking alcohol and eating beef—and even converting to Christianity.

After these juvenile excesses, some fell back into orthodoxy, but others played a significant role in the making of Bengali literature. Having imbibed western literary notions and values, they began by writing in English. But in due course some individuals felt compelled to write poetry, novels and plays in Bengali, influenced by their knowledge of western and also Sanskrit literature. The poet Madhusudan Dutt (1824–73), famous for his sonnets, and Bankim Chandra Chatterjee (1838-94), who became a hugely popular novelist, led the field because they did not merely mimic western literary forms but were inspired to recreate them in Bengali, in language that broke free of earlier literary conventions. Both writers were determined to stretch vernacular literature beyond religious folk ballads and raise it to the level of the Sanskrit classics. Between them they gave birth to a group of sophisticated readers capable of critical literary analysis through the pages of numerous literary journals, especially Bankim's own *Bangadarshan* (Mirror of Bengal). During the second half of the nineteenth century, Bengal and Bengali babus began a period of frantic literary activity, whose apogee would be the work of Rabindranath Tagore.

The Cult of the Book

Despite the international success of Indian writing in English, the Bengali literary tradition remains strong. Are Bengalis perhaps the only people to observe a ceremony for initiation into literacy—*hateh khari*—in which the infant is given a chalk and a new slate and shown the magic of drawing its first Bengali letter on a *tabula rasa*? They also gift books to friends and relatives on the birth and death anniversaries of Rabindranath Tagore (May 7 and August 7) known as *kabipoksho* (fortnight of the poet) and as wedding presents. Calcutta even has a street name celebrating a passion for books—Bishwakosh (Encyclopedia) Lane in Baghbazar. It is named for Nagendranath Basu (1866–1938), a scholar who lived there and at the age of twenty took up the task of compiling a Bengali encyclopedia, which ran into twenty-two volumes and took twenty years to complete. A friend of mine, Prasanta Kumar Paul, is currently writing a multi-volume Bengali biography of Rabindranath: he started in 1982, has so far published eight volumes, and has another eighteen years of his subject's eighty years to cover.

The annual book fair held since 1975 during the early spring on the Maidan, Calcutta's central park next to Chowringhee, is a major cultural event lasting a week to ten days. Ordinary families go on a buying spree in both Bengali and English, especially for religious books, novels and adventure and fantasy fiction. Well over five hundred temporary book stalls, including those of some major foreign publishers, and other kinds of attraction catering for the crowds, spring up along the dusty avenues, and you need a map to get around. The stalls themselves replicate gateways, ghats, temples, pavilions and famous landmarks skillfully recreated out of bamboo and canvas. Such ingenuity turns the lung of Calcutta into a fairy-tale land. Here publishers meet their buyers in the tens of thousands, writers are sometimes mobbed during a book signing, and popular poets read to capacity audiences. After dark, there is an especially festive atmosphere with special illuminations, loudspeakers announcing the evening's events, and Tagore's songs playing in between. People meet, eat, buy a bag of books at a discounted price, and return home with a warm and cultured glow.

The other place to feel Calcutta's book buzz is College Street. Its name came from Hindu College (now Presidency College), and like Hindu College, College Street was laid out in 1817 partly with funds from a lottery. (Now it is officially called Bidhan Sarani after Bidhan Chandra Roy, the chief minister of West Bengal from 1948 to 1962.) Along this narrow and crowded street are three major educational institutions: Calcutta Medical College with a Doric frontage and Corinthian pillars, the Calcutta University Senate House, almost obscured by shops and hawkers, and Presidency College with second-hand book stalls along its railings selling everything from examination-test papers to the latest English paperbacks discarded by foreign back-packers. Some of the sellers are knowledgeable and do not display their rare books but will show them on request. They also search for books for a small premium; I have been fortunate more than once. I picked up my 1885 edition of *A Compendious Vocabulary of Sanskrit* compiled by a group of English Orientalists, from one of these stalls for a mere fifty rupees ten years ago.

Books have been sold here for over a century. In 1874, there were only two bookstores, by 1899 there were thirty-six, and now there are hundreds. The shabby pot-holed lanes in the area are full of small publishing houses, printing presses and bookbinders, creating both books and the little magazines of all kinds that proliferate in Calcutta. (They took over this role from Bat-tala, where printing began.) A library-cum-museum in nearby Tamer Lane is entirely dedicated to Bengali periodicals. Stacked from floor to ceiling, it holds 25,000 items, including a rare first edition of Bankim's *Bangadarshan* (1872). The place was started as a labor of love by Sandip Dutta in 1978, and for a nominal charge he allows you to browse his collection.

Coffee House Culture

After wandering around College Street, a cup of coffee at its well-known coffee house provides a pleasant and interesting break. Across the tram track along Bankim Chatterjee Street almost facing the Sanskrit College on College Square is a small but cavernous doorway, plastered with posters and political graffiti. As you climb a flight of worn-out concrete stairs you encounter yet more bookstores and small publishers, your ears pick up the sound of ceaseless chatter, and your nose fills with the aroma of coffee mingled with cigarette smoke. The coffee house itself is fairly dark, with windows on only one side. Beneath rows of gently revolving antiquated ceiling fans sit small groups of men and women around wooden tables, lingering over cups of quite good coffee and snacks, while turbaned waiters rush around replenishing their supplies.

The place was originally built to commemorate the prince consort's visit to Calcutta in 1890, and named, without apparent irony, the Albert Hall. During the nationalist period, it became a meeting place for patriots. But when it proved too small for political meetings, it was turned into a coffee house in 1944. As coffee was much dearer than tea, the habitual drink of the local students, the place offered sophistication and was intended as somewhere for a quiet drink and chat away from the noisy and dusty roadside tea stalls. But it quickly became the haunt of the city's intelligentsia.

Each group of drinkers tends to belong to the same institution or literary and artistic group or the same political party, with their very own devil's advocate for verbal combat, or what is known as *adda*. This word is hard to define, though *adda* is integral to Bengali life. Before the 1930s, Bengalis had *akhras* where men, particularly young men, would go regularly to build up their physical fitness and discuss the issues of the day with other men. But during the nationalist period these *akhras* became hotbeds of seditious activity and were discouraged by the government. So the more informal *adda*, which could take place anywhere from a lowly tea shop to a posh drawing room, took the place of the *akhra* and became a vital outlet for influencing political opinions. Today, in a less charged political atmosphere, *adda* is closer to a session of straightforward gossip, where both men and women simply enjoy a pleasant time exchanging anecdotes, chit-chat, knowledge and information. A good *adda* is refreshing and rewarding. And they still abound. In Calcutta you just have to keep your ear tuned and join in, if you want to—be it on a bus, in a railway carriage or on a park bench. *Addas* are safety valves that protect people from the hard realities of Calcutta life.

In the past some significant projects began life in talk within the walls of the College Street coffee house. Two important literary journals—*Ekshan* and *Krittibas*—were conceived here. Signet Press, an innovative Bengali publisher, used to bring its authors here in the late 1940s and 1950s. Soumitra Chatterjee, the stage and film actor best known for his work with Satyajit Ray, used to hold court in the coffee house in the early 1960s before he became a sought-after star. And around the same time Kamal Kumar Majumdar (1914-79), a major fiction writer and a superb raconteur would pull a crowd around his table with jokes in three languages, Bengali, English and French. These *adda* sessions were witty and inspiring for my generation.

Nowadays, as ever, many of the coffee drinkers are the rebels of today who in a few years will be the conformists of tomorrow— keeping alight, more dimly perhaps, the tradition of Young Bengal. Apart from studying and politics, most of them write, act and make music and films, nurturing their creative passions and private dreams of contributing to the cultural life of Calcutta. But sadly the coffee house is no longer a place for an artistic elite. There are fewer such people; life has become faster; and there are too many other distractions, including drugs and easy sex.

Chitpur Road

The buildings around the water tank on College Square are all connected with the cultural history of the city. There are the Hindu School (1817), the Sanskrit College (1817), the Bengal Theosophical Society (1882), the Mahabodhi Society Hall (1891) with its Buddhist architecture, the Jahan Khan Mosque, the University Institute Hall (1891)—a major forum during the nationalist period—and the Baptist Mission (1911), built in the so-called Indo-Saracenic style. The variety of religions in one place is typical of Calcutta's complicated heritage.

But the place to observe this urban activity at its most atmospheric, including some of the most traditional aspects of Calcutta life, is not College Street but the Chitpur Road (Chitpore), which runs very roughly parallel to College Street further to the west, towards the river. Chitpur Road is deeply Bengali, constantly displaying a great variety of human existence and emotion. As the chief magistrate of Calcutta, a Mr. Farran, wrote in 1836 (a description that is still largely applicable): "The Chitpur Road is the great thoroughfare, but it is narrow, winding, dirty and encroached upon, while the cross-ways are all lanes, very narrow, very filthy and bounded generally by deep open ditches." In some ways, it can be a repulsive road with crowds of people and animals and every sort of transport, ancient and modern, jostling together for space, but once one knows some of its history, the road pulsates with interest. One could say that it was on the Chitpur Road that babu culture began in the eighteenth century. (Chitpur Road is now known officially as Rabindra Sarani, though it is still widely known by its old name.)

Originally the road was a track to Chitpur surrounded by dense jungle that was infested with bandits and wild animals. Then, some time after 1610, a temple of the goddess Chitteswari was discovered and the route was improved when it became a pilgrim road connecting the Kalighat temple in the south with the Chitteswari temple in the north. Decades later, Gobindaram Mitra, a tax collector for the East India Company known as the Black Zamindar built a new temple called Nabaratna Mandir in this area with a tower 165 feet high. Dubbed the Black Pagoda, it served as a navigational landmark for early European sailors on the Hugli until its tower fell down in a violent storm in 1737.

After 1756, as the White Town began to expand around the city center, the Bengali inhabitants gradually moved further north. Along this road they began to build, and then in the nineteenth century to enlarge, their mansions in a medley of baroque, rococo and native architectural styles. In due course the Tagores of Jorasanko, the Tagores of Pathuriaghat, Rajendra Mullick (the builder of the Marble Palace) and many other zamindars erected family homes in lanes just off the Chitpur Road. The buildings associated with these three Bengali luminaries are still there, though none is now a family house: the Marble Palace is a private museum; the Pathuriaghat Tagore house (known as the Tagore Castle because its style is Scottish baronial) is on long lease to a Marwari businessman and predictably much altered; and the Tagore house at Jorasanko has been turned into a museum and university, known as Rabindra Bharati, dedicated to Tagore studies.

In 1879, Calcutta Tramways started to run trams along the road. These ramshackle old vehicles still trundle along beside numerous buses, taxis, auto-rickshaws, hand-pulled rickshaws and even bullock carts, carrying all sorts of products. In addition, Calcutta is the only city in India with man-pulled rickshaws, introduced by Chinese migrants in the 1900s. People use them for short local trips because they are not allowed beyond certain areas. There are cycle rickshaws, as well. Unlike the prettily decorated rickshaws from Bangladesh, those in Calcutta are dismally plain and battered. Migrant pullers hire rickshaws from their owners at a daily rate. Most of the rickshaws carry a curious notice in archaic English—"hypothecated to"—with the name of some organization. Curiously, all paperwork regarding the registration and licensing of rickshaws is conducted in forms written in English. During monsoon when the drainage system of the city collapses, rickshaws come into their own, carrying passengers to their water-logged destinations. The West Bengal Government tried to ban them in 1996 but caved in to a massive protest.

The shops on either side of Chitpur Road sell everything from human-hair wigs, long beards and mustaches to Mughal perfumes dispensed from beautiful cut-glass containers and musical instruments. At a tiny roadside stall, a man with hennaed hair partly covered by a laced prayer cap will offer you a sniff of his *attar* or essential oil that will

knock you out for a few seconds with the concentrated fragrance of a thousand roses. Walk along a bit further, while watching out carefully on all sides for the trams and motorized transport, and you will hear the familiar tune of *Tipperary* or *Auld Lang Syne* played on some kind of wind instrument—a small brass band has assembled to rehearse for a forthcoming Marwari wedding procession. The makers of musical instruments—the sitars, the sarod, the violin, the tabla and the harmonium—continue devotedly with their craft. Famous instrumentalists buy here, including Ravi Shankar; once, on his tour of India in 1952, the Chitpur Road craftsmen repaired Yehudi Menuhin's violin. Spend a few minutes observing a wizened man's rapt attention as he adjusts an obstinate string that persistently refuses to resonate to the musical note voiced by his assistant, and see their delight when it finally does. You have just been initiated into a key feature of Indian music: its closeness to the human voice—the basis of the system of ragas.

Many of these people are Muslims. They have always been a vital part of the area; the most important and the largest mosque in Calcutta, the red-painted Nakhoda Mosque, is here at the corner of Zakaria Street. Capable of holding ten thousand worshippers, the mosque was built less than a hundred years ago on the model of Akbar's tomb at Sikandra. A little beyond the mosque is the Royal Hotel famous for its authentic Mughlai cuisine. As the month of Ramadan approaches, the Muslim shops fill with beautifully gilded and bound copies of the Koran in gift boxes with carved wooden stands, intricate and dazzling waistcoats and caps embroidered with gold and silver, gleaming hookah pipes and heaps of sweet vermicelli, nuts, dates and pomegranates. It is a good place to buy *attar* (perfume), *surma* (kohl), a *kurta* (finely embroidered shirt) and *unani dawai* (traditional Islamic medicines) —to name but a few special items. During the violent communal riots around the time of independence, loyal Hindu neighbors protected many Muslims living in Chitpur Road. Nawab Muhammed Reza Khan, who died in 1798, had his magnificent palace here, which was described by the pseudonymous Sophia Goldborne, author of *Hartley House* (1789), as follows:

The exterior of Chitpore in some degree bespeakes the grandeur of its owner, but I am apprised that few things exceed the magnificence of its interior architecture and ornaments. The apartments are immense, the baths elegant and the seraglio, though a private one, suited in every particular to the rest of the building; nor must the gardens be unmentioned, for they not only cover a wide extent of ground but are furnished with all the beauties and perfumes of the vegetable kingdom.

Other areas around Chitpur Road include Chhatawala Goli, which used to have a Chinese population. Although they have now left, there are a few shops selling authentic ingredients for Chinese cooking, right next door to the shoe shops selling handmade leather shoes. I can still vividly recall the strange mixture of smells when visiting such shops as a child at the beginning of winter to get a soft pair of warm shoes suitable for the season. The old Chinese Sea Ip temple, to be mentioned later, is there too. A narrow entrance from the Lower Chitpur Road will lead you to the arcade of Tiretta Bazar, founded by a Venetian exile, Edward Tiretta in the 1780s. Once the Armenians and the Portuguese in Calcutta used to come here to buy exotic birds and leopard cubs, but now the place is full of electronic goods and furniture. Sonagachhi (literally, gold tree), Calcutta's oldest red-light area is also here, where the city's most popular sweet, the white spherical *rosogolla* soaked in syrup was supposed to have originated. Now you can buy *rosogollas* in a can. The babus would visit the prostitutes and frequently have one or two kept women in Sonagachhi (as satirized in the Kalighat paintings). When the Tagore house at Jorasanko was converted into a museum and university in the early 1960s, prostitutes were living in the vacant back quarters and had to be evicted.

It is here that Rabindranath Tagore was born in 1861 and here that he died eighty years later. The original part of the house was built in 1785, then it was renovated and much enlarged by a British company appointed by Dwarkanath Tagore (who wanted somewhere public for his glittering receptions), and after that it underwent many further changes, with one part being knocked down altogether in the 1950s. A *son et lumière* show in the grounds of the building gives the usual romantic interpretation of the history of the Tagore family. No. 6 Dwarkanath Tagore's Lane has certainly greatly changed from the place so evocatively conjured by the adult Rabindranath in his enchanted memoirs, *My Reminiscences* (1911). It still floods in the monsoon, however, like the neighboring Chitpur Road—just as it did a hundred years ago. As Tagore noted, in an indignant lecture in 1917:

> *The moment a monsoon breeze blows, our lane gets flooded right up to the main road. The wayfarer's shoes must be carried over his head like his umbrella, and it becomes clear that the inhabitants rank no higher in the struggle for existence than amphibious beasts... The moment the rains break, they start repairing the tramway. All laws ordain that what begins must have an end. This year, when they dug up the tracks again I saw the flood of water contending with the flood of humans on Chitpur Road and at last began to ponder deeply, Why do we put up with it?*
>
> *That we need not put up with it, and that it is better not to do so, becomes obvious if we once set foot in Chowringhee. It is part of the same town under the same municipality; the only difference is that we put up with it and they [the white residents] do not.*

Chitpur Road is thus emblematic of Calcutta—both in its cosmopolitanism and in its decay.

Kumortuli: Images of the Divine

One of the lanes leading from Chitpur Road towards the river goes to Kumortuli, a small neighborhood renowned for its pottery and clay image making. Where once it supplied clay images of gods and goddesses for the puja rooms of the great houses of the babus on Chitpur Road, now it makes them for the whole of Calcutta, especially at the time of Durga Puja. Kumortuli is the only surviving colony of artisans in the heart of north Calcutta and one of the oldest anywhere in the city; the potters originally came from the nearby districts of Bansbedey, Nabadwip, Shantipur and Krishnanagar in the second half of the eighteenth century when the Black Town began to develop. Some four thousand families of *kumors* (potters) live and work in its five acres.

Raja Krishna Chandra Ray (1710–82) of Nabadwip is said to have been the first in Bengal to worship grand clay images of the Hindu deities. Prior to this, following age-old Hindu tradition, the gods were represented symbolically, with a pot, a relic or a small painted picture. The rich babus of Calcutta seized on the new idea as a way of attracting attention and filling their newly built *puja dalans*. Ironically, they may have been encouraged by seeing the large European sculptures of figures from the classical Greek pantheon in the White Town. At any rate, these European sculptures seem to have inspired the image-makers to break with the stylization of Indian sculpture and try their hands at emulating the naturalism of western classical art. If you look at the images of some of the male deities at Kumortuli, before they are painted and decorated, you may notice that they are strikingly Apollonian; but the female forms are more traditional.

There is a ghat at the back of Kumortuli from which the image-makers collect mud from the Hugli. The bamboo for the core structure and the straw for the images come by river barge. At any time in Kumortuli, rows and rows of tiny workshops are stuffed with images in various stages of completion. You walk past mounds of gray mud, heaps of straw and bamboo and piles of clay limbs. A boy of ten or eleven with a very old penknife diligently makes a fine jeweled crown out of cheap gold foil and sequins; an old man and his wife create a bunch of white roses from the pith of *sola* reed (used in large quantity in colonial days for making pith helmets, *sola topees*). The potters, dressers and frame decorators construct the most fantastic tableaux out of mundane material with basic tools. The whole colony of artisans is like a large workshop for a drama production about the gods.

Nearly all the images are made to order—and not just for Calcuttans. These days Kumortuli has a global clientele, supplying images to Africa, America, Australia and Europe, wherever there are Hindu communities. The pith weighs little, so large images are regularly sent by air. Once settled in their new homes, the images are usually preserved for years, brought out annually for diasporic devotions as the exiles reminisce about festivals back in the home country.

Potters at Kumortuli

The *kumors* are kept busy throughout the year because there are a number of important Bengali festivals, especially for Saraswati, Kali (as already mentioned in the Introduction) and Durga; and when they are not making gods and goddesses, they fashion images of illustrious Indians like Mahatma Gandhi, anatomical models for medical teaching purposes, models for museums and galleries, and cheap fairground toys and dolls. My own favorite festival, which falls in January, is that of Saraswati, the goddess of learning and wisdom, venerated by Buddhists and Jains as well as by Hindus. Her white pith or clay image, symbolizing purity and truth, carries a book and a stringed musical instrument (*vina*) in her hands and rides a swan. It is worshipped for one day in almost every home and every educational institution; in poorer homes, in place of the traditional clay image, books are placed in a sanctified area and worshipped. While the rest of India generally worships Lakshmi, the goddess of wealth, much of Calcutta reveres Saraswati—an indication of the Bengali love of knowledge. Both are daughters of Durga.

Durga Puja

The busiest time in Kumortuli is from August until Durga Puja, which falls in October or November. This is the best time to visit the place, when the potters and their fellow craftsmen shape, paint, and resplendently decorate a multitude of images. When they are finished, a special group of coolies from the neighboring district of 24 Parganas comes to transport the idols safely from the workshop in Kumortuli to a waiting truck parked away from the narrow lanes of the neighborhood. Secured with ropes to a simple bamboo frame, the heavy clay images, some more than ten feet tall, are borne on the coolies' shoulders as they deftly avoid hazardous lampposts and the maze of overhead wires. By tradition, no other coolies are permitted to do the job.

Durga Puja is Calcutta's most important festival. The run-up begins after the monsoon during September with shops advertising the latest sari designs, billboards shouting out the latest CD music compilations, special *puja* numbers of popular periodicals, and Calcutta Radio broadcasting traditional *agamani* music to welcome the goddess back. As at Christmas, during Durga Puja people throng the shops in Chowringhee's New Market, in Gariahat, in College Street and other markets, to buy new clothes for the extended family including the servants and maids. Employees receive a special *puja* bonus to help them cover the expense. Expatriate Bengalis return home on holiday to see their families. The whole city delights at the return to her parents' home of Uma (another name of Durga), the wife of madcap Shiva, the ascetic god with matted hair who dresses only in a tiger skin with a snake round his neck. Uma brings her four children—two daughters Saraswati and Lakshmi, and two sons, the valorous Kartik riding a peacock, and Ganesh, the bringer of success, accompanied by his pet rat. All of them are faithfully depicted by the clay artists of Kumortuli. Durga herself is shown, as so often in Hinduism, with two contradictory aspects juxtaposed: she is the fierce ten-armed demon slayer riding a roaring lion, and also the demure married daughter calling on her parents with her four winsome children.

Durga Puja was apparently observed as far back as 1610, before the founding of Calcutta, by the Sabarno Roy Chaudhuris of Barisha-Behala, the original landowners who negotiated with Job Charnock in 1690. The story goes that after Clive's victory at the battle of Plassey in 1757, he wanted to make a grand gesture of thanksgiving but the only church in Calcutta, St. Anne's, had been demolished during the siege of the city. Clive consulted his supporter Nabakrishna Deb, who suggested that he make an offering at the feet of Durga at his house in Sovabazar. As a result, the annual Durga Puja at 36 Nabakrishna Street is still known as Company Puja.

When the city became wealthy, the new mercantile Bengali elite, the babus, saw Durga Puja as a splendid opportunity for public relations. The ceremony was held in their newly built *thakur dalans* in increasingly grandiose style. Even today it is impressive in certain private houses, with the arrival of the potters who place Durga inside the *thakur dalan*, closely followed by the dressers who deck her with home-dyed fabric, *sola* pith ornamentation and gold and silver foil. Since foil was an imported item, which came by mail (*dak* in Bengali), the process of dressing (*saj*) is still described as *daker saj*. A film, *Utsav* (*Festival*), made in 2000 by Rituparno Ghosh, sensitively captures the modern Durga Puja ceremony as observed in traditional homes in Bengal.

The first public *puja* was held in 1910 in Balaram Basu Ghat Road in north Calcutta. It was a conscious effort to make people identify their motherland Bengal with the goddess so as to give a religious impetus to the growing nationalist movement. The promoters of the ceremony practiced and displayed the arts of stick wielding, fencing and wrestling and cultivated a martial spirit, as they prepared to fight the British rulers. One such *puja* continues in Shimulia (Simla) Street in north Calcutta organized by a local fitness club: there, in 1939, the legendary nationalist Subhas Chandra Bose unveiled a twenty-foot-high image of the goddess. At another public *puja*, in Bokulbagan in south Calcutta, the special feature is very different; each year a different leading artist is asked to design the image and the decor.

Since independence in 1947, Durga Puja has slowly changed into more of a carnival than a religious festival. The temporary shrines (locally known as *pandals*) and the images funded by local subscription compete with each other for novelty of design and decoration. Even the face of the goddess takes on the likeness of some current film actress, while theater-style lighting dramatically surrounds her with the billowing clouds at the top of the Himalayan peak, Mount Kailash, where her domestic incarnation is said to reign. Calcutta is transformed, almost unrecognizably. Shops and eateries stay open all night; the streets are cleaned and well lit and perfumed with incense; songs and mantras are chanted through loudspeakers adding to the general din from the *puja pandals*. Even the West Bengal Electric Supply Corporation goes into overdrive and there is no power shortage during the five days of this festival. Daily papers publish maps showing the most important locations with ample advice on how to travel safely with children. The festival spirit continues in a new form in the multi-story tower blocks that have been changing the skyline of the city since the 1980s. An elected committee of residents collects the subscriptions, sets up the images and conducts the ritual meticulously, and in the evenings constructs a platform for everyone to display their performing talents. Would-be singers, dancers and actors can cut their teeth here, although the overall effort is amateurish. But communal lunches of *khichuri*—a savory and spicy mixture of rice and lentil—and dinners of *luchi*—a deep-fried puffy bread (also known as *puri*) with *alur dom* (curried potato) help neighbors to get to know each other and build a network of acquaintances.

On Bijoya Dashami, the last day of the festival, the city bids farewell to its divine visitor. All the images are carried through the city with riotous pageantry to be immersed in the waters of the Hugli. At the river the image is rowed out into midstream in two boats joined together. Then the boatmen and the bearers shout their last goodbye "Jai Ma Durga!"—"Victory to Mother Durga", the boats separate gradually, and the image slowly slides into the river. Tears of emotion well up as if you are parting with a loved member of your family. The boatman returns to the bank to collect the next idol in the queue for immersion, while the worshippers return to the empty shrine and celebrate the auspicious event. All night long, the immersion ceremony continues, as hundreds of images return to the river clay from which they were made. A few weeks later, their bamboo frames are fished out of the river by the potters of Kumortuli and stored away in their workshops, until it is time to create new images for the next festival of the goddess.

CHAPTER THREE

City of the Sahibs

Government House

During the nineteenth century, as babu culture evolved in the Black Town, the Europeans, especially the British, living in the White Town turned into "sahibs"—a word fraught with just as heavy a colonial baggage, if not more so, as "babus". Trade had brought Europe to the Gangetic delta and made Bengal the richest province of the British Empire. Now the rulers began to make Calcutta not just a wealthy town but a city they thought worthy to be their imperial capital.

The process began with the arrival of the flamboyant Marquis Wellesley as governor-general in 1798. An Anglo-Irish aristocrat educated at Eton and Christ Church, Oxford, he was an out-and-out imperialist. Within a month of reaching Calcutta and without proper consultation with the Company's court of directors in London, Wellesley ordered the construction of a grandiose Government House that would be a true symbol of power and authority, a headquarters fit for a mighty empire. His ally Lord Valentia provided the rationale: that India should be ruled from "a palace, not a counting house; with the ideas of a Prince"—and not with the parochial aims of a bunch of retail traders of muslins and indigo.

The first four governor-generals—Warren Hastings, Sir John Macpherson, Lord Cornwallis and Sir John Shore—had resided in Buckingham House, a mansion to the west of Chowringhee rented from Reza Khan, the nawab of Chitpur. Wellesley kept this location and also bought the surrounding land. Hickey reported in his memoir:

> *His Lordship... determined upon building a palace suitable to his magnificent ideas, and such a one as would be proper for the residence of the British Governor-General of India. This he immediately caused to*

*be commenced, partly upon the site of the old Government House, but
taking in the Council House and about sixteen other handsome private
mansions, many of them not having been erected about five years, the
whole of which were pulled down, the ground upon which they had
stood being cleared away to create a superb open square, in the middle
of which his meditated palace was to stand.*

When completed in 1802, Wellesley's palace, designed by Captain
Charles Wyatt, appeared identical to Robert Adam's Kedleston Hall in
Derbyshire (built in the 1760s). But there were differences in the minor
details. For example, the light in the upper rooms of Kedleston Hall
comes through skylights, while the equivalent rooms in Calcutta's
Government House receive light through normal windows.
Appropriately, a century later, Lord Curzon, the owner of Kedleston
Hall, came to live in Government House as viceroy of India, and placed
urns along its roof tops to make the Bengal copy look as close to its
English original as possible.

The building was well described in 1810 in *Journal of a Residence
in India* by Maria Graham (later Lady Calcott):

*The lower storey forms a rustic basement, with arcades to the building,
which is Ionic. On the north side there is a handsome portico, with a
flight of steps, under which carriages drive to the entrance; and on the
south there is a circular colonnade with a dome. The four wings, one at
each corner of the body of the building, are connected with it by circular passages, so long as to secure their enjoying the air all around, from
whatever quarter the wind blows. These wings contain all the private
apartments; and in the north-east angle is the council room, decorated,
like the family breakfast and dinner rooms, with portraits. The centre of
the house is given up to two rooms, the finest I have seen. The lowest is
paved with dark grey marble, and supported by Doric columns of
chunam, which one would take for Parian marble. Above the hall is the
ballroom, floored with dark polished wood, and supported by Ionic
columns of white chunam. Both these fine rooms are lighted by a profu-
sion of cut-glass lustres suspended from the painted ceilings, where an
excellent taste is displayed in the decorations.*

When the "the cheese-mongers of Leadenhall Street"—Wellesley's contemptuous nickname for the court of directors in London—received bills for sums such as £71,000 (for purchase of the land), £87,000 (for construction), £18,000 (for furnishing), and more than £3,000 merely for the development of adjoining roads, they were not amused. (The chandeliers mentioned above were second-hand, from the palace tomb in Lucknow of Colonel Claude Martin, eclectic Indophile and benefactor of the La Martinière schools in Calcutta, who owned seven palaces and a harem. Perhaps they were Wellesley's concession to the Company's audit, despite his personal dislike of the French.) The decorations included not only monumental lions and sphinxes but also—Wellesley being a man of refined classical taste—twelve busts of Roman emperors, including Caligula and Nero (captured from a French ship), displayed on plinths in the marble hall. At night, apparently, the governor-general would wander alone among these eminences while contemplating the governance of India, both military and political. Government House's deliberate flaunting of imperial aspirations through its neoclassical architecture, set the style for grand colonial buildings in India.

Rajyapal Bhavan, formerly Government House

Like the pharaohs at the temple of Karnak in Egypt, most of the governor-generals of India who succeeded Wellesley put their personal stamp on their stately residence. The gravel for the paths, for instance, was imported from Bayswater by Lord Hastings; a Chinese cannon mounted on a dragon decorating the front terrace was provided by

Lord Ellenborough; gas and hot-water supplies were installed by, respectively, Lords Elgin and Northbrook; while Ladies Amherst, Bentinck and Mayo designed the gardens, which included hiding the building behind a screen of trees. So it remains to this day. The chief Indian contribution, after the ending of the British Raj in 1947, seems to have been to change the building's name to Rajyapal Bhavan, meaning "House of the State Governor", incongruously abbreviated as Raj Bhavan since the building now houses not India's ruler but merely the governor of the (Marxist) state of West Bengal. Access to visitors is restricted; five of the six gates, two each to the east and west and one each to the south and north, are usually kept closed for security, but a visitor's permit can be obtained in advance through the nearby governor's secretariat.

The false silver dome built over the roof as an added impressive feature became an apt object of satire in Sir Charles D'Oyly's verses about the life of a neophyte Company servant in Bengal (*Tom Raw the Griffin: A Burlesque Poem in Twelve Cantos, illustrated by Twenty-Five Engravings*, London, 1828):

> *One word about the dome, 'tis so superior*
> *In every way to domes of brick or stone;*
> *It covers nought below! but ripens sherry or*
> *Madeira; —a wood box, perched up alone*
> *To aid proportion, and for dumpiness t'atone.*

To celebrate the Peace of Amiens, the state rooms of Government House were illuminated for the first time on January 26, 1803 on the occasion of a grand ball. Lord Valentia had arrived in Calcutta that same day and wrote about the party in his *Voyages and Travels*:

> *About 800 people were present, who found sufficient room at supper, in the marble hall below, thence they were summoned about one o'clock to the different verandahs to see the fireworks and illuminations. The side of the citadel facing the palace was covered with a blaze of light... The rockets were superior to any I ever beheld. They were discharged from mortars on the rampart of the citadel. The colours, also, of several of the pieces were excellent; and the merit of singularity, at least, might be*

attributed to a battle between two elephants of fire, which by rollers were driven against each other.

Teachers and Missionaries

Governor-General Wellesley sincerely believed that he was bringing the torch of enlightenment to the backward peoples of India. His zeal motivated his founding of Fort William College in 1800. As mentioned earlier, its official aim was to educate young Company servants in matters of government, languages, religion and science as pertaining to India, and at the same time to segregate them from the corrupting influence of native culture. This the college effectively did for some time, while inadvertently nourishing Orientalist scholarship and, in due course, modern Indian literature, particularly in Bengali. But soon a controversy arose between Orientalists and Anglicists over the value of promoting the study of any aspect of the indigenous culture of India, given the evident superiority of western civilization. There were British supporters on both sides of the debate, but progressive Bengalis supported only western-style education. They united with the Anglicists on the British side and together mounted a successful campaign in favor of English education. During the first four decades of the nineteenth century, official support for Orientalist scholarship severely declined; its death-knell came with Macaulay's supremely confident 1835 minute on education, which declared in favor of the Anglicists that the Company should aim to create "a class of persons Indian in colour and blood, but English in tastes, in opinions, in morals, and in intellect… who may be interpreters between us and the millions we govern."

Christianity was the other major force for propagating western cultural supremacy, though with markedly less impact than English education. Unlike their predecessors, the new generation of British actively condemned Hindu practices such as the cult of Kali and suttee (the burning of widows) as idolatrous and barbaric, and some felt a moral compulsion to redeem Hindu souls through conversion to faith in Jesus Christ. Their belief—at first implicit but increasingly public—was that divine providence had granted Britain the stewardship of India, and therefore the British in India had a duty to reform Indians.

Missionaries began to arrive in droves. We have already encountered William Carey, an early missionary who left a significant legacy in Bengal by publishing works in Bengali at his Mission Press in Serampore. Brought up as a cobbler, he took to preaching and with eleven friends founded the Baptist Missionary Society in 1792, and was promptly sent to India with a neurotic wife and four children, all dependent on a meager fifty-rupee allowance from the society. When survival on this income proved too tough, he turned to farming and made assiduous efforts to till land in the marshy mouths of the Ganges known as the Sunderbans—until an indigo planter relieved him from his hopeless endeavor and put him in charge of one of his out-factories in Maldah district near Calcutta. Now, in his spare time, Carey was able to preach and translate the Holy Scriptures into Bengali.

In 1799, two other missionaries, William Ward and Joshua Marshman, a painter's apprentice and a shop boy, reached India, and the following year the three men founded the Mission Press, chiefly to print evangelical literature in local languages. Between 1801 and 1832, the Mission Press printed tens of thousands of books in more than forty languages including Armenian. It also published, in 1818, the first weekly and monthly news bulletins in Bengali: *Samachar Darpan* (News Mirror) and *Digdarshan* (General Review). In 1807, Carey was appointed professor of Bengali at Fort William College (though at a salary lower than that of his European colleagues), where in due course he produced an English-Bengali dictionary as well as many literary texts. He died in 1834 aged seventy-four and was buried in the mission cemetery at Serampore. A small museum displaying some of his publications and personal belonging exists in the college at Serampore founded by the missionaries in 1818, which was the first Christian theological college in India. But most of Carey's favorite haunts are now either covered by the Hugli or by jute mills.

The activities of the missionaries—who always came low in the imperial social pecking order—did not impinge directly on the "pukka sahibs". But the lives and attitudes of the Company's civil and military employees were changing too, in line with the increase in English evangelical fervor. Gone were the days when an Englishman smoked a hookah while watching nautch girls, kept a harem, conversed fluently in a native tongue and made his fortune out of collaborating with local intermediaries, his *munshi* and his *banian*. The new breed of Company servant, under the tutelage of Wellesley, suspected such close contact with the natives. The prospects for Indians working in the service of the Company were gradually curtailed through a series of restrictive acts.

The group that suffered most from this policy were the Eurasians, children of mixed Indo-British parentage. (Today in India they are generally known as Anglo-Indians, but during the British Raj the term Anglo-Indian was used for the British working and living in India.) Already despised by Indians for being of mixed race, the Eurasians were now discriminated against by the British too, who felt that their presence in the Company's service would diminish the Company's prestige in the eyes of the "natives". In general, Eurasians were no longer allowed to hold higher office in the army and in the civil services; and their children were no longer encouraged to go to England to study or settle.

Yet in spite of their diminished status, they continued to contribute to the maintenance of colonial authority. They remained loyal soldiers, familiar with the local languages and climate. Later in the nineteenth century, they formed the majority of staff running the developing railway system. During the twentieth century, they became an asset to Indians as teachers in the public (i.e. elite English-medium) schools of India, which continue to thrive in the subcontinent by adhering sincerely to the spirit of Macaulay's minute on education. At the La Martinière schools in modern-day Calcutta, for instance, the majority of the pupils are Hindu, but the general character of the institution is "Christian". Most pupils leave the school imbued with a Protestant ethic towards work and a fairly good knowledge of western literature, arts and science but little grasp of the Indian literary and cultural heritage (though recently efforts have been made to redress the balance). After three years at college, many of them receive offers from abroad and leave Calcutta at the earliest opportunity, mostly forever.

A Day in the Life of a Sahib
Here is a sketch of the typical life of a pukka sahib in Wellesley's time, drawn from contemporary sources. The gates of an officer's residence would be opened by his doorkeeper (*darwan*) at about 7 a.m. and his domestic staff would begin to arrive, such as the stewards (*sirkars* and

khansamas), cooks (*baburchis*), hookah bearers, messengers and errand boys (*hurcarrahs*). The manager (*jemadar*) would knock on his bedchamber door at 8 a.m., when his lady would quit his side.

As soon as he arose, he would be greeted by salaams from all quarters. After he had bathed, the servants would fuss around him with items of apparel, and the barber would attend to his beard, hair and nails. If meanwhile someone of similar rank were to arrive on urgent business, the servants would offer him a chair and afterwards the visitor might share some breakfast and a smoke with the sahib. Such sessions would continue till 10 a.m. when, attended by an entourage, the sahib would be conducted to his palanquin. There he would be greeted with more salaams from the bearers and then, riding on their shoulders, he would proceed towards his office and conduct his official duties until 2 p.m., when he would return home for a hearty lunch. During the meal a good deal of imported wine would be drunk, after which the sahib would most likely feel a strong urge to recline and take repose. According to Eliza Fay, the wife of a Calcutta barrister, writing home in a letter in 1817:

> the custom of reposing, if not sleeping, after dinner is so general that the streets of Calcutta are, from four to five in the afternoon, almost as empty of Europeans as if it were midnight. Next come the evening airings on the course, where everyone goes, though sure of being half-suffocated with dust. On returning thence, tea is served, and universally drank here even during the extreme heats. After tea, either cards or loo fill up the space till ten, when supper is usually announced. Formal visits are paid in the evening; they are generally very short, as perhaps each lady has a dozen calls to make and a party waiting for her at home besides. Gentlemen also call to offer their respects, and if asked to put down their hats, it is considered as an invitation to supper.

As for the ladies, on leaving the sahib's bed in the morning his partner would move through a private staircase either to her own apartment (assuming that the sahib was her husband) or to the courtyard (if the liaison was a casual one). The lady of the house would naturally have her own maids to help her with an elaborate toilet, after which the day would pass in supervising the servants, especially the cooks, gardeners and *ayahs* (nannies), and attending to her correspondence, as well as talking to her children and receiving visitors for gossip.

The most senior of the sahibs were as extravagant in their display of pomp and pageantry as the nawabs who had preceded the Company as the rulers of Bengal. Sir Gilbert Elliot, the first Lord Minto, governor-general from 1807-13, became irritated at the fuss and bother required of his position, as he recorded in a letter in 1807:

> *I drive out almost every evening, but the formality of this airing is uncomfortable to a degree that I cannot at all accustom myself to. Four syces [grooms] with fly-flappers ran alongside the horses until I positively rebelled against this annoyance. It is still worse with a palanquin. Thirty people go before in two lines, which extend a great way forward. They carry gold and silver maces and halberds and embroidered fans and cow's tails to keep the flies off. All these run on foot at a round trot, some of them proclaiming my titles: which, as the proclamation is rather long, I imagine must be Hindustanee for "Gilbert Elliot, Murray of Melgund and Kynymound of that ilk".*

The grandest households, when on the move, required at least half a dozen elephants, a dozen camels and several well-groomed horses to pull the carriages, some bullocks to pull the carts carrying luggage, and of course a big body of servants to manage all this palaver. On water, senior officials would travel, for both pleasure and business, in grand barges with a flotilla of lesser boats transporting their entourage. In Calcutta itself, however, no elephants were allowed, "on account of the frequent accidents which they occasion by frightening horses," according to Bishop Heber, writing in the 1820s.

Whatever Minto's reservations, increasingly impressive shows on land and water became a hallmark of the British Raj, by which the image of the sahibs as mighty governors was bolstered up and the strength of their determination to alter existing ways of life was proclaimed. Even a small English boy would be paraded on Calcutta's Maidan for exercise on a splendidly caparisoned pony with his *ayah*, coachman, umbrella bearer, watchman, a couple of *syces* and several other attendants on hand in case the little lord had any untoward encounter. While this did bring the sahibs into close contact with Indians, the relationship was always that between master and servant—which generally reinforced, rather than broke down, existing racial prejudice. The more the British became politically dominant in India, the more insular they became.

Belvedere and Alipur

You can still conjure up the arrogant atmosphere of that time by taking a tour through the exclusive area south of the Maidan named Belvedere and, beyond it, Alipur (named by Siraj-ud-Daula after his attack in 1756), reached by crossing the bridge over Tolly's Nullah beyond the Royal Calcutta Turf Club. There you will see spacious colonial-style houses set back behind tall trees in private grounds. Of course, they are no longer occupied by the British, nor even by many Bengalis: the wealthy owners generally belong to other communities, in particular the Marwari and Punjabi business elite.

The current mansion at Belvedere is believed to stand on the site of a summer house belonging to Prince Azim-us-San, the grandson of the Mughal emperor Aurangzeb. After the battle of Plassey, when Clive restored Mir Jafar to the throne of Bengal, the nawab made over his entire property at Alipur to Hastings as a gesture of gratitude for the Company's protection. Around 1778, Hastings sold his house and the garden—now called Belvedere House and clearly marked on Upjohn's map of Calcutta in 1793—to Major Tolly, who did not have the chance to enjoy his purchase because he died soon after. The property then passed through the hands of several European owners, with much alteration until it was bought by the Company in 1854 and remodeled as an Italianate palace, the official residence of the lieutenant-governor of Bengal. Its guests now included visiting British heirs to the throne (the future Edward VII and George V) and the Russian czar Nicholas II. After the capital of India moved to Delhi in 1911, viceroys visiting Calcutta would use Belvedere as a winter residence for holding glittering Christmas parties in its 114-foot-long Durbar Hall.

The National Library, current occupant of Belvedere House, took possession in 1953. Since then, regrettably, the grounds have been spoilt by the construction of an ugly towering annex for the Central Reference Library and the library staff's housing quarters. Still, the sweeping steps up to the library are impressive. This is where, in 1989, President François Mitterrand of France invested Satyajit Ray with the Legion of Honour, and where you will also see a memorial tablet for John Macfarlane, the celebrated librarian of the Imperial Library of colonial India. The reading room on the right is a beautiful colonnaded hall with galleries on either side. The library houses over two million books and some rare manuscripts and caters for a readership of more than a hundred thousand. It also has a good website.

The surrounding gardens of the Agri-Horticultural Society, founded by William Carey and Ramkamal Sen in 1820, contain some ancient trees, and the plants and shrubs are lovingly maintained by dedicated gardeners. There are pleasant paths set among aromatic plants and subtropical flowers and one can purchase specimens from a shop. The flower show held here every winter is a major social event.

Visible from the library is the small and neat entrance to the Zoological Gardens. Conceived by Sir Richard Temple, the energetic lieutenant-governor of Bengal from 1874-77, it was inaugurated by one of his royal house guests, Edward, prince of Wales, on January 1, 1876. Founded by a private voluntary society, the Zoological Gardens spread over nearly a hundred acres and house a good collection of birds, reptiles and mammals, though their past reputation for excellence has not been maintained. Even so, the place is still popular with locals for a weekend family picnic and a look at a Royal Bengal Tiger, the magnificent creature that was once such a popular quarry for imperial sportsmen. After dark, loud growls from the cages can still be disconcerting for pedestrians.

Around this area, near the west gate of the National Library, Hastings and his bitter opponent Philip Francis, a member of the governor-general's council, fought their famous but inconsequential duel on August 17, 1780, as witnessed by Colonel Pearce (who, in the manner of those earlier days, had an Indian wife and a son by her who studied in England). Around here, too, the novelist William Makepeace Thackeray, as a young child played peekaboo with his *ayah* in the cool and shady walks of his father's house (there is an inscription on the house) before being sent home to England after his father's death. Richmond Thackeray was secretary of the Company's Board of Revenue. Today, the area has been taken over by offices of the police and army; even in British times it housed the Presidency Jail, to the east of Belvedere, where most hangings were carried out during the troublesome final decades of the Raj.

Nearby, much altered, is Hastings House, now a teaching college for women. It is associated with a famous ghost story. An apparition of Hastings was for a while seen driving up every evening in a coach-and-four in search of some personal belongings, noted H. E. A. Cotton in his *Calcutta Old and New*. A curious corroboration of this story was found in a letter from Hastings to his private secretary Nesbitt Thompson dated July 21, 1785, expressing anxiety about the lost contents of one of his bureaus. In spite of a good deal of effort, the missing contents—a couple of miniature paintings and some private papers—were never found. The Hastings Chapel, built in 1855 and now overshadowed by a recently built fly-over on the approach to the second Hugli bridge (Vidyasagar Setu) and a government staff housing complex, is worth a visit for its simple but dignified appearance amidst a fast-changing cityscape. At the time of Hastings, the 70-year-old Raja Nandakumar (Nuncomar) was hanged in this area following a miscarriage of justice. Here too, Sir William Jones would walk from his home in Garden Reach to his judge's chambers.

The Race Course and the Clubs

To the east of the fly-over, in the southwestern part of the Maidan, is the Race Course. Until 1818, races were run before sunrise to avoid the heat of the day. The Bengal Jockey Club was founded in 1803 and maintained the course until 1847, when the Royal Calcutta Turf Club took over. There are three stands. You can almost forget you are in Calcutta as you look out towards the Maidan from the main viewing pavilion with its three tiers, fancy turrets and wrought-iron railings, and your gaze falls on the imposing marble monument to Queen Victoria known as the Victoria Memorial (of which more later). The original viewing stand was built as long ago as 1820, though it has been much refurbished. On race days the stand becomes full of hopeful punters, almost all of them male, ranging from rich to hard-up and flashing anything from a single ten-rupee note to wads of many hundreds of rupees while the dusty air resounds with the harsh jargon of the bookies. Gone are the days of the Viceroy's Cup when spectators were admitted by invitation only. Even as late as the 1960s, the Calcutta racing scene was still a glamorous affair, in which Indian princes in designer sunglasses arrived in shining Rolls Royces with their European guests. Here is Laura Sykes, the daughter of a British high commissioner, reminiscing about such an occasion:

As a young girl based in Delhi, I was sent by my father in best debutante fashion, to stay with some friends and 'do' the Calcutta winter season. A large part of each week was devoted to deciding what to wear at the races the following Saturday, but nothing I could come up with could beat the splendour of my competitors... I particularly remember His Highness of Cooch Behar's American wife, who looked stunning in an absolutely pale yellow chiffon sari with a magnificent choker of old Jaipur enamel work.

The colonial ambience is still precariously alive in small pockets of today's Marxist city such as the Bengal Club, the Tollygunge Club and the guest houses like Fairlawn's where English food and English speech still rule the day. Luncheon comes here with soup and sherry, while the Indian buffet is available only on Wednesdays. In his *Abdul's Taxi to Kalighat*, Joe Roberts provides a vignette of Fairlawn's:

Ted sat beside her, wearing a blazer (his handkerchief pushed up the sleeve) and cavalry twill trousers. Ted often looked startled. His eyebrows wavered constantly above his glasses and his handsome bucolic face. A native of Northamptonshire, Ted had been a Chindit, a member of General Wingate's commando force in Burma. He was, recognisably, a gentleman in the foggy manner of the shires; not a bookish man, perhaps, but unswervingly decent.

The Bengal Club, founded in 1827, is now reduced to the back of the site of Macaulay's old house in Chowringhee. Each room here comes with a bearer, and one must obtain temporary membership through another member to enjoy the privilege of this oldest survivor of colonial Calcutta's social clubs. Until 1962 it did not take Indian members. Expensive, and now a sought-after haunt for rich Indians, the club is worth a visit for its feeling of bygone days in its grand dining room, deep green leather sofas and sturdy porcelain bathtubs.

Fort William

Although the Maidan is generally regarded as a green space like London's Hyde Park, the lung that helps Calcutta to breathe, it was conceived strictly for military purposes. The space had to be large enough and level enough to offer an unrestricted field of fire from Fort William in case the fort was attacked. The original fort, started by Job Charnock and named after William III, was damaged during the siege of Calcutta in 1756. The new fort was built, not on the same spot at the center of White Town, but slightly to the south of it in Govindpore, on a site selected by Clive for strategic reasons. The thriving Bengali community there were reluctantly persuaded, with financial compensation, to move north towards Sutanuti, taking along their "tutelary deity Gobindjee and its historic shrine".

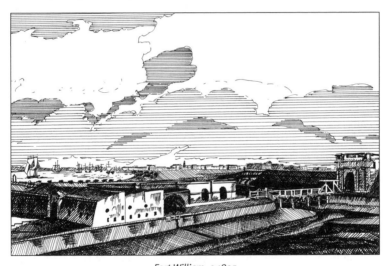

Fort William, c.1805

It took thirteen years, until 1773, and an astonishing two million pounds to complete the job. For obvious reasons, cooperation from local workers and suppliers was grudging, and eventually the Company had to use forced labor. A substantial part of the money was spent to "ward off encroachment by the river, which as it happens, has receded in exactly the opposite direction," noted Cotton in *Calcutta Old and New*. But the European residents of Calcutta were impressed. As witness, take one Mrs. Fay, who lived in Calcutta from 1780 and wrote to England about Fort William in enthusiastic terms:

> *As you come up past Fort William and the Esplanade, it has a beautiful appearance. Esplanade Row, as it is called, which fronts the Fort, seems to be composed of palaces; the whole range, except what is taken up by the Government and Council Houses, is occupied by the principal gentlemen in the settlement, no person being allowed to reside in Fort William but such as are attached to the Army. Our fort is also so well kept and everything in such excellent order, that it is quite a curiosity to see it, all the slopes, banks and ramparts are covered with the richest verdure, which completes the enchantment of the scene.*

Although the fort still impresses military historians, to most people it is not particularly striking. Its shape is that of an irregular octagon— with three sides facing the Hugli and five facing the Maidan—and seven gates, surrounded by a defensive ditch designed to be easily filled with water by opening a sluice from the river. It could apparently hold a garrison of ten thousand men. Seen from the top of the highest point on the Maidan, the 152-foot Ochterlony Monument, now known as Sahid Minar (martyrs' memorial), Fort William appears like a small walled town. The Ochterlony Monument was built from public subscription in 1828 to honor Major-General Sir David Ochterlony (1758-1825), the conqueror of Nepal. Half-Scots and born in Boston, Massachusetts, Ochterlony not only had a passion for Islamic architecture, but also embraced other native cultural practices: he had thirteen wives in his harem and is known to have paraded them on thirteen elephants. From the summit of this fine brick-built column a panoramic view of the city opens up. The architecture is Islamic, with an Egyptian-influenced plinth, a Syrian-style column and a metallic Turkish cupola. Eighty-two *sal* logs, each twenty feet long and driven eight feet into the ground, are supposed to have supported the Monument's primary foundation. A strong teakwood frame containing eight feet of solid masonry forms the base of the steps. Mark Twain in his travel journal *Following the Equator* (1897) wrote effusively about this "cloud-kissing monument". You need special permission to climb its 218 steps.

The walls of the fort are checkered with tablets commemorating British military successes in India, but Fort William itself was never besieged after 1756 and never fired a cannon at a real enemy—not even during the Sepoy Mutiny of 1857. Although on that occasion the neighboring garrison at Barrackpur was rumored to be on the march towards Calcutta, and the terrified British population of the city flocked into Fort William for refuge, in Calcutta itself the mutiny was a non-event.

The fort is out of bounds to casual visitors because it is the military headquarters for the eastern region of India. But one can obtain a permit from the army authorities with a week's advance notice. Inside, in addition to the usual network of regimental barracks and munitions stores, Hastings built a huge granary, part of a chain of stores proposed for the whole of British India, to mitigate the suffering from famines such as the terrible one that devastated Bengal in 1770. The fort was later used for a period as a military prison. There is also an army museum displaying weapons and photographs of battles; and the living quarters of Lord Kitchener, who was commander-in-chief of the Indian Army from 1902-09. On a Sunday morning, it is common to see a troop of cavalry exercising and drilling their horses in a manner reminiscent of the Company-style drawings that show scenes of life inside the fort during its early days.

Contrary to popular assumption, Fort William College was never located here, but was always housed in the Writers' Buildings (see p.13) on the southern side of BBD Bag, then a military parade ground for the Company. Nor did the college last long in the form originally conceived by Wellesley. The court of directors in London overruled Wellesley and decided that future "Indiamen" should be trained not at Fort William College but in England. In 1806, they founded a college that soon settled at Haileybury, and the college in Calcutta was quickly reduced to being merely a place for learning the Oriental languages required by the Bengal service of the Company.

Calcutta's Churches: Armenians and Anglicans
Two other buildings within Fort William are St. Peter's Church (1835), which has been converted into the fort's library, and St. Patrick's Church, which is disused. Although neither building is now used for

worship, this is not true of Calcutta's many other churches more than half a century after the end of the British Raj. While it is a fact that Christianity has made much less impression on India than many other ideas brought by the European colonizers, there is nevertheless an active Christian presence in Calcutta.

The Armenians merit first place here. They had been settlers in India from very early on, having apparently come as economic migrants from Persia. Their loyalty and integrity greatly impressed Akbar, the Mughal emperor, who took as a queen an olive-skinned Armenian, Mariam Zamani. In 1562, the community erected its first church in India, at Agra.

An old tombstone in the graveyard of the Armenian Church in north Calcutta suggests that Armenians may have been living in the area as early as 1630, and were certainly there before Charnock. They were the first local people to lend money to the Company in Bengal. Such was their keenness to show allegiance to the East India Company and later to the British Crown that the community received many favors and flourished. Hence the following generous concession made to the Armenians by the East India Company on June 22, 1688:

Whenever forty or more of the Armenian nation shall become inhabitants of any garrison cities, or towns, belonging to the company in the East Indies, the said Armenians shall not only enjoy the free use and exercise their religion, but there shall also be allotted to them a parcel of ground to erect a church thereon for worship and service of God in their own way. And that we also will, at our own charge, cause a convenient church to be built of timber, which afterwards the said Armenians may alter and build with stone or other solid materials to their own good liking. And the said Governor and Company will also allow fifty pounds per annum, during the space of seven years, for the maintenance of such priest or minister as they shall choose to officiate therein.

To celebrate one of George III's temporary recoveries from madness an Armenian merchant in Calcutta, Catchick Arrakiel, put on such a brilliant display of fireworks and illuminations in the city that Governor-General Cornwallis felt curious to know what lay at the bottom of his loyalty. Arrakiel replied that the protection of His

Majesty had enabled him to amass a vast fortune—enough for his son to maintain a standing army of a hundred volunteers to supplement the British army in times of need. Both father and son are buried in the grounds of their church.

The Armenian Church, formally known as the Church of Holy Nazareth, dates from 1724 and was erected by voluntary subscription raised under the auspices of Aga Nazar to replace a wooden chapel of 1707, built near a ghat still known as the Armenian Ghat close to the old Chinese market in north Calcutta. It is thus the oldest existing place of Christian worship in Calcutta, since St. Anne's Church, built in 1709, was destroyed in 1756.

The church is an oasis of peace amidst the frenzied atmosphere of Armenian Street, a long and winding commercial road. As you enter, you see brilliantly whitewashed walls and "Islamic" arcades along with rows of wooden chairs with cane bottoms. On Sundays there is a choir of boys dressed in smart gray suits and girls in fluttering white frocks and red bodices with red bandannas tied around their heads. They use prayer books printed in Armenian and chant in Slavonic. At the end of the service, the congregation comes out into a compound thick with mango and other tropical fruit trees growing among the old tombstones, some of which are inscribed in Cyrillic script and others in Roman script. You will notice that the church-goers leave by private cars and taxis; they stopped living in Armenian Street long ago and now have expensive houses in the wealthier suburbs, including Alipur. Their numbers have dwindled, and there are at the most some three hundred Armenians in Calcutta, including recent refugees from Iran. Most of them work in the professions or in business. As far back as the beginning of the nineteenth century, they were known for their sound understanding of the world's financial markets; they were also Calcutta's first hoteliers, owning the Grand Hotel in Chowringhee before it was bought by the Oberoi family. They are well respected for their philanthropy, too. The Armenian College in Free School Street still functions mainly as a charitable institution. Students from Iran come to study there.

Second only to the Armenian Church in age is the Old Mission Church, built while the Company's court of directors was slowly contemplating the erection of a Protestant church for their employees after the lifting of the siege of 1756. Its moving spirit was a Swedish missionary, John Zachariah Kiernander, "whose name was destined to be imperishably connected with the city," wrote Cotton. He came to Calcutta in 1757 with his wife and was cordially received by Clive, who even became a godfather to Kiernander's son. The church, known as Beth-Tephillah (the House of Prayer) was built almost entirely at Kiernander's expense and consecrated just before Christmas 1770. It could accommodate a congregation of about two hundred. But although its structure was strong and its masonry good, it remained a clumsy unplastered brick edifice with unpainted planks for pews for many years because its Danish architect died during its construction. Later on, Kiernander built a mission school with a similar capacity, in which both Indian and Eurasian children were educated jointly.

You can still see the church among high-rise office blocks not far from the Chinese quarter near Bowbazar Street on what is now R. N. Mukherjee Road (and was then Mission Row). Tall, elegant, Doric pillars at the entrance support the roof, and inside there are stained-glass windows, fine colonnaded corridors, old quarters for the clergy and a number of interesting memorials, including one for a distinguished Arab lady from Jedda who died in 1876 after becoming a Christian. Kiernander himself is buried in the mission ground. He apparently became something of a property speculator who acquired various pieces of land in the city including the site of the Presidency General (now SSKM) Hospital. As a result, he got into financial trouble. But he was clearly a survivor, for he died in 1799 at the age of eighty-eight.

Though not as old as the Armenian Church or the Old Mission Church, St. John's, at the intersection of Council House Street and Kiran Shankar Roy Street (formerly Hastings Street), not far from the north gate of Raj Bhavan, has perhaps the most interesting history. It became the Company's church, but this was hardly thanks to the court of directors. With the destruction of St. Anne's Church in 1756, rather than building a new church, the directors simply appropriated the Portuguese Chapel in Murgihata (Chicken Market) along Chitpur Road for the use of its servants. Then in 1760, part of the battered eastern gateway of the old Fort William was converted into a chapel; this makeshift church would continue to serve the British community under the name of St. John's for more than a quarter of a century.

The credit for building a proper church for the Company's servants belongs to its chaplain William Johnson—the fourth (and final) husband of the socialite Begum Johnson, an Englishwoman who had acquired her honorific after a spell living inside the women's quarters of the Mughal court. Johnson lobbied fiercely, but he did not seek to rebuild on the site of old St. Anne's, which had lain fallow since 1756. Rather, he seems to have persuaded Raja Nabakrishna Deb to make over to Hastings "for the sum of sicca rupees 10,000" the old Powder Magazine Yard and adjoining burial ground. It was a shrewd move because the Hindu businessman had been unable to find any use for the place, which he had acquired earlier at a Company auction, since it was contaminated with Christian remains. A mere week before his resignation as governor-general, Hastings made the land over to a perpetual trustee for the building of a church. The money for construction, some thirty thousand rupees, came from a lottery fund. Lieutenant James Ogg of the Bengal Engineers designed the church on the model of St. Martin-in-the-Fields in Trafalgar Square. It took three years to build, and was consecrated in 1787 at a ceremony witnessed by Lord Cornwallis.

His successor, Sir John Shore, later remarked on the event with some wryness: "A pagan gave the ground: all characters subscribed: lotteries, confiscations, donations received contrary to law were employed in completing it. The Company contributed but little: no great proof they think the morals of their servants connected with religion." As if to prove Shore's point, William Hickey attended the consecration after a lengthy Saturday-night drinking session with his chums and deliberately disgraced himself:

> [We] all stepped into Mr Keighley's coach and were rapidly conveyed to the church, the steps of which we were only able to ascend by leaning upon and supporting each other. It may easily be believed that in such a state we sadly exposed ourselves, drawing the eyes and attention of the congregation upon us as well as that of the clergyman who took occasion to introduce into his sermon a severe philippic against inebriety, against indelicate behaviour in a sacred place and Sabbath-breaking... and

directing those parts of his discourse pointedly to the pew, in which we sat.

A "person of fashion" in those days would arrive at St. John's in a gleaming black sedan chair carried by four bearers and accompanied by two running footmen—one to hold a parasol over his head, the other (depending on his official position), to carry his authorized silver mace ahead of him. There is a painting by the German-born Johann Zoffany of the Last Supper above the altar in St. John's—unfortunately in dire need of expert restoration—which is said to portray the apostles with the faces of the leading Calcutta merchants of the day, though their identities have not been conclusively proved.

The vestry record kept in the darkened vestry room, which has interesting period furniture and portraits, shows that Thackeray's grandparents and parents were married in this church. In the archives is a letter from Sir William Jones setting out the reasons why he and his brother-judges of the Supreme Court declined to contribute to St. John's building fund. Perhaps he thought the Company should have paid for it, or was he unwilling to support established religion?

The grounds are strewn with significant monuments, such as the relocated Black Hole memorial and Charnock's mausoleum. Numerous tablets on the walls testify to foreign lives—brief and not so brief—that ended in India. On a Sunday in winter, the thin congregation of mainly Indian Christians often witnesses foreigners laboriously checking the memorials in search of long-dead ancestors. For those seriously interested, there is a copy of the *Bengal Obituary* of 1818 published by a firm of undertakers in Cossitollah, which gives details of all those buried in St. John's.

The grandest church in Calcutta is St. Paul's Cathedral, at the extreme south of the Maidan. Its foundation stone is dated 1839, more than fifty years after the founding of St. John's. Another army engineer, Major-General W. N. Forbes, acted as architect, following the design of Norwich Cathedral. The style is Indo-Gothic, which according to Cotton, is "spurious Gothic adapted to the exigencies of the Indian climate". The cathedral was consecrated by the fifth bishop of Calcutta in 1847; Queen Victoria donated the silver communion plate. The original tower collapsed in the earthquake of 1897 but was replaced by an imitation of the Bell Harry tower at Canterbury Cathedral. The spacious grounds, containing old trees, give the building real grace and a feeling of tranquillity, especially in the frenetic environment of modern Calcutta.

Inside is an organ built by Joseph Willis and Sons of London with 41 stops: a fine instrument still in constant use for services and recitals. The stained glass by Burne-Jones in the west window is worth a good look. On a hot day, the breeze from the rows of quietly humming, rotating fans suspended from the wooden rafters is pleasant. Sit for a while in the beautifully carved pews and you may briefly forget that you are in post-colonial Calcutta—until you spot the pictures in the Chapel of the Holy Name showing Christ in Bengali folk style with the elongated eyes popularized by the painter Jamini Roy.

Cemeteries

To feel the weight of Calcutta's European past, however, there is nothing to match Park Street Cemetery. Located at the junction of Park Street (Burial Ground Road, as was) and Rawdon Street, it is the oldest

St. Paul's Cathedral

cemetery in the city. When the original burial ground, upon which St. John's Church stands now, was closed in 1767 for the lack of space, a new one was urgently needed to keep pace with the high mortality rate among the European residents. The first person to be buried there, on August 25, 1767, was John Wood, a writer in the Custom House, whose grave has now been leveled. All tablets similarly removed for road works have been preserved and mounted on the cemetery's entrance wall.

The cemetery is private, but one can wander around after informing the warden. Burials no longer take place, and indeed the whole cemetery was in a dilapidated, overgrown and malarial condition until the 1970s when some preservation work began. In the older part, the decaying graves, with their sarcophagi, towers, obelisks, urns and pagodas, lure the visitor along rambling paths between the bushes, like parts of London's famous Highgate Cemetery. (Perhaps Karl Marx should have had a memorial here, where people still profess faith in him, rather than in Highgate.)

There are the same long effusions about the virtues of the dead from some long-ago laboring chisel as you find in Highgate (and look out for "S. O. fecit" carved on many of the tombstones, indicating the work of the cemetery's first undertaker, Samuel Oldham, who is buried here too). Unlike in London, though, the incessant cawing of the Calcutta crows grates on any tendency to become melancholy. But then you notice the exceptionally young age at which many of the deaths occurred, young even in relation to the mortality statistics of Victorian London. No wonder, in those days, that the European residents of Calcutta would gather together annually in the cold season, just to congratulate each other on having survived. As one resident, Sophia Goldborne, noted in 1785:

> *The Bengal burying grounds… bear a melancholy testimony to the truth of my observations on the short date of existence in this climate. Obelisks and pagodas are erected at great expense; and the whole spot is surrounded by as well turned a walk as those you traverse in Kensington Gardens, ornamented by a double row of aromatic trees which afford a solemn and beautiful shade; in a word, not old Windsor Churchyard with all its cypress and yews is in the smallest degree comparable to them; and*

I quitted them with unspeakable reluctance... Funerals are indeed solemn and affecting things at Calcutta, no hearses being here introduced, or hired mourners employed: for, as it often happens in the gay circles, that a friend is dined with one day and the next day in eternity—the feelings are interested, the sensations awful, and the mental question, for the period of interment at least, which will be tomorrow's victim?

This was a time when there was virtually no understanding of tropical ailments and hygiene was basic indeed. Heat stroke, humidity, malarial swamps, alcohol poisoning and overeating were the main causes of the high death rate. Rose Aylmer was only twenty when she died in 1800 of "a most severe bowel complaint brought on entirely by indulging too much with that mischievous and dangerous fruit, the pineapple." Her grave, with a fluted pillar is probably the most famous in the cemetery, because she was adored (from afar) by Walter Savage Landor who wrote the well-known poem about her death, much loved by Charles Lamb. It appears on the tomb:

Ah, what avails the sceptred race!
Ah, what the form divine!
What every virtue, every grace!
Rose Aylmer, all were thine.

Rose Aylmer, whom these wakeful eyes
May weep, but never see,
A night of memories and of sighs
I consecrate to thee.

Close to her grave is that of Captain William Mackay, who died in 1804 at the age of 32. His narrative of the shipwreck of the *Juno* furnished Lord Byron with the details of the shipwreck in *Don Juan*.

The epitaph of "Asiatic" Jones, composed by himself, reads: "Here was deposited the mortal part of a man who feared God, but not Death, who thought none below him but the base and unjust, none above him but the wise and virtuous." Back in London the East India Company erected a handsome memorial to Jones in St. Paul's

Cathedral, in which he is depicted as a Brahmin resting his hands upon a tome of Hindu scripture with a four-armed image of god Vishnu on the pediment—an example of Britain's initial love affair with India.

The quaintest grave architecture is the black granite monument erected over the remains of an Irishman, Major-General Charles "Hindoo" Stuart, who died in 1828. It is in the shape of a temple but has a small Islamic dome with four miniature temple-shaped turrets and lotus motifs. You can enter its over-decorated interior by passing through an arch crammed with images of Hindu deities. What attracted Stuart to Hinduism is not clear, but it was so total a conversion that he took to daily bathing in the Ganges and worshipping Hindu idols at home. (Some of his private collection of deities are in the British Museum.) Curiously, this open display of allegiance to alien religious practices did not affect his military career. Over a forty-year period, he rose from cadet to major-general, and at the end he commanded his own regiment. Meanwhile, he campaigned earnestly for European women to wear saris and supported the harem as the best way to produce offspring quickly. "Hindoo" Stuart deliberately challenged his countrymen's growing racial arrogance with a mixture of seriousness and frivolity, though it has to be said with little long-term effect.

The other cemetery worth a visit is that founded by Edward Tiretta, the same man who gave his name to Tiretta Bazaar in the Lower Chitpur Road. He was a political refugee from Italy who eventually ended up in Calcutta, where he held the post of superintendent of streets and buildings for many years, and became a property speculator and lottery promoter. Here is a typical advertisement for one such lottery, published in the *Calcutta Gazette* of December 11, 1788:

> *Plan of a lottery submitted to the Public, consisting of six valuable Prizes. Tickets will be issued, entitled Tiretta's lottery, each signed by the Bengal Bank, where they are now ready to be delivered... The money to be paid into the Bengal Bank, and when the Subscription be closed, a general meeting of the subscribers resident in Calcutta will be convened, who shall appoint a Committee to direct and superintend the drawing of this Lottery. The Bank to be answerable for the amount paid in.*

All Tiretta's prizes consisted of parcels of land.

In 1797 he established his vast new cemetery beyond the Mahratta Ditch (now a major thoroughfare, Lower Circular Road) purely for Catholics and their immediate descendants, though later on the burial of non-Catholics was permitted. The oldest tomb is that of Tiretta's wife Angelica, who was only eighteen when she died in 1796. She was buried elsewhere, but when her husband acquired a suitable plot in "his" cemetery the following year, he had her remains transferred. Here Angelica lies amongst Venetians, Corsicans, Bretons, Milanese, Genoese and other Catholic Europeans.

All cemeteries remind us, whoever we are, of the transitory nature of individual existence and tend to stir up strange and conflicting feelings. But these quiet old European graves, in the grounds of Calcutta's churches, particularly those in Park Street Cemetery, in their small enclave segregated from a teeming and largely indifferent city, are a unique reminder of still-unresolved contradictions—not only at the root of Calcutta but, more generally, between East and West.

CHAPTER FOUR

City of Reformers

To the west of the Raj Bhavan (Government House), sandwiched between the Treasury Buildings and the High Court, stands the Town Hall, an impressive two-story building in Doric style with a grand flight of stairs on its south side leading to a Palladian portico. Constructed in 1813, soon after Government House, but out of funds raised by lottery rather than with Company money (as with St. John's Church), the Town Hall was intended by the British to be a place for large public meetings and functions of all kinds organized by the White Town. The very first European "fine art" exhibition—an entirely European affair—was held here during 1831-32, showing works by Canaletto, Van Dyck, Rubens and Joshua Reynolds alongside Johann Zoffany, George Chinnery, William Hodges and Tilly Kettle. In due course, it became a meeting place for Bengalis, too, and in the late nineteenth century and after, it was an important venue for some stirring political speeches against the colonial government. Although today it is not much used except for occasional exhibitions and displays, it is worth going to see its gallery of busts and fading portraits. Here you can put faces to many of the great eighteenth- and nineteenth-century British names mentioned in the last chapter. You can also see many Bengali worthies, the Tory backbenchers of their day, who need not detain us.

The most interesting portrait used to be F. R. Say's fine full-figure painting of Dwarkanath Tagore, turbaned and shawled, until it was moved to the Victoria Memorial Hall. It was painted in London and a note on the back records that "This celebrated person is painted in the full costume of Hindu condition." Here in the Town Hall, at 4 p.m. on December 2, 1846, the sheriff of Calcutta convened a memorial meeting for Dwarkanath (who had recently died in London). The aim was "to do honour to the memory of a man who set to his countrymen so noble an example of public spirit and princely munificence," in the words of a local newspaper editorial.

Dwarkanath was, as we know, a pioneer in reforming Bengali society, among the earliest of a fairly small but distinguished group of Bengalis who would stand against the orthodoxy, indolence and decadence of the typical babu, while attempting to improve the religious, social, educational and literary level of Bengalis in Calcutta. In this chapter, we shall pick out a mere five compelling individuals from the nineteenth-century Bengali "Renaissance": the thinker Rammohan Roy, the educational and social reformer Iswarchandra Vidyasagar, the poet Michael Madhusudan Dutt, the writer Bankim Chandra Chatterjee (Chattopadhyay) and the religious reformer Swami Vivekananda. (This leaves out many other interesting figures such as the religious leaders Debendranath Tagore and Keshub Chandra Sen—not because they are not key reformers, but because the reader would become confused by encountering too many unfamiliar names.)

Rammohan Roy

Probably the most notable of them all, Rammohan Roy (1772-1833), ironically has no portrait in the Town Hall. The greatest Bengali intellectual of the nineteenth century, fired with a zeal to challenge the torpor of Hindu society and its religious idolatry with new ideas, Roy had an explicit dislike for statues and personal adulation. There is, however, a posthumously painted portrait in the Victoria Memorial.

Little of Roy's early life is known, except that his father was a rich Brahmin zamindar who lost all his assets as a result of the Permanent Settlement legislated by Cornwallis in 1793. Although by the time of the death of the father, almost a complete wreck, in 1803, his son had amassed a considerable fortune as a financier in Calcutta—dealing in Company stocks and shares, speculating in land and lending money to British civilians—Roy did not bail out his father. In fact, he quarreled with his mother and stayed away from his family for eleven years. From 1803 to 1815, he worked in various parts of Bengal in collaboration with East India Company servants, including John Digby, and increased his fortune. Digby was one of the earliest students at Fort

William College and put his friend Roy in touch with the group of Orientalists and through them western thought. Around 1815, Roy settled in Calcutta and turned his mind to intellectual matters. The dilapidated house (85 Amherst Street), where he is erroneously supposed to have lived, now has a plaque stating: "This house was a family residence of Raja Rammohan Roy." The bungalow with attached grounds that he had bought and lived in was later sold to an Armenian to meet Roy's expenses in England. Much later it was turned into a government office. But when the Marxist government took over the city, old Amherst Street in north Calcutta was renamed Raja Rammohan Sarani, and some funds were set aside to restore the house.

Prior to 1815, during extensive travels in north India, Roy had studied Sanskrit in Varanasi and Persian in Patna; he also knew Hebrew and he learned English from his friends in Fort William College. This remarkable linguistic versatility enabled him to read the Hindu, Islamic and Christian scriptures in the original, to conduct informed debate on religion and law with Islamic and Christian authorities in Calcutta, and to write discourses on issues of the day. His religious views came to be based fundamentally on the Vedanta, one of the six systems of Indian philosophy, but influenced by the monotheism of Islam and Unitarian Christianity, with their well-known proscription of idolatry.

Socially, however, Roy was living the conventional life of a wealthy Calcutta babu, and inevitably he became acquainted with another babu who had done well out of the Company, the younger Dwarkanath Tagore. They discovered a mutual preoccupation with the betterment of contemporary Bengali life, and their friendship flourished. Roy began to publish books and journals denouncing idolatry; to hold erudite debates with Hindu pandits substantiated with quotations from the *Upanishads* (the source texts of the Vedanta) and also with proselytizing Christian missionaries; and, more practically, to set up schools and fellowship societies for the promotion of liberal education and rational ideas. Then in 1828, in consultation with Dwarkanath, he founded the Brahmo Sabha or Brahmo Samaj, a monotheistic Hindu sect with a liberal humanist outlook underpinned by the Vedanta and some Islamic and Unitarian ideas. In the decades after his death, it became the most influential reform movement in nineteenth-century India.

Although nowadays it is a shadow of its earlier self, the Brahmo Samaj still has a dignified, unostentatious temple, inaugurated in 1881, with tall pillars and Venetian shutters on the windows, which you can see on Bidhan Sarani (formerly Cornwallis Street), a little way past College Street heading north. As you go inside, the pulpit and pews are more reminiscent of a Unitarian church than a Hindu temple. There is a smaller Brahmo temple in Bhabanipur (Bhowanipore) in south Calcutta.

Image worship of any kind is abhorrent to true Brahmos. The trust deed of the Samaj forbids the admission of any "graven image, statue or sculpture, carving, painting, picture or portrait" into their temples. Their lengthy religious services consist of readings from the scriptures (mainly the *Upanishads*), prayers and the singing of specially composed hymns in praise of God set to tunes based on ragas. Roy was a competent musician himself, trained in the north Indian classical tradition, who composed some somber Brahmo devotional hymns that are not forgotten. But the most celebrated Brahmo songs were written more than half a century later by Rabindranath Tagore, a keen Brahmo worshipper who wrote and set to tunes some beautiful and joyous devotional lyrics. *Gitanjali,* the collection of poems in English that won Tagore the Nobel prize in 1913, contains some verses that were originally songs of this kind. Although they moved W. B. Yeats deeply, without access to their Bengali literary form as well as the accompanying melody, their real artistic quality is hard to grasp.

And of course, even for Bengalis, the pleasure depends on the quality of the singer's voice and artistic ability. The musical Satyajit Ray, a reluctant attendee of Brahmo services as a child in the 1920s and 30s, remembered feeling resentful that Brahmo festivals were much less enjoyable than Hindu ones such as Durga Puja. His mother sang beautifully, but during the service his less musically gifted relatives were encouraged to join the singing. Everyone sat on quilts spread on the marble floor of his family sitting room. "After so many years of sitting, head bent low, hearing that singing, the patterns on those quilts have become indelibly imprinted on my mind," recalled Ray.

Yet despite being a small minority within Hindu society, the Brahmos became a formidable force, determined to combat the excesses of orthodox Hinduism and the onslaught of evangelical

Christianity. As the founder of the movement, Rammohan Roy suffered much vilification for his religious views and progressive social attitudes, but he persevered, having both the intellectual and financial resources to survive the criticisms. His most famous campaign, with which his name will always be associated like Wilberforce's with the abolition of slavery, was against suttee.

Widow-burning was never as widely practiced in Bengal as in Rajasthan (where it occasionally occurs even today); Roy's mother, for example, did not have to walk onto her husband's funeral pyre. Even so, it was undoubtedly condoned by the patriarchal nature of Bengali Hindu society. In the sixteenth century, the Mughal emperor Akbar had contemplated its prohibition, but had refrained for fear of a Hindu backlash against Islam. In the 1820s, Rammohan argued vigorously that there was nothing in Hindu scripture to support suttee, and eventually Governor-General Lord Bentinck moved against the custom: suttee was made illegal in 1829. Later, Roy lobbied for the support of a woman's right to own and inherit property. Throughout his campaigns, he backed up his arguments from his wide reading of European social reformers, philosophers and jurists such as Montesquieu and Bentham.

In lobbying against suttee, Roy naturally deployed his linguistic skills by writing tracts and letters in both Bengali and English. He was a compulsive communicator through pamphlets and journals. This led to another major achievement, as he became the first Bengali to write readable, discursive prose in Bengali. He rejected the excessive use of Sanskritized language in Bengali prose, introduced by the pandits of Fort William College, who had produced a written Bengali almost inaccessible to those with no grounding in Sanskrit. By simplifying the syntax, Roy made Bengali both easier to read and more expressive, combining the fluidity of Persian with the tautness of Sanskrit. Although his prose is more distinct from spoken Bengali than Bengalis are used to reading today and certainly feels somewhat archaic, it can be read and understood without much effort.

Given his interest in his own language, it may come as a surprise to learn that Roy was also the first to plead for Indian education in English, almost a decade before Macaulay. In a letter to Lord Amherst in 1823, Roy argued that the arduous task of learning Sanskrit (like

Latin) properly took twelve years of a pupil's life and effectively killed the enthusiasm for all other forms of learning such as the sciences. A knowledge of English, on the other hand, both opened up access to scientific learning and employment opportunities.

Roy was unquestionably a genuine product of cross-cultural encounter—someone who was equally confident in speaking of European thought as of Indian thought. Although he may not be as original a thinker as was once claimed, and his concerns and enthusiasms belong to his time and not to ours, he deserves to be admired as one of the first Indians to grapple intelligently with modernity. It is typical of him that when far-off Latin America began to throw off Spanish colonial tyranny in the 1820s, Rammohan threw a brilliant dinner party where he was asked about his interest in the matter and is reported to have replied: "Ought I to be insensible to the suffering of my fellow creatures wherever they are, or however unconnected by interests, religion or language?"

He was always much interested in international political events, and in his last three years himself traveled to Europe—becoming the first Bengali to be fêted there, some ten years before Dwarkanath Tagore. Before he departed in 1830, the Mughal emperor gave him the honorary title of raja. Most of his stay was in Britain, where he wanted to be present for the parliamentary debates concerning the Reform Act of 1832 and important legislation affecting the government of India (and his patron, the Mughal emperor). But he also visited France, after soliciting permission from the French government with a letter in which he stated that "enlightened men in all countries must feel a wish to encourage and facilitate human [tendencies to travel] in order to promote the reciprocal advantage and enjoyment of the whole human race."

His reputation had preceded him, and he and his party (a son, two Bengali companions, and his trusted Muslim attendant Seikh Bokshu) were cordially received in Europe. Both Rammohan's intellectual qualities and his personal charisma won him many admirers, including Bentham. He also managed to publish his works on the Vedanta in England. But like his friend Dwarkanath, his financial arrangements with Calcutta went awry. Moving out of London in September 1833 to stay with Unitarian friends in Bristol, he caught a fever, and within a week he was dead.

It was a sad end. Yet the popular Bengali notion that Rammohan died as a lonely man in some foreign field is incorrect. In his last days he was constantly surrounded by friends and well-wishers, who tried their best to save his life. But he did specifically request not to be buried in a Christian burial ground lest this prove detrimental to his son's rightful claim to his inheritance under Hindu law. He also kept his Brahmin's sacred thread till the very end. So there is no question of claiming that he became a Christian convert, close as his sympathies may have been to Unitarianism. He was buried in an isolated spot near his friends' house in Bristol. In 1842, his remains were moved by Dwarkanath Tagore, in honor of his "friend, guide and philosopher", to Bristol's Arnos Vale cemetery and a Hindu-style mausoleum was built upon his grave. This is the place where many Bengalis come to pay homage to Roy—though very few visit the cemetery at Kensal Green in London where Dwarkanath lies buried.

Iswarchandra Vidyasagar

Moving on a generation or two, we come to a reformer who resembles Roy in many ways. As Rabindranath Tagore later noted, Iswarchandra Vidyasagar (1820-91)—whose name has been given to one of the Hugli bridges—and his predecessor looked and spoke like true Bengalis. Both had the manners and dress of Bengalis; and both had a good command of Sanskrit and of the Hindu scriptures, while also developing the expressiveness of Bengali as a literary language. And yet their boldness of character, honesty, charitableness, determination, and self-reliance can only be compared with those of the great men of Europe. Both despised the aping of the superficial aspects of European life for the sake of displaying sham progressiveness.

The younger man lacked the worldly wealth of the older, however. Born Iswarchandra Bandopadhyay into a poor but principled Brahmin family in Midnapur, he walked to Calcutta as a boy of seven or eight, learning the English numerals from the milestones. There he lived in a small rented room with his father in an alley that is now Jain Temple Road near Barabazar. At the age of nine he was admitted to Sanskrit College and for the next twelve years, until he completed his education, he obtained scholarships, earning himself the title Vidyasagar, meaning "ocean of learning". Almost immediately he was appointed as a pandit to Fort William College where he came into direct contact with English education officials before returning to Sanskrit College as its principal in 1850. You can see the college building, which now houses the Vidyasagar Museum across College Street, opposite Jahan Khan Mosque. In 1979, College Square Garden was renamed Vidyasagar Uddan.

There was no government elementary school in Bengal at that time. While the authorities were sympathetic to introducing Sanskrit and Persian education for children, they were not willing to spend the necessary money on Bengali-language teachers and textbooks. Vidyasagar began a campaign by writing graded books to teach the Bengali alphabet, which were so easy to understand that they are still used. *Barnaparichay Pratham Bhag* (First Alphabet Book) was printed on a press founded by the author at Sanskrit College in 1847, and today newly recruited Calcutta maidservants from rural areas still learn from reprinted copies of the original book with smudged woodblock illustrations on cheap paper, while children from better-off families use colorful, well-printed, glossy editions.

At a higher level, Vidyasagar began to introduce new vocabulary into the language through vivid descriptive passages, as well as new punctuation such as the semicolon. Drawing on his deep knowledge of Sanskrit literature, he wrote with new sensitivity to the sounds and onomatopoeias of spoken Bengali. As a translator, educator and original writer, he enriched his prose with clever alliteration, wit and irony, giving it a distinct style. The Bengali he created is now standard, and in his hands it became literature. At the same time colloquial and refined, Vidyasagar's prose is the earliest Bengali writing that I find is still a pleasure to read. Furthermore, he devised a simple but satisfactory Bengali syllabus for native schools, incorporating primary mathematics, history, geography, moral studies (biographies of great men and women), and the study of the physical world and hygiene.

Meanwhile, his debate with the government about elementary education was making progress. He worked on fellow Bengalis to join the campaign and recruited prospective teachers. Success came in 1854 with the introduction of the Indian Education Charter and in the following year, his appointment as inspector of schools for the south of Bengal and his setting up of a part-time teacher-training institution in

Sanskrit College. As a result of Vidyasagar's unflagging effort, enthusiasm, financial support and supervision, many elementary Bengali schools were established throughout Bengal, and the general male population of the state began to receive an education denied to those in most other areas of India.

Now he turned his attention to female education. In 1849, John Drinkwater Bethune, the law member of the governor-general's Supreme Council, had founded the first school for Bengali girls in Calcutta, with the help of Ramgopal Ghosh, Dakshinaranjan Mukhopadhaya and Madanmohan Tarkalankar. Initially known as the Hindu Balika Vidyalay (Hindu Girls' School), it became the Bethune School, located at the crossing of Bidhan Sarani and Beadon Street. In due course a college was added, where I was a student. Fittingly, Vidyasagar's house on north Calcutta's Badurbagan Street has been restored as a computer school for girls and a library; it is worth visiting to get a sense of a babu house.

Bethune knew Vidyasagar and wanted his assistance with the school, but Bethune died soon after its founding, in 1851. Despite the success of the school, which was attended mostly by girls from Brahmo and progressive Hindu homes, Vidyasagar knew from his experience of boys' education that it would be hard to expand female education further by attracting girls from conservative families, whether Hindu or Muslim. But somehow, by sheer doggedness and passionate resolve, between November 1857 and May 1858, he succeeded in persuading the government to set up thirty-five free girls' schools in Bengal with nearly 1,300 pupils, which he supervised. But the funding for such philanthropic projects soon dried up, as a result of the Sepoy Mutiny. A frustrated Vidyasagar boldly resigned his position in government service and decided that if the government would no longer extend its support to his schemes, he would appeal to rich Bengalis. They duly contributed substantial donations to his new fund for the promotion of female education and helped to save the schools. As a result, his reputation began to spread outside Bengal. When the educationalist and social reformer Mary Carpenter, who had known Rammohan Roy in Britain, came to Calcutta towards the end of 1866, she visited several schools with Vidyasagar. (During one such visit, away from Calcutta, his carriage tumbled and he was thrown out and injured, starting the severe liver damage that would trouble him for the rest of his life.)

As Rammohan had taken up the issue of suttee, Vidyasagar took up widow remarriage. In the 1850s, child marriage was still the norm among all but the most progressive Bengali families. Naturally, many women were widowed at a very young age. But under Hindu law they were prevented from remarrying. While they might no longer be expected to become suttees on their husband's pyre, they were condemned to a miserable existence with a strictly limited diet (no meat or fish) and appearance (white sari only, shaving of hair), frequent fasting without even a drop of water, social segregation at weddings, and, of course, no sexual life (although this went on in secrecy).

Ignoring serious threats to his life from some orthodox Calcutta Hindus, Vidyasagar wrote and published a Bengali treatise in 1855 advocating widow remarriage and a second one the following year in English. He then petitioned the government and succeeded in making remarriage legal. That same year, 1856, he personally supervised the first such marriage, supported by his mother and wife. Many widows fleeing social persecution took refuge at his mother's rural abode, while remarried widows who were excluded from their families' social circles were welcome in his family home. A satirical rhyme, one of several from the time, goes as follows:

Arey Vidyasagar dibere beea
Bidhobader dhore.
Tara aar felbena chul
Bandhbe benee gunjbe re ful...

("That Vidyasagar is making widows marry again. They'll shave their tresses no more, instead they'll plait their hair and tuck in flowers.")

Ordinary people nicknamed him "dayer sagar" (ocean of kindness), so numerous were his charitable acts, and in 1880 he was decorated by the colonial government for his educational work. But in later life he withdrew from Calcutta and chose to spend much of his time living among the tribal Santhals away from so-called civilized society (like the central character in Satyajit Ray's last film, *Agantuk*—not coincidentally). He had never been part of any group and was truly a self-made Bengali, independent of anyone and any one tradition. His passion for reform was instinctive. Unlike many employed in government, he never sought personal favors from his European superiors. Indeed, he resigned when there was a difference of opinion and retorted where he noticed any attempt at humiliation.

In general, Vidyasagar saw the British as partners in joint progressive enterprises, expected to be treated by them as an equal, and by doing so earned the respect of many British officials. As for the weaknesses of the Bengali character so evident around him, he despised them, like his admirer Rabindranath Tagore. At a memorial meeting in 1895, four years after Vidyasagar's death, Tagore said:

> Vidyasagar had infinite contempt for this weak, mean, heartless, lazy, arrogant, argumentative, race of men. He himself was apart from them in every way. Even as a mighty tree grows little by little until it thrusts its head skywards far above the undergrowth at its foot, so Vidyasagar, as he grew older, rose to a calm and solitary eminence far above the unhealthy thicket of Bengali society. He gave cool shade to the weary and fruits to the hungry, but he held himself aloof from the chattering, the endless speechifying, of the numerous mushroom societies and assemblies of the time.

Michael Madhusudan Dutt

Our third reformer epitomizes nineteenth-century Bengal's divided soul: "a dynamic, erratic personality and an original genius of a high order", says the *Encyclopaedia Britannica*. He became a Christian convert so as to be accepted as a writer in English—but his poetry in English is unmemorable, while his sonnets in Bengali are famous. Although he was brought up in Calcutta, the city never featured in his poetry and he spent much of his adult life avoiding the place—yet his best writing was done in Calcutta. He rejected his family and the Bengali bride they arranged for him in Calcutta and married first a Scottish woman and then a French one—yet Michael Madhusudan Dutt (1824-73) is still regarded by Bengalis as a great son of the city. According to a competent critic, J. C. Ghosh in *Bengali Literature*, "To his adventurous spirit we owe blank verse and the sonnet, our first modern comedy and tragedy, and our first epic."

Dutt was born into an aristocratic and well-off family in East

Bengal, and did not live in Calcutta until the age of seven when his father moved to the city to start a legal career. They lived in the exclusive area of Khidirpur. Madhusudan displayed early literary talent, though he chose to write in English and not in Bengali. Like the other students at Hindu College in the 1830s, he was part of Young Bengal, the westernizing movement that regarded Bengali as little more than fishermen-speak. His burning ambition was to be a poet in the English language and visit England. In 1842, while reading Tom Moore's biography of Byron, he wrote in a letter to his friend Gourdas Basak: "Oh! How should I like to see you write my 'Life' if I happen to be a great poet—Which I am almost sure I shall be, if I can go to England."

Just before this, when he turned 18, his parents had arranged his marriage to a local beauty. In desperation he had absconded and taken refuge in Fort William. No doubt it was the opportunity to escape from the marriage and the prospect of fulfilling his literary ambition that tempted him to convert to Christianity, which officially occurred on February 9, 1843 in the Old Mission Church (he took the name Michael). He composed a hymn for the occasion ending with these lines:

> I've broke Affection's tenderest ties
> For my blest Saviour's sake;—
> All, all I love beneath the skies
> Lord! I for Thee forsake!

However, he would never attend any church regularly.

The conversion caused his parents a great deal of grief, but they did not give him up. His father subsidized Michael's education for three years at Bishop's College, which had been founded in 1820 for "instructing native and other youths in the doctrine and discipline of Christ's Church" as future preachers. There Michael learned Latin and Greek and continued to write poems in English.

But when his father refused to support him any longer, Michael, in consultation with fellow students from Madras, decided to leave Calcutta and travel south to seek his fortune. There he became a teacher in a school, met the daughter of a Scottish indigo planter, fell in love, and after a great deal of persuasion received consent to marry

Rebecca. He became associated with three newspapers published in Madras. Under the pseudonym Timothy Penpoem, he also published a book of verse, *Captive Ladie*. "However creditable a performance for a non-Englishman *Captive Ladie* is a third-rate work by English standards, and gives no indication that Madhusudan would have been anything more than a third-rate poet had he continued to write in English." (J. C. Ghosh again). When Michael sent a copy of *Captive Ladie* to John Drinkwater Bethune through his Calcutta friend Basak, it drew a crucial response that changed Dutt's life. Replying to Basak, Bethune plainly advised:

> But he [Michael Madhusudan] could render far greater services to his country and have a better chance of achieving a lasting reputation for himself, if he will employ the taste and talents, which he has cultivated by the study of English, in improving the standard and adding to the stock of the poems in his own language, if poetry at all events he must write.

As Basak himself told his friend: "We do not want another Byron or another Shelley in English; what we lack is a Byron or a Shelley in Bengali literature." Without abandoning his ambition to write in English, Dutt listened to Bethune's advice and began writing in Bengali too, while at the same time studying Hebrew and Tamil in Madras.

The next few years were both troubled and productive for him. His parents died; his marriage to Rebecca collapsed and they divorced; and he began to live with a French woman named Henrietta, soon to be his second wife. In 1856 he was compelled for lack of money to return to Calcutta with Henrietta to sort out his contested inheritance. Basak and other devoted Bengali friends welcomed him back, found him a job as a judicial clerk in the police service, and ensconced him in a garden villa near Dum Dum belonging to the writer Kishorichand Mitra. Soon it was the place where everyone who mattered in contemporary Bengali writing would congregate, and it became the crucible for Dutt's most important literary works.

The group encouraged him to write plays in Bengali. He imported into the language the structure of Greek tragedy, the psychology of Shakespeare's soliloquies and the precision of Sanskrit diction, and the result was a unique creation, appreciated by both critics and the public.

His play *Sharmistha,* based on a character from the Indian epic *The Mahabharata,* was staged successfully in one of Calcutta's leading theaters. Immediately Dutt wrote two witty farces on the anomalies of babudom, but these were not staged because they were too near the knuckle for his rich babu patrons. They are Dutt's only writings about contemporary Calcutta, apart from his letters. Here is an extract from *Ekei Ke Bole Sabhyata* (We Call It Civilization), in which Naba, a babu, addresses his fellow babus in a bordello. The original is in Bengali, of course, but liberally sprinkled with English words:

> *NABA:* Gentlemen, *we are all born in the Hindu tribe, but by virtue of our education we cut the chain of* superstition *and have made ourselves free; No longer are we prepared to kneel at the sight of an idol, the darkness of our ignorance having been dispelled by the candle of enlightenment; Now I pray that all of you with united head and heart will endeavour to achieve* social reformation *for this country.*
> *EVERYBODY:* Hear, Hear.
> *NABA:* Gentlemen, *educate your women—liberate them—cast off caste division—and remarry the widows—then and only then will our darling land of Bharat [India] be able to compete with civilised countries elsewhere such as* England. *Without this, never!*
> *EVERYBODY:* Hear, Hear.
> *NABA:* But Gentlemen, *now this country is like a huge prison to us. Only these premises are our* liberty hall, *that means our courtyard of freedom: here you can do as you please.* Gentlemen, in the name of freedom let's enjoy ourselves.
> *(He sits down).*
> *EVERYBODY:* Hear, Hear,—Heep, Heep, Hooray, Hoo—ray; Liberty hall—be free—let us enjoy ourselves.
> *(Everyone now drinks wine, while the prostitutes sing and dance.)*

The achievement for which Michael is really remembered, however, is the introduction of blank-verse style into Bengali poetry. Hitherto, all Bengali verse was rhymed, as part of an oral tradition to facilitate memorization. Dutt's first experiments in this direction were not received with enthusiasm, but soon writers such as Vidyasagar began to appreciate the poetry's special quality and came out in fulsome praise. Now assured of his ability to handle literary themes in Bengali, Dutt composed an epic in 1861 entitled *Meghnadbadh Kavya* (The Assassination of Meghnad), based on the life of an anti-hero from *The Mahabharata*. It was quickly recognized as a major work, and in the manner of his time he was hailed as the "Goethe of Bengal"—and was presented with a silver claret jug. Bethune's prophecy about Dutt's Bengali had proved correct, though Bethune himself died too soon to see his success.

Meanwhile, as Dutt struggled to write, he continued to battle with his relatives in the courts for his inheritance. Having recovered some money, he traveled in 1862 to England to become a barrister and, it would appear, because he still cherished the desire to become a well-known poet in the land of his dreams. His wife Henrietta, son Milton and daughter Sharmistha remained in Calcutta. At first things went well, as he settled down to study and write. But soon his maintenance allowance sent from Calcutta ceased, as did the allowance of his wife and children, who were compelled to leave Calcutta and travel to England. The trustees in Calcutta had proved dishonest, and Dutt became the victim of deceit and family feud, like many others in Bengal at this time.

Dutt then decided to go to Paris with his young family. London was too damp and there was probably some racial prejudice, as he noted in a letter written from France to Basak in Calcutta: "[Here] Everyone, whether high or low, will treat you as a man and not a 'd—d nigger'." He must have felt very frustrated to come across such attitudes among the people of the country he held in the highest esteem for its literary achievements.

He was rescued by Vidyasagar, who had heard of his plight and borrowed a substantial sum of money from friends to tide him over. But although Dutt completed his study, was called to the Bar, and returned to Calcutta five years later, he always remained in debt through lavish living. Anxiety about repaying loans dogged him, his health began to decline, and his wife was struck with fever. His last Calcutta residence, at 22 Beniapukur Road, where he lived after his return from England, is now a listed building. When Dutt heard the news of his wife's death there, he calmly and precisely recited Macbeth's soliloquy after his own wife's death:

Life's but a walking shadow; a poor player
That struts and frets his hour upon the stage,
And then is heard no more; it is a tale
Told by an idiot, full of sound and fury.
Signifying nothing...

Two days later, Michael Madhusudan also died, in Alipur General Hospital on June 29, 1873. No Christian priest was willing to give him the last rites without special permission from the bishop of Calcutta, the head of the Anglican Church in India, until the chaplain of St. James' Church stepped forward and conducted the ceremony. A crowd of about a thousand people followed the hearse to the cemetery in Lower Circular Road.

Here, appropriately, Dutt and Bethune lie close to each other. The poet's epitaph, composed by himself, is in the form of a Petrarchan octet in Bengali—no word of English—requesting Bengalis to pause for a moment in front of his grave. Bethune has a bower to himself, courtesy of the West Bengal Government, with a memorial tablet carrying a florid inscription in English. Here, on Bethune's birthday every year, girls from the college named after him pay homage with flowers or a poem of their own dedicated to him—mostly in Bengali. Such are the paradoxes of Calcutta.

Bankim Chandra Chattopadhyay (Chatterjee)

We came across Bankim Chandra Chattopadhyay (1838-94) in an earlier chapter, where his mockery of Calcutta's babus was quoted. Novelist, essayist and editor, he was the most popular Bengali writer of the nineteenth century, whose serialized novels were as eagerly awaited in the Calcutta of the 1870s as those of Dickens had been in the London of a decade or two earlier. The reason for his success is that he shared many of the characteristics of more orthodox readers, and was able to enter their minds, while presenting them with stories strongly colored by Romanticism and Victorian sentimentality. In a sense, Chattopadhyay was a more typical Bengali than Roy, Vidyasagar or Dutt (or indeed our fifth reformer, Swami Vivekananda), both because he preferred a domestic existence in Calcutta to wandering (he hardly left Bengal except for a couple of short official assignments in Bihar and

Orissa), and because he lacked their fortitude. But he was genuinely interested in educating his readers through his journal, and his novels undoubtedly raised the general level of literary culture in Bengal. This is why, although he was more conservative than radical, he can be called a reformer

From the beginning, Bankim—as he is generally known—was closely involved with the British. At the age of six, he attended an English school run by a Mr. Tead in Midnapur, where his father was posted as a Company servant. Then he went to Hugli College, where seven of his teachers were Europeans. In 1856, he transferred to Presidency College (formerly Hindu College) in Calcutta with a scholarship to study law. After graduating, he joined government service and did well in a 33-year career, retiring as a deputy collector.

This work brought him face to face with the colonial subjugation of India, and his attitude to British rule would always be an ambivalent one. Like many of his educated contemporaries, he was exposed to English thought and literature from an early age, and admired many aspects of the colonial power. As a student at Presidency College, he read Shakespeare, Pope, Dryden, Bacon and the ethical writings of Abercrombie, as well as the Bengali version of *The Mahabharata* by Kirttibas Ojha. Like Roy, Dwarkanath Tagore and Vidyasagar, he developed a deep respect for English men of letters and thinkers, and wanted to propagate their work in India. But in his personal dealings with the British in India, he experienced some humiliation and an overt attitude of racial superiority. As a child, for example, there was a tea party at Tead's school from which he was the only boy to be excluded, being a native. As an official in government service, he saw more than enough racial prejudice to make him anti-British.

But too open an expression of this feeling would clearly have been an unwise career move. Instead, he took to writing more or less coded satires, both in his essays and in his novels. In 1883, for instance, he satirized the British community's indignant reaction to the Ilbert Bill (Ilbert was the law member of Viceroy Lord Ripon's government), which proposed to allow native magistrates and lower court judges outside Calcutta to try Europeans. The pages of newspapers like *The Englishman* were full of irate letters and reports on the bill's gross unfairness to the English. In response, Chattopadhyay wrote a *Private*

Eye-style spoof court report in orotund English on the supposed trial of one John Dickson, accused of stealing some dried fish from one Rungini Jelieni, a poor fisherwoman. I cannot resist quoting:

THE WISDOM OF A NATIVE MAGISTRATE. A story of lamentable failure of justice and race antipathy has reached us from the Mofussil [i.e. up-country Bengal, not Calcutta]. John Dickson, an English gentleman of good birth though at present rather in straightened circumstances had fallen under the displeasure of a clique of designing natives headed by one Rungini Jelieni, a person as we are assured on good authority, of great wealth, and considerable influence in native society. He was hauled up before a native Magistrate on a charge of some petty larceny which, if the trial had taken place before a European Magistrate, would have been at once thrown out as preposterous, when preferred against a European of Mr. Dickson's position and character. But Baboo Jaladhar Gangooly, the ebony-coloured Daniel before whose awful tribunal, Mr. Dickson had the misfortune to be dragged, was incapable of understanding that petty larcenies, however congenial to sharp intellects of his own country, have never been known to be perpetrated by men born and bred on English soil, and the poor man was convicted on evidence the trumpery character of which, was probably as well known to the magistrate as to the prosecutors themselves. The poor man pleaded his birth, and his rights as a European British subject, to be tried by a magistrate of his own race, but the plea was negatived for reasons we neither know nor are able to conjecture. Possibly the Babu was under the impression that Lord Ripon's cruel and nefarious Government had already passed into Law the Bill which is to authorise every man with a dark skin lawfully to murder and hang every man with a white one.

In conclusion, however, as an experienced magistrate himself, Chattopadhyay did not let his Bengali readers off with a feeling of smug complacency. He added that when the district magistrate (who was of course a European) read the above report and summoned the "ebony-coloured" baboo to explain himself, the latter cunningly lied, stating that "a European British subject cannot commit a crime and a native cannot judge honestly"—and thereby secured himself immediate promotion.

The year before this, 1882, Chattopadhyay himself had a brush with the British authorities, an episode that is well known among Bengalis, when he published *Anandamath* (*The Abbey of Bliss*), a historical novel about a religious revolt in Bengal that occurred during the time of Warren Hastings a century before. It contained a rousing anthem *Bande Mataram* (literally, "I bow to thee, Mother"), which would become the rallying cry of Bengali nationalists. The novel cost him his appointment as an assistant secretary, a position created specifically to promote able Bengali officials. In a later edition of the novel he added a foreword to the effect that the British of Hastings' time, in suppressing the revolt, had rescued Bengal from anarchy. By this compromise he continued in government service. He needed his job because he felt obliged to discharge debts imposed upon him by his father and brothers, however much he may have resented the burden. But he felt tortured by his own lack of courage.

Bankim's personal dilemmas helped to give his novels real tension. They abound in unresolved issues and somewhat unlikely compromises. They never wholly endorse a rebellion against oppressive social customs, such as the question of widow remarriage (unlike the later works of Rabindranath Tagore)—yet they show sympathy for the people caught in such dire predicaments. In his first novel in Bengali (his very first novel was written in English, but like Dutt, Bankim quickly abandoned the language), published in 1865, there is unrequited love between an aristocratic Hindu (Jagatsinha) and a Muslim princess (Ayesha), but in the end Ayesha attends the wedding of Jagatsinha to a suitable Hindu bride, suppressing her personal feelings as if to underline the moral that the greatest virtue of love is self-sacrifice. The similarity with *Ivanhoe* brought Bankim the cognomen "Scott of Bengal". Two subsequent novels lead towards the same conclusion, notwithstanding a sympathetic characterization of those who would break the taboo of widow remarriage. Although all his novels are full of sensuality, psychology and charm, they do not quite ring emotionally true. The solutions offered are nearly always restrained and platonic. The farthest Bankim went in defying social convention was in a later novel, in which the protagonist leaves his devoted wife for the charms of Rohini, a widow. Ultimately, though, he kills this *femme fatale*—not in an act of passion but as an attempt to redeem himself, and after a degree of repentance he becomes a holy man. An example, perhaps, of the fusion of Victorian and Hindu morality.

These stories were exceptionally popular with women, and Bankim was often accused of corrupting tender female minds with alien notions of romantic love and erotic desire. At the very beginning of Satyajit Ray's famous film *Charulata*, set in the Calcutta of 1879-80 at the pinnacle of Bankim's literary fame, the heroine picks a novel by Bankim out of the bookshelf—and immediately the Bengali viewer receives a subtle clue to her heightened awareness of love. Bankim was well aware of his power and reputation in this area—he even wrote a humorous sketch about it—and he deliberately maintained a moral high ground for his heroines where *dharma* (duty) ruled supreme. His descriptions of beautiful women are poetic but never sexual, and when his men and women are overcome by desire, they fall from grace and receive their just deserts. Passionate his works are, but for Bankim salvation from passion's destructive urges comes only through spiritual atonement, not physical consummation.

Yet it would be wrong to leave the impression that Chattopadhyay was always holier than thou. The monthly he started in 1872, *Bangadarshan* (Mirror of Bengal), was a stimulating mixture of witty sketches on topical subjects, religious discourses, reviews and literary criticism. He personally encouraged many capable people to write and to engage in literary, social and political debate—all of which would have a far-reaching effect in shaping the idea of what it means to be an Indian. Among his most delightful writings was a sketch after the fashion of De Quincey's *Confessions of an English Opium-Eater* entitled *Kamalakanter Daptar* (The Scribbings of Kamalakanta). In it a remarkably literate Bengali vagabond with a fondness for opium muses eclectically upon myriad matters, from the philosophy of Bentham to more subversive matters such as how far Bengalis deserve to be called members of the human race. The surreal wit, sparkling word play and general stylishness are virtually untranslatable. Bengalis owe much to Bankim for developing their acute sense of humor, a vital shock absorber for daily life in Calcutta.

Bankim Chatterjee Street, near College Square and not far from his Calcutta residence, is perhaps his best legacy, with its brisk trade in book-selling and publishing. Bankim Chandra's house in north Calcutta's Sri Gopal Mullick Lane, though now a listed building, awaits overdue restoration work. It is in a dire state, but one hopes that it will be returned to its original condition.

Swami Vivekananda

The last reformer is the most famous outside Bengal. In Calcutta, he is also the one who is associated with the most significant institution, at Belur Math. But before we come to Swami Vivekananda (1863-1902), we must encounter his even more celebrated guru, Ramakrishna Paramahansa (1836-86), the best-known Hindu saint of the nineteenth century, whose bearded image can be seen all over Calcutta's shops, institutions and homes, and whose name is attached to today's worldwide Vedantic organization, the Ramakrishna Mission, which was established at Belur by his disciple Vivekananda.

If you drive north out of Calcutta along the busy commercial Barrackpore Trunk Road and take a left towards the Hugli, you reach the Dakshineswar Temple complex on the bank of the river. It includes a tall nine-turret (*navaratna*—"nine jewels") temple of Kali, a temple for the divine couple Radha and Krishna, and a string of twelve temples dedicated to Shiva—an unusual combination of the three major Hindu cults in one precinct. Looking across the river, you can spot the even taller structure of the monastery at Belur Math. To get to Belur, a little to the north, there is the Vivekananda Setu (formerly known as Willingdon Bridge) or, like most pilgrims, you can take a ferry across the Hugli. The monastery was designed to celebrate the diversity of Indian religions. The entrance is in Buddhist style, the façade is Hindu, the windows and balconies are Islamic, and the ground plan is in the shape of a Christian cross. When I first visited the place as a child I was much taken aback to see white-skinned European and American followers of the Ramakrishna Order wandering freely in the saffron robes of Hindu holy men; and when one of them affectionately greeted me in Bengali, I could hardly believe my ears.

The Kali temple at Dakshineswar was built in the mid-nineteenth century by Rasmani, a wealthy but low-caste widow, on the site of some Muslim burial grounds. Rasmani's is a rags-to-riches tale. The beautiful daughter of a humble peasant family—where she was

Dakshineswar Temple

nevertheless called Rani (a queen) by her mother—she was married off to a wealthy Calcutta family of no pedigree. When her husband Rajchandra Marh died at the age of forty-four, she inherited his immense wealth and decided to spend it on the city. Soon she was known to everyone as Rani Rasmani, in recognition of her generosity. She seems also to have had the strength of a real Rani. For when the British government imposed a tax on all fish caught in the Hugli, adversely affecting the livelihoods of poor fishermen working on her property at the mouth of the river, she cunningly bought exclusive fishing rights in the area for a large sum and had parts of the river cordoned off. When the government protested that this was holding up shipping on the Hugli, she replied: "I have obtained these fishing rights from you for a huge sum of money. If I let the ships pass they will scare the fish away and I will lose a lot of money. If you immediately abolish the tax, I will give up my rights, but if you do not, I will sue you for damages." The government abolished the levy, and the poor fishermen regained their livelihoods.

But having completed the impressive temples spread over twenty acres of land at Dakshineswar in 1855, the low-caste Rasmani could not find a priest to perform the act of worship. Eventually she bequeathed the temples to a Brahmin in order to have them consecrated. Then, after a good deal of persuasion, a priest from Calcutta agreed to preside over the worship.

The priest's given Bengali name was Gadadhar Chattopadhyay, but he was later to be known as Ramakrishna (Paramahansa is a religious title). He had came to the city in his teens from the country village of Kamarpukur, about sixty miles northwest of Calcutta near Bardhaman junction, to help his elder brother Ramkumar with religious duties. He had very little formal education and throughout his life he spoke a simple rustic Bengali. In Calcutta, he became popular for his charming child-like manner, epigrammatic wisdom and benign sense of humor. He used simple analogies to make a point, some of which were written down and published later as his gospel, the *Kathamrita.* Here is one: "The tortoise moves about in the water of a lake. But do you know where her mind is? On the bank, where her eggs are laid. Do all your duties in the world, but let your mind dwell on thoughts of God."

Ramakrishna Paramahansa

Like St. Francis, Ramakrishna was given to beatific visions; during one such ecstasy, an English boy standing in a park appeared to him as Lord Krishna. Although he personally had hardly any contact with the British, he showed no bitterness towards British rule. He spoke of the essential unity of all religions, rejected the idea of caste and blamed sexual passion and money as the roots of all evil. As a celibate he never consummated his marriage, at the age of twenty-three to a pre-pubescent wife of five; later she was deified and regarded as a saint by the Ramakrishna Order. He called Kali "Divine Mother" and saw her as the supreme manifestation of God. His seemingly insane actions, such as dancing while holding the hand of the divine image at Dakshineswar and affectionately muttering to her, outraged the orthodox, amused non-believers and fascinated the Hindu faithful, who saw them as Ramakrishna's genuine communion with the Creator and his Creation. Only in Hinduism are the gods ritually bathed, fed, put to bed and entertained with music and dance like one's own close relatives. It happens every day at regular intervals in the morning, at noon and in the evenings at hundreds of roadside shrines and temples in Calcutta. (Recently I found myself strangely moved while watching a Bengali lady worship Kali in her north London attic by talking affectionately to the brass image of the deity—almost in the way that children talk to a teddy bear.)

Outside Dakshineswar, however, not many had heard of Ramakrishna until a leading Brahmo, Keshub Chandra Sen, paid a visit to the temple in the late 1860s. Sen was slightly younger than the holy man and as a Brahmo had little sympathy with the popular manifestations of Hinduism; but he felt intrigued enough to see for himself whether Ramakrishna's reputation was genuine or whether he might be a fake. Impressed by his unassuming manner, his ordinary appearance and his telling of simple, parable-like tales, Sen wrote enthusiastically about Ramakrishna as a saint in Calcutta's Brahmo periodicals. Ramakrishna, for his part, appreciated Sen's spirituality, attended some Brahmo prayer gatherings, and to some extent mitigated the Brahmos' abhorrence of image worship through the evident sincerity of his professed belief in a god who can have form as well as being formless. Soon a band of younger Brahmos, prompted by a mixture of curiosity and spiritual searching, began to pay visits to Dakshineswar.

One of them was Narendranath Datta, who eventually took the name Swami Vivekananda and became Ramakrishna's most famous disciple in India and abroad. His background was, however, very different from that of his guru. Narendranath was the product of a western-style education mixed with a traditional Hindu upbringing in which simple religious values were imbibed mainly from his mother, with considerable exposure to Islamic culture too. His father was trained in classical music at Lucknow; his mother learned English from a female missionary; and one of his sisters went to Bethune School. As a student at Presidency College and later in the General Assembly's Institution (now Scottish Church College), Narendranath read western literature ranging from Shakespeare to Jules Verne. In history he studied the French Revolution, Maspero's history of Egypt and the works of Gibbon. And he was a serious student of philosophy, both eastern and western, from logic to metaphysics, not forgetting some scientific thinkers of his time such as Darwin. Like most of his educated contemporaries, he knew Sanskrit well and could recite chunks of Kalidasa on demand. As a child, he recalled that he was encouraged to ask questions and taught never to show surprise—the two principles he never abandoned.

Why such a well-read and skeptical young intellectual should have been drawn to such a seemingly simple faith espoused by a rustic mystic like Ramakrishna is a complex issue. One must remember that Datta grew up at a time when concerted Christian propaganda against the Hindu rituals was creating a negative image in Europe of India's religious life. With the defeat of the Orientalists by Macaulay and others in the 1830s, very few except a handful of Oriental scholars were aware of the heritage of Indian spirituality. Understandably, as a member of the developing western-educated class in India, Datta became increasingly uncomfortable with such foreign disparagement and longed to counter it with a serious and rational defense. Intensive analytical study of the scriptures led this young Brahmo, like Rammohan Roy before him, to look afresh at the Vedanta, and the nature of the relationship between the individual self (*atman*) and the Absolute (*Brahman*). According to Vedantic philosophy, life is but an existential quest by the self to know the Absolute, where the ultimate virtues of truth, beauty and goodness reside in harmony. This inspired metaphysical theory, Datta noted, encouraged independent thinking and accommodated innovative notions and diverse forms of worship in search of God—all of which are found in Hinduism. He now regarded the Vedanta as a system of intellectually challenging doctrine, more inclusive and more profound than any western world-view.

When Narendranath first met Ramakrishna, he was dismissive of his apparent mumbo-jumbo, but in further encounters he came gradually to understand and empathize with the spiritual dimension of his personality beyond his perceived image. Here was a Hindu who held the other religions of the world including Christianity in equal reverence; a Brahmin who did not believe in caste; a *sannyasi* who had personally renounced all earthly possessions yet remained keenly interested in the domestic happiness of others; and an illiterate who could weave words of wisdom wonderfully. He now saw in Ramakrishna the essence of the Vedanta and also the continuation of the syncretistic religious tradition of the Indian Middle Ages found in Vaisnavism and Sufism. He no longer felt the need to reject his love of western writers like Milton, Wordsworth and Shelley, with their belief in a moral world of monotheistic spiritual unity. Instead, he saw the possibility of a synthesis of all that he valued—eastern and western— in the life of Ramakrishna and in the teachings of the Vedanta, and felt inspired to share this realization with the world. His mission became to transmit to the West what he saw as true Indian spirituality, beyond all the unsavory forms that had accreted over the centuries around Hinduism. Such a mission would combat Christian propaganda and would also be an honorable strategy to restore India's glory.

This is not the place to follow Vivekananda's world career after the death of Ramakrishna in 1886 in more than barest outline. In 1893, he made his famous speech on Vedanta at the World's Parliament of Religions in Chicago, and the American press gave this charismatic orator tremendous applause as the "greatest figure at the Parliament". Lecture tours followed in the United States and in Britain, attracting large audiences and making converts. He stayed three years in the West, mainly in America, and worked hard to found the Vedanta Society, preaching the ethics of self-perfection and service to humanity; he was able to adapt the highest ideals of the Vedantic religion and make it relevant for a progressive world. On his return to Calcutta in 1897, he founded the Ramakrishna Mission with some western disciples at Belur Math, which today runs a charitable hospital in Calcutta, a cultural center at Gol Park in the south of the city, and many educational institutions in and around the city. In 1899 he again left India for further lectures and established another branch of the Vedanta Society in San Francisco. Returning in 1900, he died in Calcutta two years later aged only thirty-nine, burnt out by his efforts. In 1911, the Calcutta Improvement Trust built a new road in the north of the city close to

Swami Vivekananda

where he lived and named it Vivekananda Road. His family home in north Calcutta's Gour Mohon Mukherjee Lane is now a heritage building and work to restore it is well under way. It is also a fine example of a babu house, solidly built and incorporating traditional and western features.

In the West Vivekananda projected Vedanta as the basis of all religion, and eastern spirituality and western materialism as complementary to each other. His Absolute was man's own higher self, and man's noblest endeavor was to work for the benefit of mankind. For better or worse, he successfully replaced the profane nineteenth-century image of India with a sacred twentieth-century one. It is mainly because of Vivekananda that yoga, transcendental meditation and other Indian forms of spiritual self-improvement were later enthusiastically received in the West.

Rammohan Roy, Iswarchandra Vidyasagar, Madhusudan Dutt, Bankim Chandra Chattopadhyay and Swami Vivekananda—all five men of Calcutta admired western intellectual integrity but also valued their eastern heritage of spiritual and moral ideals. They desired to make a synthesis of the two in their respective fields of work. Their encounter with western knowledge excited them, while their clash with western preconceptions about India infuriated them. But they battled on, dealing with the anomalies in their own way, and in the process shaped much of modern Bengali identity. Today, with British rule long gone from Calcutta, Bengalis remain divided in their opinions as to how much of a product of cultural mixing they really are—or should be. I have often wondered what sort of people we would have become, had we not been forced into our thought-provoking encounter with the West. Certainly, it is hard to imagine individuals such as these five reformers without such an encounter.

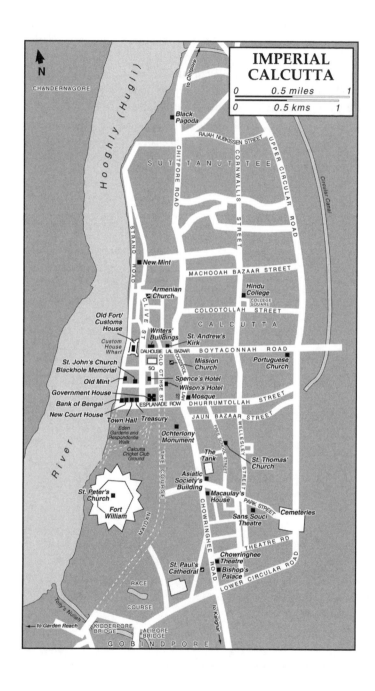

IMPERIAL CALCUTTA

| 0 | 0.5 miles | 1 |
| 0 | 0.5 kms | 1 |

CHANDERNAGORE

Hooghly (Hugli)

to Chitpore

Circular Canal

Black Pagoda

RAJAH NUBKISSEN STREET

SUTTANUTTEE

CHITPORE ROAD

CORNWALLIS STREET

UPPER CIRCULAR ROAD

STRAND ROAD

New Mint

MACHOOAH BAZAAR STREET

Hindu College

Armenian Church

COLLEGE SQUARE

CLIVE ST

COLOOTOLLAH STREET

Old Fort/ Customs House

C A L C U T T A

Custom House Wharf

Writers' Buildings

St. Andrew's Kirk

DALHOUSIE

LAL BAZAAR

BOYTACONNAH ROAD

OLD CT HSE ST

COSSITOLA

St. John's Church
Blackhole Memorial

SQ

Mission Church

Portuguese Church

Old Mint

Spence's Hotel

Wilson's Hotel

Government House

LAL

Mosque

Bank of Bengal

New Court House

ESPLANADE ROW

DHURRUMTOLLAH STREET

WELLESLEY STREET

Town Hall

Treasury

JAUN BAZAAR STREET

FREE SCHOOL STREET

Eden Gardens and Respondentia Walk

Ochterlony Monument

Calcutta Cricket Club Ground

The Tank

St. Thomas' Church

THE COURSE

Asiatic Society's Building

Macaulay's House

PARK STREET

River

St. Peter's Church

Fort William

Sans Souci Theatre

Cemeteries

CHOWRINGHEE ROAD

MAIDAN

THEATRE RD

Chowringhee Theatre

LOWER CIRCULAR ROAD

RACE

St. Paul's Cathedral

Bishop's Palace

COURSE

to Kalighat

Tolly's Nullah

to Garden Reach

KIDDERPORE BRIDGE

ALIPORE BRIDGE

G O B I N D P O R E

CHAPTER FIVE

Imperial City

One of the ironies of Calcutta's history is that reform, of the kind described in the previous chapter, went hand in hand with imperialism—indeed the reform movement among Bengalis was at its most vigorous when imperialism among the British rulers of Calcutta was at its most formidable, during the half century or so following the Sepoy Mutiny of 1857.

This pivotal event in Indian history was the revolt of traditional, caste-based Indian society against westernization. It broke out in May among the troops (sepoys) stationed at Meerut, when some sepoys refused, on religious grounds, to use the newly introduced Enfield rifle because this involved biting off the end of its cartridge, which was lubricated by grease supposed to be made from pig and cow fat. The sepoys were severely punished and imprisoned; their comrades mutinied in support, shooting their British officers; and the revolt quickly spread across northern India to Delhi, Agra, Cawnpore and Lucknow though not into Bengal (Calcutta remained quiet throughout). It was not finally put down until July 1858, after much barbarity on both sides, including the shooting of hundreds of sepoys from cannons in a frenzy of British vengeance.

The mutiny, the subsequent revolt and its suppression by the British effectively put an end to the East India Company (though it was not formally disbanded until 1873). Instead of Company rule, India came under the direct rule of the British government, with the governor-general appointed as viceroy of India, the personal representative of Queen Victoria, who in 1877, at the first imperial durbar, was made queen empress of India. Viceroys would rule India, first from Calcutta, later from New Delhi, until Indian independence in 1947; the viceroyalty soon came to be regarded as "one of the more lucrative plums in the crown's personage orchard" (*Encyclopaedia Britannica*).

Victoria immediately tried to improve relations between the rulers and their Indian subjects. In her proclamation of November 1858 she declared: "We hold ourselves bound to the natives of our Indian territories by the same obligations of duty which bind us to all our other subjects." This, followed by the admission of an Indian-nominated element to the viceroy's executive council and a few Indian officers to the civil service, and the granting of dominion status to Canada in 1867, generated expectations in India. The growing number of western-educated Indians—universities were founded in Calcutta (based around Presidency College), Madras and Bombay in 1857—put great faith in the British sense of fair play and justice. They believed that if they could present a just case for at least partial self-government, progressive Britons would support them. But what had been possible in a few individual relationships between Indians and British, such as those of Dwarkanath Tagore and Iswarchandra Vidyasagar, would prove impossible at the official level for many decades to come: colonial reality and British idealism were irreconcilable in the government of Victorian India.

Lord Canning, the last governor-general of India and the first viceroy of India (1856-62), was known as "Clemency" Canning—a derisive name given to him by the British in India for his tendency to pardon rebel leaders of the mutiny. Indians, of course, looked upon him more generously. But it is his dear wife who has been immortalized in Bengal—in the name of a popular sweet, the *ladikani*. Apparently, she challenged the master confectioner Bhimchandra Nag to create a new sweet for her birthday, whereupon he produced a dark-brown spherical fried delicacy made from milk solids oozing fragrant sugar syrup, which she adored. (In taste *ladikani* is very similar to the Punjabi *gulab jamun* served in most Indian restaurants; try the authentic *ladikani* served at the branch of the Bhimchandra Nag sweet shop at Gariahat in south Calcutta.) Lady Canning died in Bengal in November 1861 and was buried in her favorite spot in Barrackpore Park, some miles upriver from Calcutta on a lovely bend of the Hugli. In reaction to her death, her husband resigned the viceroyalty and returned to Britain in 1862, but died that same year; he is buried in Westminster Abbey.

Calcutta—and the Bengal Chamber of Commerce—began to prosper as never before from the late 1850s. Trains carried coal to the capital from neighboring Raniganj, power-driven factories beside the river turned raw jute into gunny sacks, auction houses busily traded in tea from Darjeeling and Assam. In 1853, the total value of exports and imports from Bengal was some £28 million; by the turn of the century, it had quadrupled to £111 million. The first bridge across the Hugli, a pontoon type linking Calcutta with Haora, opened in 1874; horse-drawn trams appeared in the streets in 1880, bicycles in 1889, and motor cars in 1896. Telephones arrived in 1882, and in 1898 the first moving picture, showing Queen Victoria's 1897 Diamond Jubilee, was shown at the Star Theatre (destroyed in a fire a few years ago).

A view of Calcutta in the 1820s

But there was hardly any notion of town planning. The rapid commercial expansion took its toll on the physical appearance of the city and its environs. Industrial equipment, factory chimneys, underground pipes for water and sewage (connected to the pumping station at Entally, now gone) and a network of overhead telegraph cables, brutally transformed the City of Palaces into the second city of the British empire. From the roof tops of north Calcutta's four-story houses, the Black Town came to look even more like a total jumble—whatever may have been the appearance of the Maidan, with its rows of carefully tended trees and shrubs along clean avenues surrounded by majestic neoclassical buildings.

As Rabindranath Tagore recalled of his childhood in Calcutta in the 1860s and 1870s:

> *My grandfather [Dwarkanath] belonged to that period when amplitude of dress and courtesy and a generous leisure were gradually being clipped and curtailed into Victorian manners... I came to a world in which the modern city-bred spirit of progress had just triumphed over the lush green life of our ancient village community. Though the trampling process was almost complete... something of the past lingered over the wreckage.*

The Beginnings of Nationalism

Many other Bengalis, by contrast, welcomed the "Victorian manners" that made Tagore uneasy. In 1875 one of them placed a book of Hindu music at the foot of Her Majesty's throne, so to speak, as an offering. *Victoria-Gitika, or Sanskrit Verses, celebrating the deeds and virtues of Her Most Gracious Majesty, Queen Victoria, and her predecessors* is a quaint example of the conflicting national loyalties experienced by most educated Bengalis of the time. Its author was Sourindra Mohan Tagore (1840–1914), a member of the more orthodox branch of the Tagore family. Since 1899 the Royal College of Music in London has remembered Sourindra Mohan annually in its award of the prestigious Tagore gold medal to western classical musicians. In his preface to *Victoria-Gitika*, Sourindra Mohan wrote that, "To impart to

Dwarkanath Tagore

Englishmen an insight into the nature of our Rags and Raginis these pieces have been set to Hindu music." But when he tried to translate the Indian modes into western staff notation, he saw the impossibility of rendering them accurately. Undaunted, in 1879 he produced another collection containing thirty genres of Hindu music, from classical to folk, again written in western staff notation and with a short introductory note in English; the book concludes with the author's "Loyal Song of Bengal" written in Bengali based on the raga Bhup-Khambaj—*khambaj* is the raga and *bhup* means "sovereign"—which had been performed at his Calcutta house on the occasion of the queen's assumption of the title empress of India. He translated the chorus into English as follows:

> *Victory! Victory! Victory!—*
> *Success to our Empress!—*
> *To-day is a day of perfect joy*
>   *For thee, O Land of Bengal!*

Such was the sycophancy of this Pathuriaghat branch of the Tagores that when in 1940 Rabindranath Tagore received an honorary doctorate from Oxford University, he requested there be no mention of the fact that in 1896 Oxford had awarded an honorary doctorate—the first to be awarded to an Indian—to his distant musicologist relative Sourindra Mohan.

Yet in spite of appearances, Sourindra Mohan was a fervent nationalist. He really believed in the greatness of Hindu music derived from Sanskrit aesthetics, and he diligently searched for an appropriate notation, so that it could be recorded and shared without degradation. His aim was to establish a distinct genre of national music that would be widely regarded as being as rich and sophisticated as western classical music. To this end, he founded the Bengal Music School in 1871 and the Bengal Academy of Music in 1882, and financed them until his death. He also donated native musical instruments and miniature paintings depicting several ragas and raginis to museums in Europe and America. Perhaps his sycophancy towards the British monarchy was at least partly motivated by the desire to seek artistic recognition for the musical wealth of Her Majesty's Indian empire, as well as its dissemination and conservation.

Other forms of nascent Bengali nationalism were less genteel. As the balance of Indo-British trade swung in favor of imports to India over exports to Britain, Bengalis became increasingly perturbed. In 1861 a small group of them launched a Society for the Promotion of National Feeling, which advised Bengalis to speak and write Bengali not English, to wear the dhoti rather than western clothes, to eat Bengali food, to take up indigenous games and exercises such as yoga, and to depend on traditional medicine such as the Ayurvedic system. An ardent Brahmo nationalist, Nabagopal Mitra, started the Hindu Mela, an annual cultural-cum-political festival promoting traditional village handicrafts to boost national pride. Although the aims of the festival were initially somewhat confused—it once included a specially commissioned "nationalist" painting "depicting the people of India in supplication before the figure of Britannia"!—the festival became a fixture in the calendar and helped to prepare the way for the Swadeshi movement after 1900.

The most dramatic resistance to British rule took the form of a revolt by peasants against the indigo planters, which occurred upcountry but had an immediate impact on Calcutta. The indigo industry had been founded in the 1820s by John Prinsep, a Company servant, and quickly became the most important industry in the province, attracting Bengali as well as European factory owners. Many, including the Tagores, thought that the cultivation of indigo improved the quality of rural life. In a meeting at Calcutta Town Hall in 1829 Rammohan Roy boldly stated:

> *I found the natives residing in the neighbourhood of indigo plantations evidently better clothed and better conditioned than those who lived at a distance from such stations. There may be some partial injury done by the indigo planters; but on the whole, they have performed more good to the generality of the natives of this country than any other class of Europeans whether in or out of service.*

Dwarkanath Tagore supported Roy, claiming, "I have several zamindaris in various districts and that I have found the cultivation of indigo and residences of Europeans have considerably benefited the country and the community at large."

But in due course the dominant attitude of the planters became little better than one of extortion and total indifference towards the peasantry. A law passed in 1845 protected their monopoly. The foreign planters formed their own political association and through all kinds of graft and malpractice got the magistrates on their side. The situation became increasingly volatile, and the Indigo Revolt, or Blue Mutiny, of 1859-60 was the direct result of the planters' oppression of their labor force.

Dinabandhu Mitra (1830-73), a postal employee who traveled among the areas worst affected, was moved to write a polemical play in 1860 entitled *Nildarpan* (*The Mirror of Indigo*). The following year, it was published in English translation (the translator was anonymous but was in fact Michael Madhusudan Dutt) by the Rev. James Long, an Irish missionary in Bengal, who introduced what was the first political Bengali drama with an emotional preface:

> *[The play] describes a respectable ryot, a peasant proprietor, happy with his family in the enjoyment of his land till the Indigo System compelled him to take advances, to neglect his own land, to cultivate crops which beggared him, reducing him to the condition of a serf and a vagabond. The effect of this on his home, children, and relatives are pointed out in language plain but true; it shows how arbitrary power debases the lord as well as the peasant; reference is made to the partiality of various Magistrates in favour of Planters and to the Act of last year penally enforcing Indigo contracts.*

Then Long made a fervent moral appeal:

> *Oh, ye Indigo Planters! Your malevolent conduct has brought a stain upon the English Nation, which was so graced by the ever-memorable names of Sydney, Howard, Hall and other great men. Is your desire for money so very powerful, that through the instigation of that vain wealth, you are engaged in making holes like rust in the long acquired and pure fame of the British people?*

Copies of the play went to influential people, both in India and Britain, and raised a storm. The planters hit back, supported b

Europeans in Calcutta, and Long was tried, imprisoned and fined; a Bengali writer paid the fine. *Nildarpan* had become a *cause célèbre*, as important in raising awareness of oppression as *Uncle Tom's Cabin* or *Oliver Twist*. Mitra's depiction of the planter sahibs, who speak to their workers in a mixture of ungrammatical Bengali and Hindi, even now has the comic brilliance of, say, Peter Sellers' portrayal of the Indian-English accent. On stage, the play's popularity grew from its first performance in 1872 to a peak during the nationalist movement of the early twentieth century.

Victorian Viceroys

In 1872 Lord Mayo, who had become viceroy in 1869, was assassinated by an Afghan prisoner while visiting the Indian government's high-security jail in the Andaman Islands in the Bay of Bengal. A statue was erected on the Maidan bearing the following inscription: "To the honourable and beloved memory of Richard Southwell, 6th Earl of Mayo, Humane, Courteous, Resolute, and Enlightened, Struck down in the midst of a Patriotic and Beneficent career on 18th February by the treacherous hand of an assassin. The people of India, mourning and indignant, raise this statue." It stood there in the middle of the Maidan for ninety years until, like most of the other statues of British figures, it was taken away by the West Bengal Government after independence. (Very recently, however, as the colonial period gradually becomes history not living memory, a pressure group has grown in Calcutta for the preservation of colonial heritage, lobbying for the return of removed statues of the Raj to their original location. Nothing much has yet happened, however: the statues still lie in the Lat Bagan at Barrackpore.)

Bengal itself remained remarkably peaceful during the second half of the nineteenth century, especially when compared with its turbulent and violent twentieth-century history, but beneath the surface there was a gradual deterioration of the relationship between rulers and ruled. The British passed a series of repressive legislative acts aimed at stamping out "sedition"—including even legitimate criticism of the cost of the imperial durbar of 1876-77—such as Lord Lytton's Vernacular Press Act (1878) directed against newspapers in Bengali; and they encouraged trade policies beneficial to foreign not indigenous companies. The opening of the Suez Canal in 1869 and the shorter navigational route to Europe, coupled with the growth of the telegraph, brought Bengal closer to Britain and yet further loosened the already-fragile ties between British and Bengali. Something of a siege mentality took hold among most of the British, in which segregation from the natives gradually intensified along with a fear of terrorism.

But as ever with Britain and India, there was a countervailing, if weaker movement towards integration. The Indian Civil Service, the senates of the newly founded Indian universities and the bar and bench of the high courts all began to accept a few suitably qualified Indians. The viceroy who followed Lytton, Lord Ripon (1880-84), was a Gladstonian and a man of idealism. He repealed the Vernacular Press Act and began to implement Indian representation in government, at both the municipal and the national level. Although Ripon is not as famous a viceroy as Curzon or Mountbatten, his popularity in India is unequaled by any other viceroy.

It was Ripon who asked the law member of his council Sir Courtney Ilbert to draft the controversial bill, mentioned earlier, intended to permit Indian judges to try Englishmen. The furious agitation against it masterminded by the European and Anglo-Indian Defence Association took a nakedly racial form. A barrister acting for the association, Mr. Branson—the object of Bankim Chandra Chatterjee's satire—stirred a packed meeting at the Town Hall in March 1883 with the following speech:

Gentlemen, it is asked that you should give up your right to be tried by your own countrymen. Now this is notoriously a country in which the utmost ingenuity is ever trying to concoct and bring false charges (cheers). What the stiletto is to the Italian, the false charge is to the ordinary Bengali. He loves it, it is his weapon which he ever carries with him, and the facility with which false evidence can be procured out here enables him to use this weapon with the most fatal effect: and we are called cowards forsooth, because we have asked that we shall not be tied hand and foot, and left in the hands of these men with their stilettos of false charges; and not we alone, but English ladies, in the remote district of Cachar, may be brought up before a native commissioner when their husbands are away, and there has been some quarrel with the coolies of

some neighbouring garden. They may be carried before a native Magis-
trate and there tried at his hands, and subjected to all the indignities
which you can picture for yourselves before a man who has not the small-
est knowledge of their natures (loud and continued cheering)... Gentle-
men, it is more than sentiment, it is a sacred charge, a sacred duty, you
have cast upon you. Many of you have brought from your far English
home a fair girl, entrusted to you by a fond father to be your wife; and
if you abandon their rights now, you break your faith with those who gave
that girl to you.

The introduction into the speech by Branson of what a Bengali historian Rajat Kanta Ray called "an explosive sexual element" carried the day.

Ironically, European protest over the Ilbert Bill had the inadvertent effect of demonstrating to Bengalis the lobbying power of an educated minority. It would not be long before they themselves began to lobby the viceroy and the government for various causes, both selfless and self-serving. Practically all the men who petitioned were political moderates, with trust in British good faith. They worked by appealing to fair play using a mixture of hope and flattery. Most eventually ended their careers with a title such as Rai Bahadur (roughly equivalent to OBE) which they wore with some pride, not to mention arrogance. A couple of faded nameplates of Rai Bahadurs in our family still exist near the entrance to my ancestral home in north Calcutta; both were civil servants.

It was obvious, however, even to the most moderate Indian in the 1880s, that only limited concessions were possible as a result of such lobbying. Some therefore decided to found an avowedly political organization, the Indian National Congress, which nevertheless proclaimed its loyalty to the queen empress and regarded the British connection as beneficial to India. Although its first meeting in 1885 was held in Bombay, and its first general secretary was an Englishman, a retired civil servant and ornithologist with sympathy for the cause of greater Indian participation in government, Allan Octavian Hume—son of the great English radical politician Joseph Hume, who had made his fortune in India—the Congress quickly became attractive to Bengali orators. (All the speeches were in English, however.) But it had no significant impact on British policy until the twentieth century. In 1898, for example, following a major earthquake in Bengal the previous year, and during a famine and a period of some political insurgency including the assassination of a British officer, Viceroy Lord Elgin (1894–99) pushed through an anti-sedition bill to control the political activity—against the opposition of the Indian National Congress and an impassioned speech by Rabindranath Tagore. No doubt Elgin wanted Bengali babus to stick to loyal celebration of Victoria's Diamond Jubilee, and leave real politics to himself and his council.

Romesh Chunder Dutt

Romesh Chunder Dutt (1848-1909), president of the Indian National Congress in 1899, was a politically moderate Bengali of the kind Hume would have approved of. His family, the Dutts of Rambagan, were traditional and fairly well off. After studying at Presidency College in the University of Calcutta, he went to Britain without parental consent to sit the civil service (ICS) examination, passed with flying colors and was called to the Bar in 1871. At this time his Christian female cousins Aru Dutt and Toru Dutt were living in London, and were already young poets of some repute in French and English, amazingly at home in these two literatures (Toru was the better known and the more talented) until they returned to Calcutta, where both died prematurely, aged barely twenty.

You can still see the sprawling mansion of the Dutt family on what used to be Maniktola Street, part of which is now Romesh Dutt Street, very close to a red-light area. There, all the year round, the low-caste Dom community, in between their traditional tasks of burning corpses at Nimtola Ghat, also skillfully create bamboo structures showing fantastic objects—a huge winged swan or a gorgeous Oriental palace for a wedding or a festival. In a couple of hours they can transform an ordinary taxi for transporting the bridal party into a beautiful peacock boat or a mini-temple. Like the potters at Kumortuli, the Dom craftsmen make beautiful forms out of cane, bamboo, string, tinsel and tissue paper. Watch their nimble fingers creating reality out of ephemera. Or should that be the other way around—creating passing fantasy out of mundane reality?

While staying in Britain, Romesh Chunder Dutt read extensively in English literature and history, and also traveled on the Continent. He was impressed by the enthusiasm of the voting public in the British elections of 1868, which followed Parliament's extension of the male franchise the previous year. Returning to Bengal, he served in the ICS from 1871 to 1897 and worked with tremendous efficiency throughout his career; he always despised the Bengali babu's dilatory tendencies. He also wrote extensively, frequently quoting from English literature, beginning with the first notable socio-economic history of India, *The Peasantry of Bengal* (1874). In due course he produced a three-volume history of ancient India, several translations of Hindu scriptures and Sanskrit poetry, school texts and a short history of Bengali literature, among other works—and was made a fellow of the Royal Society of Literature. As a historian, Dutt reinvented a glorious Hindu past to lend support to the burgeoning Indian nationalism of his later years. His admiration for British good government correspondingly diminished as he grew older. In his *Economic History of India* (1897), he tried to show systematically that colonial economic policies were formulated to protect the economy of Britain and had crippled India. But he continued to value the positive contribution of British rule. In his *Literature of Bengal* he wrote: "The British conquest of Bengal was not merely a political revolution, but brought in a greater revolution in thought and ideas, in religion and social progress. The Hindu intellect came in contact with all that is noblest and most healthy in European history and literature, and profited by it." Indians, he believed, would not rise in revolution against foreign rule because this would be against their traditions. In *The Peasantry of Bengal*, he claimed that colonial subjugation would have provoked a general revolution "among any other people than the Bengalis, who are so tenacious to order, so persistent to their inactivity, so strong in a passive resistance, that nothing ever produced or shall produce a social explosion among them." Dutt would live just long enough to see such claims disproved after 1905.

Lord Curzon

Lord Curzon, who succeeded Elgin in 1899 and stepped down as viceroy six years later in 1905, was the most articulate, passionate, arrogant, effective and important of all the viceroys. Much of what he achieved has no direct relevance to Calcutta, but it is worth dwelling on his personality because it influenced the city profoundly.

Curzon undoubtedly saw India, in Kipling's 1898 phrase, as the "white man's burden", and with zealous high-mindedness he set out to impose his imperial ideals on the subcontinent, believing himself to be the leading trustee of the welfare of the Indian people. He confessed to being "an imperialist heart and soul", but "very far from being a Jingo", and someone who "cared not a snap of the fingers for the tawdry lust of conquest." The Indian Civil Service, which he streamlined, he regarded as "the proudest and most honourable" service in the world. In 1900 he wrote to the Liberal politician John Morley justifying his mission in India:

> *I do not see how any Englishman, contrasting India as it now is with what it was, and would certainly have been under any other condition than British rule can fail to see that we came and have stayed here under no blind or capricious impulse, but in obedience to what some (of whom I am one) would call the decree of Providence, others the law of destiny— in any case for the lasting benefit of millions of the human race. We often make great mistakes here: we are sometimes hard and insolent, and over-bearing: we are a good deal strangled with red tape. But none the less there is no government in the world (and I have seen the most) that rests on so secure a moral basis, or that is more freely animated by duty.*

Despite India's ancient civilization, which interested him, to Curzon India was really a vast mass of diverse peoples that had at various times been forcibly united by a powerful ruler. He maintained that the end of British Raj, if it ever came, would destroy this unity. But Indian self-government "will not come in my time," he said, adding philosophically: "I cannot say what may happen in the future." Yet Curzon did not think Indians by nature dishonest, just a little immature and often aggravating. "If I were asked to sum up in a single word the most notable characteristic of the East—physical, intellectual and moral—as compared to the West, the word 'exaggeration', or 'extravagance', is the one that I should employ", he loftily told the convocation of Calcutta University in 1902. But he was not racially prejudiced: he was genuinely anguished to see the maltreatment of Indians as a result of such prejudice among the British in India, including some of his officials, and openly declared such attitudes to be a danger to the survival of British rule.

Well-traveled and with a strong sense of history, Curzon was especially interested in the monuments of India, going so far as to call them, without exaggeration, "the most wonderful and varied collection of ancient monuments in the world". He revived the moribund Archaeological Survey of India and carried out a great work of preservation at Agra, his favorite place in India, costing nearly fifty thousand pounds as an "offering of reverence to the past and a gift of recovered beauty to the future". Repairs to Mughal mausoleums at Fatehpur Sikri, to the minarets of Akbar's tomb at Sikandra and to the gardens of the Taj Mahal at Agra, were all personally supervised by Curzon, despite his suffering constant pain from the curvature of his spine. As he explained to the Asiatic Society of Bengal:

> *If there be anyone who says to me there is no duty developing upon a Christian Government to preserve the monuments of a pagan art, or the sanctuaries of an alien faith, I cannot pause to argue with such a man. Art and beauty, and the reverence that is owing to all that has evoked human genius or has inspired human faith, are independent of creeds, and, in so far as they touch the sphere of religion, are embraced by the common religion of all mankind.*

Jawaharlal Nehru was probably right when he remarked: "After every other viceroy has been forgotten, Curzon will be remembered because he restored all that was beautiful in India."

Although he loved the pomp and pageantry of the viceroyalty—despite his criticism of eastern "extravagance"—and planned the second imperial durbar for Edward VII in Delhi in meticulous detail, Curzon was not a gregarious man. Among the British in India, he had only one friend, a fellow Old Etonian J. E. C. Welldon, the bishop of Calcutta, whom he felt was his intellectual equal (and whom he once bluntly informed that the spread of Christianity should not happen in India). But though he was a loner at heart, Curzon thrived on official work. His keen involvement with politics, his prolific correspondence with individuals on many issues, and the personal attention he gave in emergencies, contradict the popular perception of him as aloof and despotic. During the famine of 1899, ignoring his wife's considerable anxiety, he plunged into the thick of disease and death in western India, protecting himself with only a jab of Haffkine's serum. As he grandly told his audience in his last official speech before leaving India: "Let India be my judge." So be it.

Curzon and Bengal

Curzon's view of educated Indians was formed through personal contact with Bengali babus, many of whom were undoubtedly vain and self-seeking. From time to time he would seek their opinions on agriculture, commerce and industry. He never appointed a native to his Executive Council (the first, a Bengali, was appointed in 1909) on the grounds that in an emergency "[he would] not attract the respect of his subordinates." Curzon believed that the babus did not understand the principles of good governance and were interested only in securing themselves executive positions. It is a pity that he never got to know a Bengali of Dwarkanath Tagore's stature to cure him of this misconception, and that he developed no personal contact with the unsycophantic members of the Tagore family of his own time. In public Curzon complimented the Bengalis of Calcutta on their superb handling of the English language and advised them to cultivate the power of thinking. But in private he was disdainful. After he left office, he wrote to Lord Hardinge, the viceroy from 1910-16, that the Bengali had an incurable vice, the "faculty of rolling out yards and yards of frothy declamation about subjects he has imperfectly considered, or which he does not fully understand." His view of the Indian National Congress, too, was biased by the preponderance of the Bengali "chattering class"; the only Congress delegate he admired was G. K. Gokhale, a Brahmin from western India. Curzon's basic attitude was that a tiny minority of educated Bengalis should not be permitted to exert power over the millions of "real" Indians, mainly peasants; the native aristocracy under the patronage of the British were better placed to serve India's interests, he thought.

Thus, when in 1901 Romesh Chunder Dutt, now safely retired from the ICS, wrote a series of open letters arguing that the major cause of the recent Indian famine was the high assessment of land revenue by the British, the viceroy himself wrote a severe rebuttal. Of course, he had the benefit of official statistics to bolster his arguments, to which poor Dutt had no access. But having made his case against Dutt, Curzon then went on to favor a reduction in the revenue assessment. It appears that he was prompted to respond to Dutt not so much by the criticism of the government's handling of the famine as by his dislike of educated Bengalis.

Again, in 1912, while chancellor of Oxford University, Curzon quashed a proposal to award an honorary doctorate to Rabindranath Tagore. "I question whether he is up to the standard," he wrote privately to an Orientalist friend while requesting advice on Tagore's work as a writer. But for this obduracy, Oxford would have had the signal honor of being the first western institution to recognize Tagore before the Swedish Academy's award of the Nobel Prize in 1913. In this case, Curzon must also have been irritated by Tagore's political stance regarding his government's 1905 partition of Bengal into two provinces and the tremendous impact of Tagore's patriotic songs in rousing Bengali nationalism against the partition—which we shall come to at the end of this chapter. At any rate, it was pleasant to see Curzon's grandson, the writer Nicholas Mosley, redressing the earlier wrong in a different age, with his remark in 1995 that "[Tagore] never lost the magic of his presence and the extraordinary fecundity of his art."

As for the architecture of Calcutta, Curzon made a number of alterations and additions, some small, some very substantial. As described in earlier chapters, he made Government House (Raj Bhavan) into almost a spitting image of his own family house Kedleston Hall (he also installed the first lift). He also resurrected—as only he could—that imperial icon, the Black Hole monument, adding some new names of supposed victims and commenting in his opening speech that Calcutta was a "great graveyard of memories".

More significantly, Curzon supported the idea of an Imperial Library in Calcutta. The site he chose was Metcalfe Hall (now restored), which had been built in the 1840s in the fashion of the Tower of Winds in Athens at the junction of Strand Road and Hare Street but which had fallen into disuse and been "given up to pigeons, plants and ploughs". The library was opened in 1903, with Curzon's remark that "after two years of incessant work we are introducing our child, I hope a robust as well as a learned child, to the Calcutta public and inviting them to take notice of her and patronise her now that she has made her bow to the world." The library remained there until 1953, when it was moved to its present building at Belvedere.

When the capital of India was moved from Calcutta to Delhi in 1912, Curzon was an outspoken critic of the decision. Delhi was a "cemetery of dead monuments and forgotten dynasties", and an inappropriate seat for government, given that its non-military British population was then only 84 persons as against Calcutta's 12,080, he said. As for the argument that Delhi was geographically central, he observed that none of the capitals of Britain, France or the United States is centrally located.

The fact is, that unlike most other viceroys, Curzon liked Calcutta and found the city stimulating. He hated the hill station of Simla, the viceregal summer resort, preferred by most of his countrymen. In his speech to the fiftieth anniversary banquet of the Bengal Chamber of Commerce in 1903 he praised the place with all his imperialist heart:

To me, Calcutta is the capital, nor merely of a province, great as the province is, but the Indian empire. As such it appears to me fitly to symbolise the work the English have done, and are doing, in this country. For though, of the enormous population of over 1,100,000 souls that make up the city on both banks of the river, not much more than 30,000 are returned as Europeans or Eurasians, yet a glance at the building of the town, at the river and the roar and the smoke, is sufficient to show that Calcutta is in reality a European city set down upon Asiatic soil, and that it is a monument—in my opinion one of the most striking extant monuments, for it is the second city to London in the entire British Empire—to the energy and achievements of our race.

The Victoria Memorial Hall

But without any question, Curzon's greatest contribution to Calcutta was the Victoria Memorial Hall. The city's spontaneous expression of mourning on Queen Victoria's death in January 1901 must have moved the viceroy deeply. There was a huge turnout by her ordinary Indian subjects who sat on the Maidan grieving all day without food,

The Victoria Memorial Hall

while her British subjects thronged to tailors and jewelers (especially Bama Churn Bhur and Co. and J. Boseck and Co., who advertised in *The Statesman*), in order to buy a suitable mourning outfit. Curzon knew of the queen's personal concern for the people of India from the thirty letters she had addressed him in her gradually deteriorating handwriting, imploring him to govern India for their benefit. And since his arrival in Calcutta in 1899, he had experienced the charismatic effect of the distant but benign queen on the minds of his Indian advisers.

The suggestion for a building in memory of the queen came within the days of her death from Curzon's secretary and future biographer, Walter Lawrence. Curzon took it up and quickly decided that the building should be on a scale worthy of both her memory and the munificence of British rule. He floated the idea with these words: "Let us, therefore, have a building, stately, spacious, monumental and grand, to which every newcomer in Calcutta will turn, to which all the resident population, European and Native, will flock, where all classes will learn the lessons of history, and see revived before their eyes the marvels of the past."

Predictably, he met opposition. British detractors of the proposal suggested that a charitable foundation in Victoria's name would be more appropriate than a mausoleum. Indians, chiefly Bengalis such as Gurudas Banerjee, a lawyer who would often irritate Curzon, quite liked the idea of a grand building, but wanted it to be dedicated to Sita, the wife of Rama in the epic *The Ramayana*—an idea that was obviously going to be anathema to the British viceroy. But, as usual, Curzon got his own way and settled down to plan an edifice of empire "more eloquent than any spoken address". His conception was of a magnificent public building, severe in its simplicity yet grand in structure, with galleries and corridors radiating from a circular central hall dedicated to the queen. He rejected the Gothic style because, he said, that would be like putting "the Taj in Hyde Park". He also turned down the Indo-Islamic style for its inappropriateness to a European city and after due deliberation opted for an Italianate or Palladian building (though this style was later abandoned, except for some details). Then he set about raising the funds required and collecting the treasures appropriate for the galleries.

To the amazement of his opponents, given the costs already being incurred for the Delhi Durbar planned for 1902-03, Curzon raised £400,000, to which he substantially contributed. The rest came mainly from Indian princes and the British government in London. An impressive collection of memorabilia from the entire colonial period came from nearby sources such as the Town Hall and the Asiatic Society and also from far-off Indian royal houses such as Bikaner, Mysore and Patiala, as well as the late queen's son, Edward VII, who was a major donor. In 1904, Curzon had the treasures exhibited in the Indian Museum on Chowringhee.

For principal architect, Curzon chose Sir William Emerson, president of the Royal Institute of British Architects. Since Emerson was then nearing sixty, he needed an assistant. Curzon selected Vincent Esch, who was experienced with large-scale construction in India, on the strength of Esch's design for the Delhi Durbar. (Esch was also architect of the present Bengal Club off Park Street and the headquarters of the Bengal-Nagpur Railway Company at Garden Reach.)

In January 1906, the Victoria Memorial was inaugurated. The prince of Wales, later George V, laid the foundation stone, and Martin and Co. began work. The building would take some sixteen years to complete, during which the five construction cranes were to become a Calcutta landmark. The writer Nirad C. Chaudhuri, who arrived in the city from East Bengal in 1910, remembered "these impressive architectural ancillaries" as being "no less decorative and monumental than architecture itself, and for many years these magnificently arranged objects, imprinted as they were on the southern sky of Calcutta, created the illusion of a vast Brangwyn etching overhanging the city or some colossal ghost working its derricks in the upper air." In December 1921, another prince of Wales, later Edward VIII, opened the building to the public by turning a golden key. Ironically, at the inauguration, the project's progenitor Lord Curzon was no longer viceroy (he had left India in November 1905 after his dispute with Lord Kitchener, the commander-in-chief), while at the completion, the seat of the Indian government was no longer at Calcutta (it had formally moved to Delhi in April 1912).

The style adopted by Emerson was a mixture of English Baroque and Indo-Saracenic with some Islamic and Hindu features. "The Victoria Memorial owes a lot to contemporary British civic classicism and not a little to Belfast City Hall, as well as earlier Indian works by Emerson," remarks Philip Davies in *The Penguin Guide to the Monuments of India*. Indian corbels in the frieze of the entablature, stone fretwork (*jali*) and the faintly Mughal-style corner domes are marks of Emerson's appreciation of Indian architectural beauty. Davies gently mocks the building as an "Imperial Valhalla", and it is undoubtedly the Taj of the Raj. But whether or not it pleases purists, it is now, with its many acres of adjoining green space for relaxation, a dominant feature of Calcutta, even an icon of the city. In 1992, Penguin India chose a photograph of the Victoria Memorial for the jacket of an anthology of Bengali short stories, *Noon in Calcutta*, that I translated with Andrew Robinson—to our considerable surprise (and indeed dismay). A couple of years after that, in 1994, New Delhi's Bengali community built a splendid white cloth-and-bamboo model of the building (after the fashion of Rambagan's bamboo craftsmen) as a shrine for their celebration of Durga Puja!

The principal dome is faced in white Makrana marble from Jodhpur in Rajasthan, that is, from the same quarries used to face the Taj Mahal. During the heat of the day the dome dazzles, while at night its illumination (courtesy of Tata Steel) gives the dome a mellow resplendence. (Lady Alexandra Metcalfe, daughter of Curzon, inaugurated the illumination of the Victoria Memorial in the 1990s.) When the heavens open during the monsoon in July, the sixteen-foot-high revolving bronze Angel of Victory on top of the dome looks like a serenely beautiful deliquescent waxwork. Coachloads of pilgrims in colorful clothes from outside Calcutta heading for the temple at Kalighat stop to prostrate themselves and offer marigolds and hibiscus flowers at the foot of Victoria's statue. They call her Toria Mai, meaning Victoria the Mother, and appeal for her blessings with the same religious fervor as they do to Kali. In a sense, the Bengali critics of Curzon who wanted an Indian goddess as the centerpiece have finally got their way.

The charming life-size statue shows the young Victoria, sculpted by Sir Thomas Brock. It stands at the center of the memorial set amidst marble inscriptions of her imperial proclamations of 1858 and 1877. Around the hall, lunettes by Frank Salisbury depict the major events in the queen's life, rendered with colonial symbolism, for example a Bengal tiger at the feet of Britannia alongside a British lion. A more elderly queen in bronze by Sir George Frampton sits enthroned outside, and around the building are statues of governor-generals, viceroys, and other luminaries of empire: Hastings, Cornwallis, Clive, Wellesley, Dalhousie, Ochterlony, Burke, Kipling (by Burne-Jones), and many more. Curzon still stands before the north entrance, but his second statue, originally in the forecourt, has been replaced by an awkward statue of Sri Aurobindo, the Bengali revolutionary-turned-mystic-sage (more of him in Chapter 6). His beard and robe look rather incongruous among the British figures, historical and allegorical—an example of confused post-colonial political correctness.

In the galleries themselves, Curzon was liberal enough to place images of "those who have fought against the British, provided that their memories are not sullied with dishonour or crime." Hence he included a painting of Tipu Sultan, the ruler of Mysore, who died fighting the British. (Naturally, many other nationalist leaders have been added since independence.) But the main value of the collection is in the way it documents, through period costumes, sculpture, paintings, drawings, caricatures, engravings, half-tones, photographs, maps, wills, testaments, minutes, gazettes and other historical papers, the history of the British in India. A high proportion of those who were significant in British art during the heyday of the Raj visited Calcutta; at least one of their works can be found here. The world's largest collection of works by Thomas and William Daniell, uncle and nephew who painted and engraved Indian scenes in the late eighteenth century, are housed here, along with works by other painters of the Orient such as Johann Zoffany and William Hodges.

Unfortunately and as so often in Indian museums, the displays are haphazard, with Mughal manuscripts and European survey maps and technical drawings lying irrelevantly together, or a portrait of the Brahmo Samaj leader Keshub Chandra Sen mingling meaninglessly with portraits of a governor-general or British admiral. More satisfactory, at least in this respect, is the gallery of national leaders containing portraits and memorabilia of persons of national importance, added since 1947, and—the most recent addition to the Victoria Memorial—a Calcutta gallery established in 1992, showing paintings and other papers specifically about the growth of the city to 1911 and beyond.

A serious attempt to conserve the decaying paintings in the collections started in 1990, during the tercentenary of Calcutta's founding, as a unique East-West project. Money was raised and well-known museums in Britain, continental Europe and the United States provided expertise, conservation materials and training of local museum personnel. The success of this collaboration is one of the reasons for the recent movement to restore colonial buildings and statues of British officials to their original sites around the city.

As intended by Curzon, the Victoria Memorial is today very much a people's palace—although no bathing in the pool and no movie cameras are allowed. In the exterior spaces, lorry drivers from Rajasthan rub shoulders with serious scholars of Calcutta as both take tea in unfired clay cups served by an itinerant seller and relax after a day's toil while watching a free dance recital; a foreign visitor browses a contemporary art display by local artists in the Durbar Hall alongside a bewildered village woman who is visiting Calcutta for the first time. The garden and the open space beyond are popular places for a romantic rendezvous after dark, in a city where lovers find it hard to discover private space away from crowded homes and prying families.

Partition, Swadeshi and Terrorism

Earlier, we referred in passing to the partition of Bengal by Curzon in 1905. From the time this was announced in 1903 until the formal division became a political reality in October 1905, the month before Curzon left India, Calcutta was at the center of continual agitation against partition through petitions, speeches, publications, plays and patriotic songs by Tagore and others—the first open rebellion against British rule since the Sepoy Mutiny of 1857. Curzon had intended the partition as a way to "divide and rule" Bengal by splitting it into a Hindu-majority province (the western part, including Calcutta) and a Muslim-majority province (the eastern part, which became East Pakistan in 1947 and Bangladesh in 1971). But the inevitable backlash from the Bengalis he disdained would eventually prove too much for the British, and the partition was rescinded in 1911.

On the eve of the formal division, at a public meeting in the Town Hall, Bengalis decided to boycott all foreign goods and pledged to use only indigenous manufactures. The rallying cry of the time was now *swadeshi*, meaning "made in our country". Very soon, the Swadeshi movement, like Ireland's Sinn Fein (also founded in 1905), led to the first cries for *swaraj*, "home rule", which were given a resounding ovation at the 1906 Indian National Congress session held in Calcutta. Soon after this, the movement turned violent and bombs began to be thrown—both between Hindus and Muslims and at British officials. From 1907, terrorism became a fact of life in Bengal, as powerfully evoked in the volatile atmosphere of Rabindranath Tagore's novel *Ghare Baire* (*The Home and the World*), published by Tagore in 1915-16 and made into a film by Satyajit Ray in 1984.

Meanwhile in Britain the Liberal Party's electoral victory of 1906 marked an apparent shift in the governance of India. Lord Minto became viceroy after Curzon, and began to implement some of the late lamented queen's proclamations offering equal opportunities to all imperial subjects, with the long-term aim of encouraging parliamentary democracy in India. Two Indians, a Hindu and a Muslim, were appointed to the India Office in London, and in Calcutta the first Indian member, Satyendra Prasanna Sinha, was appointed to the viceroy's executive council in 1909, as part of a number of reforms within the Indian government. But these changes were insufficient to calm the rebellious spirit ignited by the partition of Bengal. Young Bengalis in underground groups continued to learn about explosives; some even went to Paris to learn terrorist techniques. Women secretly donated gold jewelry for the patriotic cause. Tensions in Bengal continued to run high when Minto left office in 1910.

The new viceroy, Lord Hardinge (1910-16), received advice from Curzon but decided to accept his predecessor Minto's recommendation that Bengal be reunified and a separate neighboring province of Bihar and Orissa be created. This was announced in person by George V at the third and final Delhi Durbar in December 1911, along with the official proclamation that India's capital would in due course move to Delhi, following the construction of a new city there. The second announcement infuriated the European community in Calcutta, who regarded it as a betrayal. Yet on the day of the durbar, five thousand troops paraded on the Calcutta Maidan, and as King George spoke in distant Delhi a royal salute of one hundred guns followed by a bugle call marked the moment. In addition, the monarch granted clemency to 651 native prisoners in Calcutta's jails, and awarded a knighthood to a Bengali, Sir Ashutosh Mookerjee, vice-chancellor of Calcutta University.

Bengalis, of course, regarded the reunification of Bengal as a moral victory, but they were surprisingly indifferent to the transfer of the capital. Nirad C. Chaudhuri recalled their reaction in his autobiography published in 1951 just after independence:

In 1911, unknown to all of us, the shadow of death had already fallen [on Calcutta]. I still remember my father reading with his friends the news of the transfer of the capital to Delhi. The Statesman of Calcutta was furious but was thinking more of the past than future and was not inspired to prophecies in the spirit of Cassandra. We, the Bengalis, were, but not in the spirit of Cassandra. We were flippant. One of my father's friend dryly said, "They are going to Delhi, the graveyard of empires, to be buried there." Everybody present laughed, but none of us on that day imagined that although the burial was the object of our most fervent hopes it was only thirty-six years away.

But the political tranquillity of a decade earlier could not be restored by royal proclamations. In December 1912, there was an attempt to assassinate Hardinge in Delhi masterminded by a Bengali revolutionary, Rashbehari Bose. The viceroy and his wife escaped death almost miraculously, since the guard standing close behind them was killed by the bomb thrown at the viceregal procession.

The First World War interrupted any further moves towards giving Indians greater political power. Indian forces fought bravely in Europe and elsewhere on the Allied side; the Indian National Congress supported the war effort on the assumption that the British would repay its loyalty with substantial political concessions after the war; and even Gandhi toured Indian villages urging peasants to join the British army. In Calcutta, sporadic anti-British terrorism continued in spite of rigorous intelligence surveillance and severe punishment. A Bengali public prosecutor, Ashutosh Biswas, was shot dead in the courthouse at Alipur while prosecuting a terrorist. Surreptitious bomb-making went on in some respectable north Calcutta homes. Indian papers published a cartoon of the viceroy as Hercules killing the Hydra of anarchism.

The next viceroy Lord Chelmsford (1916-21) along with Edwin Montagu, the secretary of state for India, worked out a formula for devolution of power in India. Montagu's "Report on Indian Constitutional Reforms" of July 1918 stated that "nationhood within the empire represents something better than anything India has hitherto attained." But after the end of the war, repressive emergency legislation was passed, against the express opposition of Indian members of the viceroy's council, and the political situation deteriorated rapidly. In the Amritsar massacre of April 1919, in the Punjab, troops under the command of General Dyer fired indiscriminately into a crowd of civilians killing some 350 and wounding 1,200 others. The massacre was later described by Winston Churchill (no lover of freedom for India) as an event "without precedent or parallel in the modern history of the British Empire... a monstrous event, an event which stands in singular and sinister isolation." Dyer defended himself, saying that he was trying to "produce a moral and widespread effect... throughout the Punjab" in order to fight terrorism.

When, despite heavy government censorship, news of the killings reached Tagore in Bengal, he traveled to Calcutta to call a public protest meeting. But not even the most firebrand Bengali politicians would support him for fear of reprisals under the government's emergency legislation, and Gandhi himself kept silent. Tagore decided he must act alone. On May 30, he sat up all night in his house at Jorasanko in north Calcutta, and eventually wrote a letter of protest to Lord Chelmsford. In a gesture of solitary defiance he asked to be relieved of the knighthood conferred on him four years before by Lord Hardinge. To quote his own famous words:

> *The enormity of the measures taken by the Government in the Punjab for quelling some local disturbances has, with a rude shock, revealed to our minds the helplessness of our position as British subjects in India... Considering that such treatment has been meted out to a population, disarmed and resourceless, by a power which has the most terribly efficient organization for destruction of human lives, we must strongly assert that it can claim no political expediency, far less moral justification. The accounts of the insults and sufferings undergone by our brothers in the Punjab have trickled through the gagged silence, reaching every corner of India, and the universal agony of indignation roused in the hearts of our people has been ignored by our rulers—possibly congratulating themselves for imparting what they imagine as salutary lessons... The time has come when badges of honour make our shame glaring in the incongruous context of humiliation, and I for my part wish to stand, shorn of all special distinctions, by the side of those of my countrymen who for their so-called insignificance are liable to suffer a degradation not fit for human beings.*

Although Tagore was never officially relieved of his title, his gesture had a subtle impact. His letter was printed in the newspapers and widely read within India. The Amritsar massacre, meanwhile, converted patient and loyal supporters of the Raj into nationalists, who would never again trust the official British protestations of fair play and justice in India—especially when they heard that Dyer was a hero to many in Britain, including Kipling, who welcomed him back to Britain after he was relieved of his Indian command with a purse containing thousands of pounds and a jeweled sword inscribed "Saviour of the Punjab".

In Calcutta, although political power had left the city, and the viceroy was soon to be substituted with a mere governor, life went on largely unaffected, both in the White Town and in the Black Town, at least on the surface. In December 1911, the London Repertory Company played *The Rivals* at the Grand Opera House in Lindsay Street (now Nelly Sengupta Sarani). The second Swadeshi Mela was a success, displaying 234 home-spun exhibits and making a profit for the first time. English-language newspapers printed resentful letters on Calcutta's fall from grace in favor of Delhi. Bengali newspapers reported the success of the Bengali race in diverse fields of activity. The poor entertained themselves by watching pigeon racing from roadside bird tables. But beneath the surface, a decline in the city's fortunes had begun, which only now, almost a century later, is perhaps showing signs of a reversal. Imperialism was beginning its long retreat, leaving the second city of the empire with a growing sense of conflict and a tendency towards self-destruction.

CHAPTER SIX

The Struggle for Independence

For a century and a half, between the defeat of Nawab Siraj-ud-Daula by Clive in 1757 and Curzon's partition of Bengal in 1905, Muslims played little part in the life of Calcutta. There was no noteworthy Muslim businessman like Dwarkanath Tagore, no Muslim writer like Bankim Chandra Chatterjee, and no Muslim religious and social reformer like Swami Vivekananda in nineteenth-century Calcutta. But after the 1905 partition, Muslims began to assert themselves, politically at least. By the time of independence, in the 1940s, Hindu-Muslim hostility was in danger of tearing the city apart.

According to the census of 1872, nearly half of the total population of Bengal was Muslim. They were mainly peasants living in the Gangetic plain of East Bengal (now Bangladesh); very few were landlords and moneylenders. In Calcutta itself, Muslims were in a distinct minority, not more than perhaps 20 percent. Of these the majority were day laborers—cooks, coachmen and stable boys—in European households, while others were tailors, boatmen, poultry and beef butchers, tobacco and perfume sellers, lascars (sailors), bookbinders and carpenters. Very few held government jobs or professional occupations; indeed, literacy levels were much lower among Muslims than among Hindus. The proportion of Muslims in government service rose from 4.4 percent in 1871 to 10.3 percent in 1901 while for Hindus the figures were 32.2 percent rising to 56.1 percent during the same period. Most Muslims had come to the city leaving behind their families in rural East Bengal. They congregated in the Zakaria Street, Mechuabazar and Park Circus areas between the White and the Black Town, which Nirad C. Chaudhuri named the "Muhammadan belt". In his autobiography he observed:

One of the typical sights of these quarters were the butcher's shops with beef hanging from iron hooks in huge carcasses, very much bigger than the goat carcasses to whose size we the Bengalis were more used. These wayside stalls were redolent of lard, and were frequented by pariah or mongrel dogs of far stronger build and fiercer than the dogs of the Hindu parts of the city.

Chaudhuri also noted—and here his experience was typical of educated Calcutta Hindus—that during the three decades he lived in Calcutta (from 1910 to 1942), Hindus and Muslims lived separately:

I hardly met any Muslims and became intimate with none... I found an arrogant contempt for the Muslims and a deep-seated hostility towards them, which could have been produced only by a complete insulation of the two communities and absence of personal relations between their members. This inhuman antagonism could not exist in East Bengal, where, owing to the number of the Muslims and also to the fact that they were Bengali-speaking, the economic and social life of the two communities was interwoven.

Religious Divides

It was the 1905 partition that made the split between the two communities unbridgeable. Hindus were generally against the partition, Muslims generally in favor because they were in a majority in East Bengal. From 1906, under the guidance of the nawab of Dacca (Dhaka), Salimullah, Bengal's Muslim population began to organize itself politically and seek separate representation from the Hindus in the councils of the British Raj. This growth of Muslim solidarity in Bengal had a significant impact upon the rest of India. At one level, it consisted of an intensified devotion to Islam and its prayers, rituals and festivals, but at another level, the faithful were actively encouraged to interfere with Hindu practices by, say, touching a sacred water pot, taking water from a Brahmin's well or defiling the image of a Hindu deity. Sporadic incidents of this kind gradually increased in number and violence, though they did not threaten the overall political stability of Bengal until the 1940s. The British did little to discourage communal friction, which served the purposes of "divide and rule", and they even fanned the sparks.

Spiritual Visitors and Secret Societies

Strangely enough, as Bengal and India became more politicized, the country struck many foreigners as increasingly spiritual. After Vivekananda's 1893 success at the World's Parliament of Religions in Chicago, India began to be seen by more than merely scholars and philosophers as the home of a unique and lofty idealism based on ancient Hindu wisdom, not as a mere British colony. Foreigners started to arrive in search of enlightenment.

Among the early ones was an Irishwoman, Margaret Noble (1867-1911), who heard Vivekananda speak in Europe and became his disciple. In March 1898, he introduced her to Bengali society at an inaugural meeting of the Ramakrishna Order in the Star Theatre. She spoke of the spread of Indian spirituality in Britain and won the hearts of the audience. Rabindranath Tagore dubbed her Lokmata, meaning Mother of the People, though he would always dislike her dogmatism. She herself took the name Sister Nivedita (the Dedicated), dressed herself in a white robe with a string of *rudraksha* beads (the rosary of the Indian sadhu) around her neck, and soon became both a ferocious champion of Hinduism and a friend of the nascent Bengali political revolutionaries, even corresponding with the Russian anarchist Kropotkin. Although it was religion that apparently first attracted Noble to India, Indian nationalism quickly got a grip on her emotions.

A second visitor was the Japanese art critic and historian Okakura Kakuzo (1862-1913), who in the late nineteenth century helped to rescue Japanese traditional art from the onslaught of western painting. Speaking in 1902, Okakura chided a well-attended Bengali gathering at the Indian Association Hall: "You are such a highly cultivated race. Why do you let a handful of Englishmen tread you down? Do everything you can to achieve freedom, openly and secretly. Japan will assist you." On another occasion he proclaimed: "Political assassinations and secret societies are the chief weapons of a powerless and disarmed people, who seek their emancipation from political ills." Coming from the scion of a Japanese samurai family, such advice influenced Bengal's revolutionaries. But when Okakura tried to motivate Rabindranath Tagore's nephew with a violent description of the bloody decapitated head of his uncle who had sacrificed himself in the noble cause of Japanese patriotism, he got only a lukewarm response.

Secret societies had existed among educated Bengalis, especially students, since the 1870s, after the fashion of Italian revolutionaries like Carbonari and Mazzini. One of Rabindranath's elder brothers, Jyotirindranath Tagore, was in charge of such a society. The adult Rabindranath recalled its atmosphere with gentle mockery in *My Reminiscences*:

It held its sittings in a tumble-down building in an obscure Calcutta lane. The proceedings were shrouded in mystery. This was its only claim to inspire awe, for there was nothing in our deliberations or doings of which government or people need have been afraid. The rest of our family had no idea where we spent our afternoons. Our front door would be locked, the meeting room in darkness, the watchword a Vedic mantra, our talk in whispers. These alone provided us with enough thrills, and we wanted nothing more. Though a mere child I was also a member. We surrounded ourselves with such an atmosphere of hot air that we seemed constantly to be floating aloft on bubbles of speculation. We showed no bashfulness, diffidence or fear; our main object was to bask in the heat of our own ardour.

The fad did not last long. But, a generation or so later, around the end of the century, secret societies were back in fashion, now with an added emphasis on physical culture and military training. A niece of Rabindranath Tagore, Sarala Devi (1872-1945), who admired Miss Noble and was exposed from an early age to the cultural and political movements of the time, founded a society. She had traveled widely, obtained a degree and left marriage until she was well past thirty—unconventional behavior for a Bengali woman of her time. While in western India, in Maharastra, she had seen a demonstration of fencing with swords and medium-sized wooden poles, known locally as *lathis*. This is the traditional weapon of the Indian martial arts, but in Bengal a century or so ago, its users were mainly Muslims and lower-class Hindus. (Today, it is Calcutta's policemen who are often seen brandishing their *lathis* at the slightest provocation.) Sarala was so impressed that she wanted to introduce lessons in *lathi*-play to the feeble and passive young men of Bengal. She employed a Muslim circus performer, "Professor" Murtaza, as a teacher, and swiftly the lawn of her

Calcutta home in Ballygunj was filled with enthusiastic young men swinging wooden poles. As queen bee of this hive, Sarala inspired her male followers with uncompromising patriotism, which she stimulated with chauvinistic events of her own devising, such as Birastami (Felicitation of the Heroes) and Pratapaditya Utsab—a festival to commemorate a Bengali (Hindu) ruler who fought gallantly against Akbar. Sarala Devi and Sister Nivedita became goddesses for Bengali revolutionaries: apparitions of *shakti*, the female power, found in Kali and Durga.

The Revolutionaries

Similar societies and clubs began to mushroom all over Calcutta. They were known as *akhras*, and as already mentioned in relation to College Street and its famous coffee house, these *akhras* were highly politicized in the early part of the twentieth century. (Today, in roadside *akhras* the ordinary youth of a locality can be seen working out in a sandpit or claypit, while better-off people go to well-equipped gyms for exercise.) In Nirad C. Chaudhuri's words:

> *These [* akhras*] became a feature of the nationalist agitation of 1905. They were not pure and simple institutions of physical culture, but were, like the Prussian gymnastic clubs organised by the poet Jahn before the war of liberation against Napoleon, institutions for giving training in patriotism, collective discipline, and the ethics of nationalism, with the ultimate object of raising a national army to overthrow British rule.*

The most prominent secret society, the Anushilan Samiti (Work-out Association), was led by Jatin Banerjee, nicknamed "Bagha" (Tiger-like) Jatin because he had once single-handedly killed a leopard with a knife. Jatin procured a house at 108 Lower Circular Road (now Acharya Jagadish Chandra Bose Road) and started an *akhra* on the plot opposite the house. The members concentrated mainly on developing physical strength and stamina through martial arts, horse riding, cycling and wrestling. They also exercised their minds by attending lectures by Margaret Noble and other rousing nationalists on the French Revolution and Mazzini, and reading Hindu scripture, especially the *Bhagavad Gita*. They had no guns (and only one bicycle and one horse) to begin with, but in due course they started to consider armed robbery as a way of obtaining political funds—despite the definite opposition of Sarala Devi. Meanwhile, throughout this period of training, Banerjee continued to work as a stenographer in the government's finance department; none of his colleagues knew of his anti-imperialist activities.

Banerjee was a disciple of Aurobindo Ghose, also known as Sri Aurobindo (1872-1950), whose statue appears in the Victoria Memorial. In 1903 Aurobindo and his firebrand brother Barin arrived in Calcutta from Baroda (Vadodhara) to observe the organization of the Anushilan Samiti. Unimpressed by its amateurishness, the two brothers took over the leadership, which led to a feud between Barin and Jatin. Although the society more or less dissolved, it would soon regroup under Aurobindo's influence and become more effective.

The trigger was the proclamation of partition in October 1905. The outburst of feeling in Calcutta went well beyond the earlier stirring speeches and printed appeals. The *swadeshi* pledge to use only home-produced goods, however poor these might be, led to huge bonfires of heaped-up Lancashire cotton and silk and other foreign consumer goods, and the boycott of everything British-made, even matches. Attempts were made to start industries to substitute Indian-made products for foreign ones, and new institutions were set up to provide banking and insurance services with Indian finance. Although considerable credit must be given to these pioneering *swadeshi* entrepreneurs, they could not achieve much due to lack of leadership, capital and commercial expertise. In most cases their quixotic efforts were thwarted by the nationalist ideology of austerity, by terrorist activities and by British competition. By 1907 the boycott movement had more or less fizzled out, leaving hardly a dent on British financial interests. But it nurtured a spirit of independence which developed into a burning desire to be treated as equals, not subordinates, in business and commerce, both among Bengalis and among Indians in other areas where the movement spread, such as Poona (Pune), Bombay and Madras.

Muslims, however, were generally alienated by the Swadeshi movement. At a meeting in Dhaka, the new post-partition capital of East Bengal and Assam, Muslims headed by Aga Khan III demanded from the British safeguards for their special interests. In December 1906, they formed the All India Muslim League, which pledged loyalty to the British government, supported partition and denounced the nationalist movement.

Aurobindo shrewdly gave Hindu sentiment against partition a strongly religious tinge by writing a political pamphlet ("Bhabani Mandir") in which he deliberately conflated Mother India—awaiting reinstallation in her rightful temple—with the goddess Bhabani (Kali). His partisan mixing of politics with Hinduism, so much deplored by Tagore at the time, sowed poisonous seeds of discord that would later destroy the relationship between Calcutta's Hindus and Muslims forever. It was nurtured by Aurobindo and his brother Barin in a weekly Bengali paper, *Jugantar* (The New Age), which they started in March 1906 without printing their names, and in their writing for another existing English paper, *Bande Mataram*, founded by Bipin Pal and later edited unofficially by Aurobindo. (The name, *Bande Mataram*, was chosen to provoke, being that of the nationalist song by Bankim Chandra Chatterjee.) Although both papers were published in Calcutta, they were widely read throughout Bengal, especially among the Hindu young men of East Bengal, who were sturdier, better organized and more devoted to the cause of revolution than the youth of Calcutta. Both papers were prosecuted many times by the government for sedition, and were closed down in 1908.

Apart from writing fiery articles and traveling to meet fellow revolutionaries, Aurobindo and his brother set up a training center in Calcutta. They had access to a deserted ancestral property in the suburb of Maniktola, beyond the circular canal. It consisted of a small one-storied building and some land with fruit trees and a couple of small slimy ponds. Barin enthusiastically set about turning this obscure place into a seminary for martyrs. The cadres followed a strict physical and ideological regime and lived on a frugal vegetarian diet; they also cooked and cleaned. Funds came from a few anonymous backers among the babus of the city. The police had no inkling of the place and its purpose until the backers asked to see some tangible results.

To attract major attention to the cause, the Maniktola *akhra* decided to kill Sir Andrew Fraser, the lieutenant-governor of Bengal. Ullaskar Dutta, a competent chemist, managed to stockpile dynamite (supplied by a Bengali who owned a mine in north Bengal), while others obtained firearms, probably from the French enclave in nearby Chandernagore. After a couple of abortive attempts to blow up the governor's train while he was on tour, they succeeded in derailing it in December 1907, but he miraculously escaped injury. Next they targeted Douglas Kingsford, a well-known judge, with a parcel bomb hidden inside a huge legal tome sent to his Calcutta address, which fortunately for him he did not open. This was followed by a bomb thrown mistakenly at the carriage ahead of the judge's when he was on his way home from a local bridge club at Muzaffarpur. On this occasion two Englishwomen were killed.

Police suspicion now fell on the Maniktola garden house. A Muslim *lathi* instructor and trusted associate of some of the revolutionary *akhras* had turned police informer. But rather than moving immediately to catch the group, plain-clothes policemen tracked their every movement between north Calcutta addresses in College Street, Harrison Road (now Mahatma Gandhi Road) and Grey Street (now Aurobindo Sarani). The police watched them buy chemicals and store them for future use. Sensing the surveillance, the group hurriedly gathered their weapons from various locations and buried them in the grounds of the Maniktola house. Having worked all night, they were about to disperse when armed police suddenly appeared and arrested the thirteen exhausted terrorists; they had no chance to offer resistance. The police dug up the ground again and found three sporting rifles, two double-barreled shotguns, nine revolvers, fourteen boxes of cartridges, and three bombs primed to explode, plus twenty-five pounds of dynamite, large quantities of chemicals, an explosives manual from Paris and coded documents. This enabled the police to raid premises in north Calcutta and make further arrests. The raided premises included the house of Aurobindo, who was living with his wife and sister at 48 Grey Street, where the police were disappointed to find no weapons. The conspirators were all sent to Alipur Jail, where they were kept in nine-by-six-foot cells with only a tar-coated basket for a latrine.

Meanwhile, a spate of bomb explosions rocked the city. Police found bombs in places like the steps of a Native Christian church in Acharya Prafulla Chandra Roy Road. A municipal dust-cart ran over a bomb on a tram track in Grey Street. Several cases of injury from attempted bomb-making were known to Bengalis but hushed up for fear of police reprisals. For weeks everyone in the city could talk of nothing else but bombs. From now on, ordinary Bengalis had brushes with the police, who perceived them as allies of the terrorists. Often Bengali boys looking for fun in a tense city would harass them. My father used to tell me of a seven-year-old schoolmate who frequently teased the police by walking suspiciously with a bump under his shawl, which was actually a mango or guava.

Khudiram Bose, who had undoubtedly thrown the bombs in Muzaffarpur, was hanged. His cool composure when the noose was tied around his neck would inspire many more youths of the city to die for the cause of freedom. The other conspirators were committed for trial; Barin Ghose, by virtue of being born in England, was given the option of trial by jury, which he turned down. A jailbreak was planned. Despite the heavy security, the prisoners managed to smuggle firearms into the jail and organize a quick getaway with the help of sympathizers in the city. But the plot was not put into operation because two of the revolutionaries, Kanai Dutta and Satyen Bose, decided to settle scores with a third, Narendranath Goswami, who had turned against the cause in jail and given evidence against the others. Having murdered the traitor, a month later in September 1908, both Dutta and Bose were sentenced to be hanged. The public response to the announcement was almost totally anti-British. The Bengali press reported how merrily Kanai laughed on hearing his sentence and how bravely he refused the right to an appeal. A European witness of the hanging in November asked Barin Ghose: "How many boys like this do you have?" An hour afterwards, Kanai's body was handed over to relatives waiting with a flower-strewn bier. As they carried him to the burning ghat, thousands of barefoot mourners joined in. When they passed the nearby temple at Kalighat, although Kanai was from a weaver caste, a Brahmin priest came out and decked the corpse with a garland as a tribute to a hero. Many housewives from respectable families anointed it with sandalwood paste and vermilion powder. Kanai's hair was shorn and the locks distributed as relics; so were the ashes. As a direct result of such scenes, when Satyen Bose was hanged eleven days later, the authorities compelled his relatives to cremate him within the prison yard.

The day of judgment on the remaining prisoners from the Maniktola group was kept secret for fear of a riot. Around mid-morning on May 6, 1909, five hundred military policemen took up position on the roads and lanes between the jail and the courthouse. The English judge in the case, who had been a contemporary of Aurobindo Ghose at Cambridge University in the 1890s, pronounced two death sentences, on Barin Ghose and Ullaskar Dutta. According to the report in *The Bengalee*—an English newspaper run by a Bengali but certainly no supporter of terrorism—Ullaskar responded to the sentence by singing:

> *Before the court sat, in fact before the clattering of the hand-cuffs and creaking of boots were stopped, a voice, at once melodious and powerful issued forth from the prisoner's dock… All the "golmal" [hubbub] in the room—even on the verandah—was at once hushed into perfect silence. Even the European sergeants—to whose ears an Indian tune would not naturally sound very sweet—adopted the posture of attention and began to listen with undivided attention.*

The song was by Rabindranath Tagore, one of many that had been sung throughout the city in protest against partition. *The Bengalee* printed the words—probably the first published translation of a Tagore patriotic song—which showed how Rabindranath eschewed jingoism in favor of adoration of Bengal's natural beauty and nourishing quality:

> *Blessed is my birth—for I was born in this land.*
> *Blessed is my birth—for I have loved thee.*
> *I do not know in what garden,*
> *Flowers enrapture so much with perfume;*
> *In what sky rises the moon, smiling such a smile.*
> *…Oh mother, opening my eyes, seeing thy light,*
> *My eyes are regaled;*
> *Keeping my eyes on that light*
> *I shall close my eyes in the end.*

The judge then handed down further sentences of life imprisonment in the Andaman Islands. But there was no conclusive evidence against

Aurobindo and he was unexpectedly released. His acquittal delighted Bengalis and annoyed the British who criticized the judicial process for letting the ringleader get off scot-free. The judge, however, maintained that "No Englishman worthy of the name will grudge the Indian the ideal of Independence."

On appeal, after political lobbying both in India and in Britain, the death sentences were repealed. Both prisoners were also sent to the Andamans. Barin was released ten years later but Ullaskar lost his mind as a result of the hard labor in the penal colony. He was sent to an asylum in Madras, later released cured and lived till 1965. Aurobindo left Calcutta and went to French territory, first to nearby Chandernagore and then to Pondicherry in south India. Here he founded a now-famous ashram and became a spiritual leader. His conversion to mysticism had come from his hours of meditation during solitary confinement in Alipur Jail.

I recall being driven past the forbidding perimeter walls of Alipur Jail as a child and listening to one of my uncles—a gentle man but a terrorist sympathizer—telling me all about the young revolutionaries who had once bravely paid the price for our independence. I remember a feeling of something like gratitude. Much later, I came to feel that the lives of these young men certainly exonerated Bengalis from the common charge of having no courage.

Hindu-Muslim Confrontation

If the Swadeshi movement and its violent fringe was largely ineffective against the British, its effect on Hindu-Muslim relations in Bengal was sadly all too influential. By 1907 the goal of *swaraj* (home rule) had captured the minds of eighty percent of Bengali Hindus, but had left unmoved all Muslims bar a tiny Calcutta-based group known as the Bengal Mahomedan Association. This group tried in vain to persuade Bengali Muslims to unite with Hindus in the cause of national freedom, while the viceroy Lord Minto appealed to their self-interest and courted them as a counterbalance to the anti-partition movement.

Trouble soon broke out between the two communities in the early months of 1907 in Comilla and Jamalpur in East Bengal, where a nationalist boycott of foreign goods had the effect of forcing poor Muslims to buy *swadeshi* goods at a higher price than their foreign equivalents. Itinerant mullahs, preaching in village mosques against the nationalists through sermons and pamphlets, heightened the tension. Rumors of communal atrocities in remote villages printed in sectarian newspapers made the situation worse. Aurobindo Ghose, writing in *Bande Mataram*, called blatantly for confrontation with Muslims: "The Mahomedans may be numerically superior in some districts, but in India as a whole Hindus outnumber the Mahomedans. And is not this an occasion for all India to take up the cause of dishonoured religion?" The fact that the landlords in East Bengal were mainly Hindu, while their tenants were Muslim, contributed further to the discord. All over Bengal, there grew an atmosphere of pervasive mistrust between Hindus and Muslims.

In Calcutta, following Minto's government reforms introducing Indian members into the legislature, competition between the two communities for official posts was fierce, creating resentment between the educated classes. But the first violent clash arose from a different kind of rivalry, between Muslims and Marwaris.

The Marwaris and Barabazar

The bulk of the Marwari community in Calcutta had come late to the city, chiefly around 1890, from their home state of Rajasthan, escaping its desert and drought conditions, although some arrived even in the 1830s. Traditionally, Marwaris were money-lenders who worked extremely hard, took business risks, and looked after their own, while mostly following Jainism in religion. They soon established a thriving business in money-lending and petty trading in north Calcutta's Barabazar. They also embellished the showy Jain temple at Badridas Temple Street, designed and built by Rai Bahadur Badridas, a court jeweler, in 1867 and described by Geoffrey Moorhouse as "a shrine of filigree delicacy and sherbet sweetness... with mirror-glass mosaic smothering its interior"—a place well worth visiting.

Nowhere in Calcutta are the sights, sounds and smells of the city more vivid than in the labyrinth of Barabazar. This is where the starving protagonist of Dominique Lapierre's sentimental bestseller *City of Joy* (1985) arrives in search of survival and, maybe, a fortune. To reach its alleys full of an amazing collection of goods, you have to dodge all manner of overloaded vehicles, coolies with huge loads precariously balanced on their heads, and thousands of people.

The British established the market on the site of an old bazaar in the late eighteenth century for trading in jute and textiles because the location was close to river transport. With the building of Haora Station in 1854 and Haora Bridge in 1874, Barabazar expanded into the biggest wholesale market in India with a stock ranging "from pins to elephants," as they say in Bengali. In the sari section alone, the astounding range of designs, textiles and colors runs into thousands. Most of the traders are Marwaris and Punjabis with only a scattering of Bengalis. The main form of currency is hard cash; it is impossible to miss the traders licking their index fingers and counting huge bundles of rupee notes.

Here you may feel choked by the smell of burning fuel, rotten food debris and organic excretions of various kinds. But you will also be assailed by savory smells wafting from roadside food stalls frying samosas, onion bhajis and delicious omelettes. Around the area of fresh produce, the smell of ripe mango or jack-fruit will overwhelm you, and the heady mixed fragrance of flowers, sandalwood paste and incense from some small shrine nearby will entice you to take a peep.

Sprawling over five square miles and catering for more than a million people every day, Barabazar is a dingy, rackety, overcrowded, daunting and yet oddly orderly place, with each trader owning at least a desk space and a letter box. Larger traders have a private showroom for their wares, while others work with sample goods. Deals are done in a relaxed manner over a cup of tea or a bottle of Thums Up (a highly sweetened cola manufactured by the Coca-Cola

Pavement peddler in Barabazar

company specifically for sweet-toothed Indians). Traditional trading offices exude a social atmosphere, featuring a low-level sitting area (known as a *gaddi*) scattered with bolsters. Most traders have been here for over decades and are resourceful types. Although computers have arrived, it is mobile phones that are the most popular technology; mobiles allow the traders to keep in continuous contact with Lyons Range in central Calcutta, the city's stock exchange.

The big business of the city is not done in Barabazar. It occurs in the network of streets around the Writers' Building, lined with trading offices and company headquarters. During the day the area heaves with clerks, male and female, who weave their way between the vehicles and the street merchants. The Birlas, an all-India Marwari-run family company, are the biggest players, owning a diversified business empire that ranges from agricultural tools to shipping and automobiles. The Birlas are often compared to American dynasties like the Fords and the Rockefellers, both for their business acumen, their wider influence in society and their somewhat dubious early history.

The state government is currently encouraging trade and commerce to spread out from this hectic commercial hub around BBD Bag (Dalhousie Square) to other areas of the city like Park Street and Salt Lake (see p.192). The modern district of Salt Lake now hosts several hi-tech industries and is home to a thriving software export business. The "hottest" spot for business is now fittingly Camac Street, named after William Camac, a senior East India Company merchant in the days of Cornwallis and Wellesley (no name change here yet!). Camac Street runs from Park Street to Lower Circular Road and has been the haunt of the rich and classy for over two hundred years or so. However, the rising cost of maintenance, disputes over inheritance and ever-escalating tax bills are forcing the present owners of crumbling grand houses to sell up to property developers who are building multi-story complexes that they can rent out to business houses. The government's commerce department is here and more departments from the Writers' Building are due to transfer to the area. There are also expensive shopping arcades, restaurants, cafés and bars where Calcuttans in designer clothing like to hang out.

Communal Riots and Non-cooperation

During the economic turmoil of the First World War, Marwaris made a killing out of speculative buying and selling, not to speak of adulteration of foodstuffs such as ghee (clarified butter)—while at the same time attempting to outlaw the Muslim slaughter of cows for beef. It was not long before they were detested by both Hindus and Muslims for making money unscrupulously while living in a world of their own in large houses protected by armed guards from Rajasthan. When, soon after it was founded in 1911, the Calcutta Improvement Trust began to clear the slums inhabited by poor Muslims, the land was sold to wealthy Marwaris who built ostentatious mansions on roads like Zakaria Street and Chittaranjan Avenue (now rented out because their original inhabitants have moved to more sought-after addresses in Park Street, Alipur and Khidirpur). The dislodged Muslim tenants were duly aggrieved.

Calcutta's Muslims were already disappointed by the rescinding of the partition and the reunification of Bengal in 1911. Then, during the First World War, there was a sharp increase in the price of essentials like rice, wheat, salt, cooking oil and clothes because of speculative hoarding by Marwaris—which hit poor Muslims in Calcutta hardest and further fueled their resentment. By the second half of 1918, the scene was set for the first of several major communal riots in Calcutta.

By then a fair number of wealthy Muslims—exiled princes (like the descendants of the nawab of Oudh and his entourage settled in Metiaburz, a southwestern suburb inhabited now mainly by Muslim tailors), landlords, and merchants—were living in the city. At the same time, as we know, the labor force contained a large Muslim element, which was increasing with the industrial development of Calcutta. The two groups would meet regularly at the Nakhoda Mosque.

The Muslim elite provided the oppressed poor with the leadership required to rebel against their conditions. Their growing disaffection was easily manipulated when Turkey joined the First World War against the Allies. Although the vast majority of Calcutta Muslims had no understanding of international politics, the pillars of their community presented the war against Turkey as a war on Islam. Weekly sermons at the Nakhoda Mosque drove the message home and gradually the congregation came to see a connection between their personal grievances and the alleged international conspiracy to undermine their faith. They were ready for a *jihad*, a holy war, not only against the Marwaris but also against the British.

For three days, from September 9-11, 1918, the Muslim mob damaged or destroyed civic property, the public transport system and some Marwari houses including the Jain temple, without touching any of the Hindu temples and shrines in the area. Marwari-owned shops were ransacked and set on fire. Several traders were stabbed and killed. In the final count, forty-three civilians died—thirty-six of them Muslims—and four hundred people were arrested. The stock exchange was closed because of the absence of the Marwaris; there was a food shortage, and north Calcutta's streets had to be cleared of debris before the city could function again. But Bengali Hindus were unharmed and not a single Hindu among the police force was hurt. Even so, the riot was the start of the labor unrest that has dogged the city ever since. Most of the mill workers in the industrial suburb of Garden Reach were upcountry Muslims, who were politicized by agitators calling on them to attend a rally instead of going to work. When they went on strike, they found themselves pitted against their European employers, with serious consequences.

The first big communal riot severely disrupted normal life, especially in north Calcutta. Law and order was gradually restored— only to be disrupted again by an unprecedented demonstration of temporary solidarity between Hindus and Muslims, as Gandhi launched his movement of civil disobedience. From 1920 onwards, until independence and after, Calcutta would be in an almost constant state of tension.

The repressive legislation that had provoked the Amritsar massacre in April 1919 was known as the Rowlatt Act; it became law in late 1918. Not long after, Gandhi issued a rallying call against the measures in the act, and this received a response from Calcutta's Hindu population, led by Surendranath Banerjee, Chittaranjan Das and Subhas Chandra Bose. In 1919 Hindus and Muslims took to the streets shouting "Bande Mataram!" and "Ali Ali!" in unison, under the unlikely joint banner of Gandhi's *satyagraha* (truth force) and the Muslim Khilafat (Caliphate) Movement, which was agitating to retain the sultan of Turkey, defeated in the war, as the caliph or religious head of the Islamic world. A joint meeting of Hindus and Muslims was held inside the Nakhoda Mosque in the same year, chaired by Gandhi's son Hiralal. Soon, educated Bengalis threw themselves into a flurry of political activity, raising funds, holding meetings, preaching temperance, and of course spinning and weaving. The cult of the spinning wheel, known as the *charka*, was Gandhi's pet project, and it caught on even in Calcutta, despite the opposition of Tagore, who rightly regarded it as an ineffective activity for nation building. As he wrote scathingly to a Bengali friend in 1929: "The *charka* does not require anyone to think: one simply turns the wheel of the antiquated invention endlessly, using the minimum of judgement and stamina. In a more industrious and vital country than ours such a proposition would have no chance of acceptance—but in this country anything more strenuous would be rejected." But Tagore was here in a small minority; virtually every household in Calcutta acquired at least one *charka* which family members would take turns to spin solemnly each day and then send the threads to the weavers. The act of spinning generated a warm patriotic glow in the new era of mass politics.

The climax of this first phase of non-cooperation came with a nationwide general strike on November 17, 1921 against the prince of Wales' visit to India. In response to Gandhi's call, Calcutta that day looked like a deserted city with empty streets, closed shops and offices, and no switching on of electric lights at night. It was seen as a national day of mourning, according to *The Statesman's* editorial on the following day.

But as the newly politicized masses slowly became addicted to the excitement of patriotic activity and relative anarchy on the streets, communal discord simmered below the apparently harmonious surface of nationalist politics. Inflammatory political leaflets continued to circulate underground in both communities. Hindus felt that the majority community had a right to impose itself on the minority communities; mullahs continued to incite anti-Hindu animosity at weekly sermons in the mosques.

On April 2, 1926, a group of Hindus belonging to the Arya Samaj led a procession singing devotional music which passed noisily outside a mosque in north Calcutta while the Muslims were engaged in prayer. This provoked the city's second major communal riot. Marwari houses and warehouses were again vandalized and looted, and these acts of violence were followed by attacks on Muslim property and persons. The violence was supported on the Muslim side by the deputy mayor of Calcutta, H. S. Suhrawardy, and on the Hindu side by the terrorist *akhras*. Although statements were issued by both communities ostensibly condemning the incidents, street brawls and stabbings now became regular occurrences in certain parts of the city.

A new group of troublemakers, known as *goondas*, embarked on a savage spree of damage and destruction, including places of worship. Such hoodlums were originally commandos in the service of the East India Company, who were later retained by wealthy landlords for protection and dirty work. Now they were hired by political factions to extort money from supporters and beat up political opponents. After the 1918 riot, Marwari merchants brought in *goondas* from neighboring Bihar, uneducated but strong and macho young men willing to do almost anything for money and power. They became such a nuisance to ordinary citizens that the government passed a Goonda Act in 1923 to control them. After independence, ordinary Calcuttans suffered increasingly under their tyranny; people spoke casually of "Congress *goondas*", "Marxist *goondas*" and other types of *goonda*. Today, they form the majority population in Calcutta's prisons with criminal records ranging from pilfering to contract murder.

There was an important difference between the riot in 1926 and that in 1918: the communal polarization had become much sharper. Hindus were organized in the second riot, driving out Muslim marauders with bricks hurled from roof tops; while Muslim pockets near the Nakhoda Mosque and in Mechuabazar and Kalabagan became no-go areas for Hindus. Nevertheless, there were instances of mutual cooperation in quelling the violence. Many Muslims protected their Hindu neighbors, and vice versa.

But in general, from the time of the 1926 riot onwards, Calcutta became a city of processions and demonstrations with an increasingly chaotic work culture. At the feeblest excuse, half a dozen people would begin a march with a makeshift banner and shout slogans; and many more would quickly join in, disrupting traffic and becoming rowdy. The first target would usually be a tramcar. The bewildered passengers would be forced off, and the car would be set alight. The fire brigade would then arrive, almost always in time to stop the conflagration getting out of hand. In due course, the tramways authority no longer bothered to repaint and repair the vehicles, and Calcutta's once-gleaming and elegant trams (as I remember them even as late as the 1960s) came to look like battered and burnt cooking pans. Perhaps the communist government that has ruled the city since the late 1960s decided to indulge this culture of protest as being a safer outlet for people's frustrations than the armed revolution of the early 1970s. Anyway, Calcuttans have grown to tolerate such civic hazards—just as they must tolerate the floods during the monsoon that annually turn parts of the city, such as Jorasanko, into a shabby Venice with half-drowned rickshaws plying the streets instead of gondolas.

The Rise of Subhas Chandra Bose

In 1927, a Trade Union Act came into force enabling employees to form their own union. As it lacked effective provisions against irresponsible strikes and picketing, Calcutta's labor force grew steadily more militant. Dock and transport workers, railroad workers, mill hands, garbage collectors, sweepers—all began to use their clout to paralyze economic and civic life. Agitators from both the political right and left infiltrated the unions; by 1930 the communists had established a firm hold, working at the grass-roots and organizing popular campaigns through small meetings and simply written handouts.

This atmosphere provided fertile ground for a return of revolutionary terrorism, which had been relatively dormant during the 1920s. In December 1930, three terrorists entered the Writers' Building—the administrative center of the Government of Bengal—and managed to obtain an interview with Colonel Simpson, the inspector-general of prisons. Having shot him dead, two of the assassins, Badal Gupta and Dinesh Chandra Gupta, took cyanide and escaped capture; the third, Binay Krishna Basu, survived, and was tried and hanged for murder the following year. All three were young men (Badal was only 18) from respectable families, following the earlier tradition of educated terrorists at the time of the 1905 partition. Their memories were preserved when, after independence, Dalhousie Square, the north side of which is occupied by the Writers' Building, was renamed Binay-Badal-Dinesh Bag. This is usually shortened to BBD

Bag, using the English initials of the martyrs—although there exists another version based on their Bengali initials pronounced *Bibadi Bag*, which means roughly "garden in dispute"!

There were also women revolutionaries from respectable families. Calcutta's women had played a major role in the marches and picketing carried out by the non-cooperation movement, and had received the same violent treatment as men, along with prison sentences. By emerging from their homes and joining politics in large numbers, they gave a distinctive coloring to Bengal's and India's freedom movement. Better than the men at social organization, the women founded primary schools and maternity and child-welfare centers in Calcutta that would continue to benefit the city after independence, though the city women made little contact with the impoverished women of the villages, especially the Muslims who continued to observe purdah. Of the relatively few Calcutta women who went further than civil disobedience and actually joined the revolutionaries, the most famous was Bina Das, who fired a shot at the governor of Bengal during the 1932 convocation of Calcutta University. (She survived, and lived until 1986.)

Massive police surveillance and military operations crushed the revolutionary activities in Calcutta and various parts of Bengal during 1931-33; a whole battalion of British infantry and six battalions of Indian infantry—all Gurkha regiments (as used at Amritsar in 1919)—operated from two brigade headquarters in Bengal at this time. Much later, during the cold war, British intelligence officers who had experience of counter-insurgency work in Bengal, would be regarded as particularly valuable assets by the Special Branch and MI5—such was the reputation of Bengali terrorism in the 1930s. The repression continued under the governorship of Sir John Anderson (later Viscount Waverley) from 1932-33. So severe was it that the terrorists of Bengal would play no part in the ending of British rule in the 1940s.

Subhas Chandra Bose (1897-1945), the undoubted political star of Bengal at this time, was a regular inmate of British prisons. His incarcerations helped to ensure his popularity in Calcutta, where he became known as Netaji (Revered Leader). Even Tagore offered his support, dubbing Bose *Desanayak* (Leader of the Nation) and asking faction-ridden Bengalis to rally round him in a speech given in 1939:

"More than anything else Bengal needs today to emulate the powerful force of your determination and your self-reliant courage." In vain: Bose failed to unite his people, fell out with Nehru and Gandhi (and even Tagore), and during the Second World War misguidedly turned to the fascists in Germany and Japan for help in fighting the British Raj. (He founded the Indian National Army with Japanese support, and fought the Allies in Burma.) As Nirad C. Chaudhuri, who in the 1930s was secretary to Bose's elder brother, the Calcutta politician Sarat Bose, perceptively commented: "Since Subhas Bose was challenging what might be called the nationalist Establishment in India, he needed a party all the more. Yet he never had one. His following was always floating, shifting from year to year to different factions."

Yet no other Indian political leader so captivated Bengal, with its revolutionary romanticism, as Subhas Chandra Bose. His patriotic ardor and explicit hatred for the British are legendary. The letter he wrote in 1919 as a student at Cambridge University to a Bengali friend is often quoted approvingly in Calcutta: "Nothing makes me happier than to be served by the whites and to watch them clean my shoes." Political parties of all types—the Congress, the Marxists, and the Bharatiya Janata Party (BJP)—have each claimed Bose as a political godfather. Most major Indian cities have streets named after him, while the central government in Delhi, in addition to allocating generous funding for research into Bose's life, issued a commemorative two-rupee coin on his birth centenary in 1997. In Calcutta, despite Bose's fascist connections, the Left Front government named the city's new international airport not after Rabindranath Tagore, Bengal's greatest son, but after Subhas Chandra Bose—Bengal's Netaji.

The Netaji Bhavan, his ancestral home on Lala Lajpat Road (formerly Elgin Road) in Bhabanipur in south Calcutta, is now a museum celebrating his life and achievements through photographs, statues and other approved memorabilia. Beneath the porch is a replica of the Singapore memorial to the martyrs of his Indian National Army blown up by the British in 1945. Outside in the yard is Bose's get-away car, in which he escaped from house arrest in January 1941, dressed as a Muslim upcountry gentleman. Having reached Delhi, he boarded the Frontier Mail to Peshawar, and from there, disguised as a mute Pathan pilgrim, went by mule across the Afghan border and was eventually smuggled to Nazi Germany, from where he went by German submarine to Japan.

Many Bengalis still revel in the story of his great adventure; for them Bose retains the charisma of a Che Guevara, untarnished by his later career. In fact for several decades, until the 1980s, many people in Calcutta refused to accept the official Indian account of Netaji's death in a mysterious plane crash in Taiwan at the end of the Second World War, and insisted that he was still alive and would return to India. In Calcutta's *addas* they still like to speculate about how Bose would have solved the Indo-Pakistan and Indo-China conflicts which have dogged the country since independence. Around 1970, I was in the College Street coffee house when a group got into a violent disagreement about the precise nature of Bose's relationship with Hitler. In 2001, while chatting with some young men gathered near my family house in north Calcutta on Independence Day (August 15), I found that most of them believed their revered Netaji had marched on Delhi with his army in 1947 and driven the British out of India. When I told them Netaji had died in 1945, that he drank alcohol and ate beef, and had a daughter by an Austrian women named Emilie Schenkel, they laughed me away in disbelief.

Skepticism about his wartime role apart, Bose had genuine concern for Calcutta. He worked tirelessly for civic improvement as chief executive of the Calcutta Corporation from 1923 until he left India in 1934. He was elected as mayor in 1930, and put forward a program for education, medical care for the poor, and transportation, and visited other cities of India and Europe to seek out models for improving Calcutta. But as Nirad C. Chaudhuri has observed, instead of doing something concrete and far reaching for his beloved city, he "became more and more a prisoner in the hands of the hard-boiled and worldly middle-class of Calcutta, to whom civic welfare meant the welfare of their class."

Bose's moon-faced, bespectacled image in army uniform can always be spotted on Calcutta's walls in drawings and posters. He is often shown as a mythical hero riding ahead on a horse like an avatar of Kalki, the final incarnation of Vishnu, savior of the world, or as Shivaji, the Maratha leader who successfully resisted the armies of the Mughal emperor Aurangzeb in the seventeenth century. For Bose loved uniforms. His own was designed and made, ironically enough, by a firm of British tailors, Harmans. He gave himself the rank of General Officer Commanding and set up a volunteer corps with a women's contingent dressed in trousers. Gandhi caused much offense to Bengalis when he said that Bose's volunteer corps reminded him of the Bertram Mills Circus.

Three times a year in Calcutta—on January 23, Bose's birthday, on January 26, Republic Day, and on Independence Day in August—countless small memorial shrines with images of Bose and bunting in the colors of the national flag spring up in the streets of the city. The

Subhas Chandra Bose

potters of Kumortuli keep a permanent stock of clay busts of Bose. Early in the morning on these days, youths gather locally to sing the marching song of the Indian National Army, *Kadam Kadam* ("Forward Forward"). The tune is uncannily similar to the English nursery song about Noah's ark, *The Animals Went In Two By Two*.

The cult of Bose, for that is what it certainly is, is partly the result of his memorable anti-British sound bites, and partly because (unusually for a Bengali) he had some prowess as a military leader. He and his army were certainly courageous, even if he led them to total disaster in the jungles of Burma. He did his best to undermine the British view of Bengalis as effete babus by training his followers in disciplined activities, though with limited success; and in the Indian National Army he united all communities, including Hindus and Muslims, with greater success. But more important than anything else, the cult has flourished because of an absence of moral leadership in today's India—no Gandhi or Nehru or Tagore to set an example— which has created a psychological necessity to idealize Netaji Subhas.

The Bengal Famine

During the war, in 1943-44, Bengal was struck by a terrible famine that claimed somewhere between three and five million lives through starvation and epidemics. Generally regarded as man-made, the famine has long been the subject of much discussion, analysis and some controversy over the particular contributions of the Allied war effort, hoarding and profiteering in causing it. Although the worst effects were to be found in the villages, the famine had a major impact on Calcutta.

H. S. Suhrawardy was the food minister of the provincial government throughout the famine. In May 1943, just as it was beginning, he gave a public assurance that there would be no shortage of food in Bengal. Although there were rumors about lack of rice supplies due to hoarding and profiteering, the Bengal Government— which was by then almost entirely Indianized—did nothing to prepare Calcutta for the invasion to come. Villagers walked into the city in search of scraps, some dying by the wayside, the rest arriving half-dead. There they dragged their emaciated bodies from door to door begging for *phyan*, rice water, the starchy liquid left after boiling rice that is usually poured away or used for stiffening clothes.

My mother and my aunts used to keep *phyan* for these beggars. If any of it slopped over while being poured into their battered containers, they would immediately lick it up from the floor like a cat. Starvation had weakened their digestion so much that if they were given any food more indigestible than *phyan*, they would vomit. My father, who taught anatomical dissection at R. G. Kar Medical College, used some of the unidentified corpses of famine victims. He told me they had eaten dogs, rats and snails and garbage scrounged from domestic refuse. Malnourished babies were dumped at the doorsteps of Calcutta families and children were sold in exchange for food. A reporter spotted the body of a child half-eaten by a dog in Cornwallis Street (now Bidhan Sarani), one of the city's main thoroughfares. Calcuttans began to go to work stepping over an occasional corpse. By September 1943, there were clusters of dead bodies in the streets, mostly of women and children, but still the government did not officially admit to the desperate situation. Only in October was the Bengal Destitute Persons Ordinance passed declaring Calcutta to be famine stricken, and the police were instructed to clear the corpses from the streets and issue food to the starving.

Nevertheless, there was a concerted effort to suppress the exact statistics of fatalities from starvation and related diseases, such as cholera, dysentery and typhoid. At the height of the famine, around 11,000 people were dying every week in Calcutta. Jackals and vultures had a field day. The burning ghats of Nimtola in the north and Keoratola in the south filled the city with the smell of charred human flesh. One of the Doms—who organize cremations—told my uncle wryly that at least starved and dehydrated bodies saved on wood because they burned better and quicker than well-fed ones.

Otherwise, the harsh truth is that middle-class Calcutta life carried on pretty much as normal. There was no food shortage for government workers and professionals. Although many of the starving lay in front of shops and warehouses stuffed with food—there was even a bumper crop of wheat in the spring of 1944—they never raided any Calcutta shops. There was none of the disruption caused by communal riots. The famine victims were more or less resigned to their fate: they were simple village folk, confused by their unprecedented predicament.

Thus most better-off Calcuttans failed to grasp the severity of the famine—or at any rate closed their eyes to it.

They could not close their ears, though. The unforgettable whining of the beggars addressed to the ladies of a house, "Phyan dao Ma" (Give us rice water, Mother), was heard all over the city, as the novelist Bhabani Bhattacharya remembered: "You heard it day in and day out, every hour and every minute, at your own house door and at your neighbours', till the surfeit of the cry stunned the pain and pity it had first started, till it pierced no longer, and was no more hurtful than the death-rattle of a stricken animal. You hated the hideous monotony of it." Although *The Statesman* published some distressing photographs of the dead and dying, they made little impact in the city. Of course, there was no television. The desperate rural beggars were treated more as a civic nuisance than as pathetic victims; they became a race apart. "There was stink in the air but not much anger," recalled Mrinal Sen, the film director. Satyajit Ray, then starting out as a commercial artist, looked back and confessed that he had been "a little callous" about the famine: "one just got used to it, and there was nobody doing anything about it. It was too vast a problem for anyone to tackle." A quarter of a century after the famine, both film directors made sensitive, and to some extent conscience-stricken films about the period: *Baishey Sravan* by Sen, and *Ashani Sanket* (*Distant Thunder*) by Ray. The economist Amartya Sen, then a boy, witnessed this suffering with bewilderment, which spurred him as an adult to study famines. He recalled, "It is hard to forget the sight of thousands of shrivelled people—begging feebly, suffering atrociously, and dying quietly."

The Great Killing
In the run-up to independence in 1947, Calcutta was shaken by an intensification of communal violence. Never before had the city experienced such a tremendous outburst of primordial hatred between Hindus and Muslims. It was, of course, the wrangle between the Congress, led by Nehru, and the Muslim League, led by Mohammed Ali Jinnah, about how to divide India, that provoked the fury. Jinnah gave a call to all Muslims to suspend business on August 16, 1946. By then, Bengal was being ruled by a Muslim League-dominated ministry, headed by the famine-denier Suhrawardy. He

decided to declare August 16 a public holiday despite Congress opposition.

The Muslim League called a mass meeting at the Ochterlony Monument on the Maidan—now known as the Sahid Minar, the martyrs' minaret, at which Muslims still gather for prayer meetings. Streams of people converged on the monument. In the heat and humidity of a monsoon afternoon, they heard inflammatory speeches including one by Suhrawardy and became increasingly volatile.

For weeks they had been sharpening their knives and daggers for a *jihad.* Now, at the end of the meeting, they were uncontrollable and let loose their animosity on anything that came in their way, looting, stabbing, and burning. Slum dwellers in Kalabagan and Rajabazar were burnt alive or hacked to death with axes and swords. By evening a curfew had to be imposed, after which violators would be shot on sight. The night echoed with chants of "Allah ho Akbar" and "Bande Mataram".

The next morning a train, the 36 Down Parcel Express, was forcibly stopped just outside the city and its crew butchered. Families now took to sheltering in a single house, leaving looters to ransack their other houses. The mob had gone berserk. The area most affected was bounded on the north by Vivekananda Road, on the south by Bowbazar Street, on the east by Acharya Prafulla Chandra Roy Road and on the west by Strand Road. A downstairs room in my ancestral home in north Calcutta facing the street was let to a Muslim shawl mender. When the rioters broke into it, my uncles helped him to escape into our house through a service door. He shaved his beard and wore a dhoti instead of a lungi and hid in our house for some days, lucky to be alive. The rioters may well have guessed where he was but they left us alone. In those parts of the city like ours where Hindus and Muslims had lived together for a long time, there were many instances of trust and loyalty between neighbors. Even the house of the Tagores was attacked on suspicion of sheltering local Muslims. But mostly it was a story of senseless slaughter. Many Bengali short stories capture those terrible days. Perhaps the best one is "Adab" ("Farewell") by Samaresh Basu, written in 1946. Two terrified strangers, ordinary men, confront each other in a deserted nighttime street while sheltering on either side of a large rubbish bin. Rioting can be heard in the near-distance. Are the two men Hindu or Muslim? They do not know each other's identity and have no easy way of telling. Naturally, they suspect the worst. Basu portrays their wild oscillation between fear and fellow feeling with emotional power and concision, as they finally reveal themselves to be a Hindu and a Muslim. In the end they decide to help each other, but one of them, the Muslim boatman, is shot by a British policeman while trying to escape across the river to his wife and family.

In the event it took a week for the police and the army to restore some order. The Muslim League and the Congress tried to impose a catchy slogan "Hindu Muslim ek ho" (Hindu-Muslim unite)—but it was futile. The *goondas* were in charge, manipulating a combination of *jihad* and the cult of Kali. Hideous violence continued for three more days.

The Statesman blamed Suhrawardy's ministry for the carnage—with much justification. On August 20, it commented:

> *Maintenance of law and order is any Ministry's prime obligation... But instead of fulfilling this, it undeniably, by confused act of omission and provocation, contributed rather than otherwise to the horrible events which have occurred... It has fallen down shamefully in what should be the main task of any Administration worth the name. The bloody shambles to which this country's largest city has been reduced is an abounding disgrace...*

It added: "This is not a riot. It needs a word found in mediaeval history, a fury. Yet, 'fury' sounds spontaneous, and there must have been some deliberation and organisation to set fury on its way."

There was a massive exodus from the city. More than 100,000 people left by road and rail that week. About the same number lost their homes. So many people went missing that *The Statesman* published a poignant notice on August 21: "Information would be welcome about those Indian members of *The Statesman* staff in Calcutta who have not been in the office since 16 August. Would those whom the recent events still preclude from returning from duty please send news of themselves?" Meanwhile, the Hugli River was awash with rotting and mutilated bodies, and the city's sewers were blocked by bloated corpses.

Exactly how many people were killed during those ten days in August 1946 is difficult to ascertain. By August 27, 3,468 bodies had been identified; the total number of dead may well have been twice that figure. Small-scale butchery continued in Calcutta for a year. When Gandhi visited the city in mid-August 1947—he felt himself to be needed more in Calcutta than in the official celebrations of independence in New Delhi—in desperation he announced that he and Suhrawardy had agreed to live together in a troubled area, to stop the killing. They moved to a large house in Beliaghata belonging to a Muslim businessman which was surrounded by Hindu slums. The police protected it while Gandhi received admirers, mostly women, wishing to hear him say something about the forthcoming independence of India. But Gandhi's presence did have some calming effect on Calcutta during this period.

Despite the poisoned atmosphere in the city, Independence Day itself passed off peacefully in Calcutta, the streets thronged with people singing and embracing across the communal and caste divides, watched by huge posters of Gandhi, Nehru and Bose. (Not everyone was stirred, however: Satyajit Ray had absolutely no recollection of what he did that day.) At the stroke of midnight on August 14/15, 1947 women all over the city blew conch shells and lit ceremonial lamps. It was a time of joyousness—but for Calcutta the joy would be short-lived.

CHAPTER SEVEN

City of Strife

After 1947, Calcutta increasingly became a city of migrants—mainly coming into the city, but also leaving it. The Chinese community, for example, which was about 50,000 strong in 1947, first grew—following the Chinese revolution of 1949—and then slowly shrank, as its members emigrated to Canada, Australia, the United States and Hong Kong. By the end of the century, there were only ten thousand Chinese in Calcutta.

Like the Armenians, the Jews and the Marwaris, the first Calcutta Chinese were economic migrants. Around 1780, Yong Atchew received a grant from Warren Hastings of some land and money to set up a sugar plantation. More than 100 countrymen came to work it, and a subsidiary business sprang up distilling arrack. Soon these early immigrants were joined by deserters from ships, while a group of shoe-makers and tanners from Hakka district in China settled in Old China Bazaar Street at Barabazar, where their descendants still make cheap but satisfactory shoes. Today, most of the community are Indian citizens, hard working and prosperous, though forming a relatively closed community with its own mini-Chinatown, like expatriate Chinese the world over. As mentioned earlier, this Chinatown was once in Chitpur Road—where it even had its own opium dens—but it is now elsewhere. The post-independence Calcutta Corporation made a concerted effort to develop that area with multi-story business premises, and so the Chinese moved to Tangra in the east on the way to the airport, where they set up tanneries. Tangra has a Chinese school, social clubs, specialist shops and two newspapers, and restaurants that serve savory and clean food at a reasonable price. Only the Sea Ip Temple in Chhatawalla Goli remains in the Chitpur area, marking the original Chinese connection. It is difficult to locate, being hidden by taller buildings, but it can be recognized by its curved roof with two huge porcelain fish standing on their tails. Inside is a dusty collection of old Chinese weapons.

Yet the commercial basis of Calcutta's Chinatown is now under threat. In 2002, the state government ordered the closure of 530 tanneries in Calcutta on environmental grounds, more than 150 of them Chinese-owned, and their relocation away from the city in the neighboring district of 24 Parganas. But the new location lacks adequate infrastructure, and the Chinese leather-makers are furious; they say they will move right out of West Bengal, to Kanpur or Madras (Chennai), and that could mean the end of the leather industry in West Bengal and the loss of half a million jobs. However, it will not mean the end of the Chinese in the city, who have moved into pharmaceutical production and food processing, producing sauces and sea food for a global market. Calcutta will continue to celebrate Chinese festivals with illuminations, dragon dances and fireworks in Tangra, and paper lanterns and bunting in the Chinese restaurants of Park Street, along with the preparation of special dishes like *sau chu* (roasted whole pig). On the fifteenth day of the Chinese New Year, the Calcutta Chinese will continue to visit the gleaming tomb of Atchew in Achipur, an eastern suburb close to Diamond Harbour, and the Taoist temple nearby. The community, though small in number, will go on thriving as it has for over two centuries.

The same cannot be said of the Jewish community, which was much depleted after 1948 when most of its members left for the new state of Israel; even the bakery Nahoum's in New Market closed down. The city's original Jews arrived soon after Charnock and gradually grew in number until they were two thousand strong in 1900. The earlier migrants came mainly from Baghdad, with a later group coming from Romania during the Second World War. During the nineteenth century, they prospered by dealing in jute, tobacco, coal, and property, and became notably westernized, speaking English in public. Their contribution to Calcutta's hospitals was substantial. Elias David Joseph Ezra, the first Jew to become sheriff of Calcutta, erected the Maghen David Synagogue on Canning Street in 1884, where it still stands with resplendent colored glass windows, a vaulted roof and an ornate altar.

Refugees from East Bengal

By far the biggest migration into the city consisted of Hindu refugees from East Bengal, fleeing from discrimination and persecution in what had become East Pakistan. Although there are no reliable statistics on this exodus, by the time of the 1951 census a mere one-third (33.2 percent) of the inhabitants of Calcutta were recorded as having been born in the city, with everyone else being an immigrant: 12.3 percent were from neighboring villages, 26.6 percent from other Indian states, and 26.9 percent—more than a quarter of the population—were from East Pakistan, as a result of the communal troubles that had raged since 1907 and the 1947 partition.

The big migration began in the early 1940s, a steady flow of middle-class people who already had family and business ties with Calcutta and therefore could look after themselves financially. These people gradually bought houses from Muslims who were moving out of the city in the opposite direction, and settled down fairly well despite imposing a strain on the city's resources of housing and employment.

Then came an uncontrollable wave of refugees. Three quarters of a million of them washed up in Calcutta during 1948-49. In 1950, well over a million entered West Bengal. They included both the middle class and the rural poor, who had been forcibly uprooted, unlike the earlier migrants. Some—about a quarter of the 1950 influx—settled in relief camps known as "colonies". In 1949, there were more than 40 colonies in southeast Calcutta and some 65 in the north. Their "housing" consisted of temporarily built thatched huts, water drawn from a standpipe, and sanitation arrangements that were insufficient. Conditions were severely overcrowded and squalid. Yet these shabby clusters of shelters had grand names like Adarsha Nagar (Ideal City) and Bijoygarh (Victory Town)—the second of which still exists, though no longer as a shanty town but as a busy southern suburb. An original resident of the Bijoygarh colony told me stories of remarkable human resilience, resourcefulness, good neighborliness and compassion in those early days. When a tropical storm blew down some of the flimsy shacks in the middle of night, their occupants would be welcome to huddle under the equally vulnerable ones of neighbors, and as soon as the storm had passed, everyone would get busy rebuilding the demolished shacks. If there was a malnourished baby in the community, people would club together to buy milk for the child. There were long queues to collect a single bucket of water from the standpipe and to use the communal lavatories. But in general the refugees never lost patience and hope. Half a century on, my elderly informant was living in a decent brick house with his family who knew little of the plight of the first generation. "We were survivors. We coped," he said very quietly, almost as if speaking to himself. His sons and daughters, born in Calcutta, have no trace of an East Bengal accent, unlike their father.

Not content with the inadequate facilities of the colonies, some of the more enterprising refugees started to squat in empty houses in the city's suburbs. This is the first time the word "squat" and its new pan-Indian equivalent, *jabar dakhal*, came into ordinary conversation. There were a substantial number of such empty properties following partition, including the grand colonial houses of the departed British. So great was the tide of potential squatters that the police could not prevent them from taking over many of these empty buildings.

In addition, the West Bengal Government's ministry of rehabilitation opened empty warehouses and berthed steamers on the Hugli as temporary shelters. The platforms and concourses of the two main railway stations at Haora and Sealdah filled up, too, with bewildered refugees. Still more came after the dispute over Kashmir in 1951, and the entire city became a refugee relief center. The refugees were camping in the streets, scratching a living by setting up tea shops and tiny kiosks selling cigarettes and *pan*. Listless and bored, they spat the blood-red juice from chewing *pan* all over the city's walls and pavements, not bothering with a spittoon. Lacking any kind of sanitation, they defecated in the open gutters. Babies were born on the railway platforms and open streets without much ado, let alone medical treatment. The streets were alive with rats, cockroaches and flies, and scavenging dogs and vultures. Refugees who were near death were sometimes carried by relatives to the Kalighat temple for the last rites. They were the lucky ones.

Mother Teresa

These were the conditions that gave birth to the legend of Mother Teresa. On August 22, 1952, a feast day dedicated to the Immaculate

Heart of Mary, she opened her famous home for the dying, Nirmal Hriday (Sacred Heart) next to the Kalighat temple, in a house that was once a pilgrims' hostel but at the time was occupied by local *goondas*. She had obtained the property from the Calcutta Corporation through her personal contact with Bidhan Chandra Roy, the chief minister of West Bengal from 1948 until 1962.

As mentioned in the Introduction, the Albanian-born Sister Teresa (1910-97) had been in the city since 1931. She knew very well of its vulnerability to disaster such as the famine of 1943-44, and of its oppressive climate. Walking the streets in 1948, she saw the human catastrophe of the refugees and was moved to pity. Although her request to Rome for permission to found a new order in Calcutta was not immediately granted (the pope sanctified the order in 1950), she bided her time, contemplating her religious duty and working out an action plan. With an uncanny understanding of the psychology of charity, she knew that the images of dying human beings on the streets of Calcutta would trouble an affluent West and generate massive support for her Missionaries of Charity.

For two decades, she worked quietly in Calcutta, unheralded by the world. The famous image of Mother Teresa of Calcutta—her wrinkled face hooded in a blue-bordered simple white cotton sari with her hands folded in a *namaskar*—dates from the late 1960s. In May 1968, a BBC television Sunday-night program, *Meeting Point*, presented by Malcolm Muggeridge (who had known Calcutta as a journalist on *The Statesman* in the 1930s), beamed appalling images of Calcutta's poverty into British homes along with the dedicated work of the Missionaries of Charity. Muggeridge even claimed that a miracle had occurred in the filming; despite the low light level inside Nirmal Hriday, his cameraman had been able to work successfully—presumably (implied Muggeridge) because of Teresa's divine light. (The cameraman had a different explanation!)

Over the years since then, thousands of mainly British and American young men and women have traveled to Calcutta to serve Mother Teresa's cause. They were full of enthusiasm to do good to the Indian poor, and most returned home with a life-changing experience. Mother Teresa became a photo-opportunity for celebrities, the rich and the powerful from all over the world, from the Indian painter M. F.

Husain and Princess Diana to Senator Edward Kennedy and President Ronald Reagan. Like the pope, she became something of a globetrotter, rubbing shoulders with political and religious leaders, along with some decidedly dubious businessmen. In 1979, she was awarded the Nobel Peace Prize. At the beginning of the new millennium, despite considerable controversy, the Catholic Church seems determined to canonize her as a contemporary saint who ministered to the humble.

When she died on September 5, 1997—less than a week after Princess Diana—there was a massive funeral procession in Calcutta organized by the government, with Mother Teresa's body borne rather inappropriately on a gun carriage. Her order, the Missionaries of Charity, carries on in Calcutta under Sister Nirmala, a timid Hindu convert who has refused to call herself Mother and is reluctant to give interviews. Nor does her institution, Nirmal Hriday, lack inmates: I saw 85 people lying on mattresses during a visit in 2001. But the city whose name Teresa took to herself is distinctly uncomfortable with her glory. Her death anniversary is hardly commemorated and no street has yet been named after her, nor is there a statue of her (though a proposal is pending), even if there is a larger-than-life mosaic of her on the wall of the metro station at Kalighat. If you drive around the city, you will most likely see her image only in the form of old and tattered posters with her slogan "Calcutta is my workshop".

The main reason for discomfort is that Mother Teresa made Calcutta synonymous with poverty and slums in the mind of non-Indians, obliterating all other characteristics of the city, including its artistic life. In other words, her work gave new currency to the colonial notion of the Black Hole of Calcutta and Kipling's City of Dreadful Night. Secondly, many people who worked at Nirmal Hriday, especially foreign volunteers with medical knowledge, were dismayed by the lack of training available to the helpers—newcomers, for example, might be asked to bathe a leprous woman without receiving advice as to how to protect themselves—and even more by the lack of commitment to scientific medical treatment. Unlike some other Calcutta charities, the Missionaries of Charity did not care to nourish those with malnutrition or to nurse the diseased back to health; Mother Teresa apparently wanted only those who were about to die. Although they would scarcely be treated medically, they would be assured of an afterlife of eternal peace. When none of the city's hospitals could find space for a dying patient, they knew they could drive the poor soul to Nirmal Hriday in the dead of the night. There the dying person would lie on a foam mattress of green or blue plastic and receive a last rite, however alien it might be.

Furthermore—and here I have much less sympathy for Calcuttans' criticisms—Mother Teresa and her mission were a disturbing challenge to Calcutta's administrators, both because of her admirable determination and because she tried in her own way to improve the city. Without doubt she demonstrated how an individual with vision and persistence could draw world attention to a local humanitarian failure. With only five rupees and no training in business, she built a chain of 755 centers throughout the world—no mean feat. The Missionaries of Charity now run some 600 homes of various kinds in 125 countries besides India. Since her death, as with the Ramakrishna Mission, funds and volunteers continue to arrive freely. But still, if her order wishes to reconnect her name with the city that made her famous in a positive way, it should devote itself to looking after the poor as well as the dying by offering proper medical care. The Missionaries of Charity owe that to Calcutta.

The City in Crisis
The refugees camping in the streets received a subsidy from the government, however small. But the squatters had no means of subsistence. Everyone was forced to take whatever work was on offer simply to survive. The men became casual domestic servants, porters, sweepers, hawkers, rag pickers, and rickshaw pullers; the women became domestic helpers and often turned to prostitution. Others took to petty crime, while still others became *goondas*. When house owners tried to evict the street dwellers and remove the shacks of bamboo, straw, plywood, cardboard boxes, plastic sheeting, corrugated tin and newspaper that had sprung up on the pavements outside the boundary walls of respectable properties, these menacing *goondas* would turn up to defend the shanty dwellers and throw bricks through the windows of the houses.

Politically the refugees identified with the left. Bengali intellectuals pre-1947 were already oriented towards Marxism and social revolution

Bengal Famine, 1943, photographed by Sunil Janah

(notwithstanding the mass appeal of the fascistically inclined Subhas Chandra Bose). Now millions of ordinary people were destitute and felt they had nothing to lose, so they became easy fodder for agitators. Supported by the left-wing political parties, they became more and more voluble. This was the time when Calcutta's infrastructure not only became more squalid and crowded, but its walls also became covered in graffiti. The writings on the walls, indeed on any available surface, asked "Why are we here?" and "Are we not humans?" The questions demanded answers. The government of Chief Minister B. C. Roy did not know how to reply.

Most of the refugees had no identity card, passport or ration card. Visible everywhere in the city, officially they were invisible. The undernourished children who saw their first light lying on the pavements of Calcutta quickly became props for an army of beggars. With one arm outstretched, and the other clutching a deformed baby, mothers infested the streets, pestering for alms. Calcutta had never seen persistent and itinerant beggars like these before; hitherto, mendicants had congregated mainly near the temples and mosques and at the cremation grounds by the river.

The refugee invasion was too big for the city—any city—to handle. It scarred Calcutta and Calcuttans. Most residents had some link with East Bengal and felt a natural affinity with Bengali Hindus fleeing Pakistani persecution. As for the central government in Delhi, it did not offer much funding, busy as it was trying to sort out the administrative nightmares of a newly independent country of great complexity. Nor was any help forthcoming from the former colonial masters, occupied with Britain's own recovery from the Second World War. Calcutta was left alone to pick up the pieces with totally inadequate resources and no experience of coping with disaster on such a scale. No wonder slums multiplied throughout the city with a naked display of human misery, while anger, frustration and desperation unbalanced people's minds.

The city's writers and artists responded. Many of them joined the Indian People's Theatre Association or were sympathetic to it. Founded in 1943 as an anti-fascist group, the IPTA produced and toured plays about the plight of ordinary people, including the refugees. Poets of the time like Samar Sen and Subhash Mukhopadhyay and novelists such as

Tarashankar Bandopadhyay and Manik Bandopadhyay wrote about the refugees. The artists Zainul Abedin, Chittaprasad and Adinath Mukherjee painted and sketched them, and the photographer Sunil Janah, who had taken some of the most harrowing photographs of the famine in 1943-44, depicted the refugees in numerous images. The film director Ritwik Ghatak, who came from East Bengal, was deeply moved by their plight and a little later made a poignant melodrama, *Subarnarekha*, set in a Calcutta refugee colony, using a wonderful new actress, Madhabi Mukherjee, playing a woman forced to sell her body to survive.

Thus the 1940s and after were certainly troubled years for Calcutta, but culturally they were fruitful. In 1952, for example, there was a week-long All India Peace Conference in Calcutta attended by major artists and intellectuals from all over India including the painter Jamini Roy, the musician Ustad Allauddin Khan, the dancer Uday Shankar and the actor Prithviraj Kapoor. Calcutta also hosted the first international film festival (which included Akira Kurosawa's new film *Rashomon*); and the shooting of Satyajit Ray's first film, the classic *Pather Panchali*, began. Ray, Ravi Shankar and the actor and theater director Shambhu Mitra all began their careers during what was a hopeful time in Bengal, artistically speaking. We shall return to all this in Chapter 9.

Under Western Eyes

As Calcutta became a byword for human degradation, it began to attract foreign visitors with a taste for observing such horror. Although many of them could occasionally be intelligent, sensitive and balanced, the general trend of their observations was anything but. Some of their criticism may be excused by their ignorance, but much of it was clearly motivated by arrogance and disdain; they did not bother to do any research on the city, apparently feeling that their uninformed personal impressions had their own raw validity.

Perhaps the most interesting examples are the social anthropologist Claude Lévi-Strauss, the film-maker Louis Malle and the writer and Nobel laureate Günter Grass. Lévi-Strauss's *Tristes Tropiques* (1955), Louis Malle's *Calcutta* (1969), a prelude to his series of films *Phantom India*, and Grass' two books referring to Calcutta, *The Flounder* (1977) and *Show Your Tongue* (1988), have exerted considerable influence on western perceptions of post-colonial Calcutta.

Lévi-Strauss visited the city fairly briefly during the chaotic period of the early 1950s and was overwhelmed with disgust. But in expressing his horror, he shows little awareness of the city's history and complex culture. His implication is that fundamentally Calcutta has always been like this—for Indian cities are "the urban phenomenon, reduced to its ultimate expression":

> *Filth, chaos, promiscuity, congestion; ruins, huts, mud, dirt; dung, urine, pus, humours, secretions and running sores: all the things against which we expect urban life to give us organised protection, all the things we hate and guard against at such great cost, all these by-products of cohabitation do not set any limitation on it [i.e. the urban phenomenon] in India. They are more like a natural environment, which the Indian town needs in order to prosper. To every individual, any street, footpath or alley affords a home, where he can sit, sleep, and even pick up his food straight from the glutinous filth. Far from repelling him, this filth acquires a kind of domestic status through having been exuded, excreted, trampled on and handled by so many men.*

Lévi-Strauss saw the interaction of these individuals with himself as equally atavistic:

> *Every time I emerged from my hotel in Calcutta, which was besieged by cows and had vultures perched on its window-sills, I became the central figure in a ballet which would have seemed funny to me, had it not been so pathetic. The various accomplished performers made their entries in turn: a shoeblack flung himself at my feet; a small boy rushed up to me; whining 'One anna, papa, one anna!' a cripple displayed his stumps, having bared himself to give a better view; a pander—'British girls, very nice…'; a clarinet-seller; a New Market porter begged me to buy everything, not because he himself could get any commission but because the annas he earned by following me would allow him to eat.*

After mentioning "a whole host of minor players", such as rickshaw touts, shop keepers and street hawkers, Lévi-Strauss concludes that in the "grotesque gestures and contorted movements" of the ballet, he was witnessing the "clinical symptoms of a life-and-death struggle":

> *A single obsession, hunger, prompts this despairing behaviour; it is the same obsession which drives the country dwellers into the cities and has caused Calcutta's population to leap from two to five millions in the space of a few years; it crowds refugees into stations, although they cannot afford to board the trains, and, as one passes through at night, one can see them sleeping on the platforms, wrapped in the white cotton fabric which today is their garment but tomorrow will be their shroud...*

But this conclusion is simply wrong, however poetic its morbid imagery. Hunger was indeed what drove people into Calcutta during the famine in 1943-44, but it was history and politics, not hunger, that drove them there in greater numbers post-1947. By conflating the famine and the partition into one episode, Lévi-Strauss reduces Bengal and Calcutta to a primitive stereotype in which individual behavior plays no part. No wonder that he took no interest in the work of that great Bengali individualist, Satyajit Ray, whose film about the famine, *Distant Thunder*, humanized the catastrophe by focusing on a handful of individuals, and whose last film, *The Stranger*, about an anthropologist, was ironically enough based partly on the anthropological works of Lévi-Strauss.

Louis Malle and Günter Grass: Images of Horror

I saw Louis Malle's *Calcutta* when it was first shown in 1975, along with his seven-part *Phantom India*, to a packed London audience, following the sensational banning of the entire documentary in India. The Calcutta film struck me as a collage of random repulsive images: pigs snuffling in a sewer while slum children are at play; dying people at Mother Teresa's Nirmal Hriday; buses packed with people like sardines while others cling to the doors and windows like crabs; a cripple sitting in the middle of a public thoroughfare while traffic dodges around him; a leper with rotting flesh; and much more. Relentlessly the camera rolls and captures scenes shockingly at odds with normal life in a developed western metropolis. Who gave Malle the right to do this? And what was his purpose? I was confused and helplessly enraged by his Calcutta film.

Much later I read a letter written at the time by Satyajit Ray to Marie Seton, his first biographer, which clarified for me what was wrong with Malle's attitude. Ray had talked to Malle at length in Calcutta in 1967 and showed him some of his own work, but he was unsympathetic to the French director's whole approach to India, described by Malle as "the perfect *tabula rasa*: it was like starting from scratch." In Ray's view:

> *The whole Malle affair is deplorable. Personally I don't think any director has any right to go to a foreign country and make a documentary film about it unless a) he is absolutely thorough in his groundwork on all aspects of the country—historical, social, religious etc., and b) he does it with genuine love. Working in a dazed state—whether of admiration or disgust—can produce nothing of any value.*

There is a story told in Calcutta that while Malle was busy shooting a demonstration in Calcutta, an infuriated Bengali policeman came up and threatened to smash his camera, shouting "Who do you think you are?" On hearing the name "Louis Malle", the policeman smiled, said *"Zazie dans le Metro!"* and left Malle alone to work. The encounter is typical of a city in which ordinary people sometimes spring a surprise with their lovingly garnered knowledge of western cultural life. But Malle's film, with its preoccupation with the exotic and the bizarre, fails to capture Calcutta's genuine aspiration towards art and culture as a response to harsh realities. Malle was explicitly distrustful of 'westernized' Bengalis, and deliberately excluded Bengali artists and thinkers from his film; not even Mrinal Sen (who joined Malle in at least one of his shoots) is permitted a voice. Hence the fact that the film amounts to "nothing of any value", as Ray perceived, despite western acclaim for the documentary's truthfulness. Once again, as with Lévi-Strauss, history and perspective are signally absent. Indeed, it is very much as if Malle had taken Lévi-Strauss's fascination with Calcutta's filth and grotesquerie and set out to illustrate them on film.

For Günter Grass, too, the place is, finally, an embarrassment to civilization. His first visit was in 1975 as a state guest staying at the Raj

Bhavan. He visited Nirmal Hriday but did not meet Mother Teresa, went to one of her leper colonies, saw the Kalighat temple, visited the Ramakrishna Mission at Narendrapur and its cultural institute at Gol Park, and met writers, artists and intellectuals, including Sen but not Ray. Then he went home and wrote a novel, *The Flounder*, which contains a section on Calcutta, "Vasco returns", in which Grass' alter ego Vasco (named after Vasco da Gama, the fifteenth-century Portuguese explorer), visits India.

Here is Vasco's view of a Bengali writers' group:

> *They read one another (in English) poems about flowers, monsoon clouds, and the elephant-headed god, Ganesha. An English lady (in a sari) lisps impressions on her travels in India. Some forty people in elegant, spacious garments sit spiritually on fibre mats under a draft-propelled fan; outside the windows, the bustees [slums] are not far away.*
>
> *Vasco admires the fine editions of books, the literary chitchat, the imported pop posters. Like everyone else he nibbles pine nuts and doesn't know which of the lady poets he would like to fuck if the opportunity presented itself.*
>
> *Why not a poem about a pile of shit that God dropped and named Calcutta.*

Apparently the writers' sophistication vexed Grass. Like Malle (and Lord Curzon before him), he perhaps presumed that the middle-class babus and their women were deliberately out of touch with the realities of Calcutta. When writing of his meeting with Mrinal Sen, Vasco casually ponders: "In 1943... two million Bengalis had starved because the British army had used up all the rice stocks in the war against Japan. Had a film been made about it? No, unfortunately not. You can't film starvation." If we leave aside the simplistic economics, Grass was obviously ignorant of Sen's own film on the famine, not to speak of Ray's celebrated famine film, which won the top prize at the Berlin Film Festival in 1973.

Yet Grass was moved by the "cheerfulness" of the poor in spite of their misery. They prompt Vasco to make a highly emotional statement:

Send a postcard with regards from Calcutta. See Calcutta and go on living. Meet your Damascus in Calcutta. As alive as Calcutta. Chop off your cock in Calcutta (in the temple of Kali, where young goats are sacrificed and a tree is hung with wishing stones that cry out for children, more and more children)... Recommend Calcutta to a young couple as a good place to visit on their honeymoon. Write a poem called "Calcutta" and stop taking planes to far-off places. Get a composer to set all the projects for cleaning up Calcutta to music and have the resulting oratorio (sung by a Bach society) open in Calcutta. Develop a new dialectic from Calcutta's contradictions. Transfer the UN to Calcutta.

But his final line about Calcutta makes all this sound merely like delirious babble: "Let's not waste another word on Calcutta. Delete Calcutta from all guidebooks."

Having ignored his own advice, Grass visited the city again in 1986-87, now with his wife Ute, arriving with the professed intention of settling down in the place for a year to observe, write and draw (though in fact the pair stayed only for six months). They rented a garden bungalow in Baruipur within commuting distance of the south of the city. From there they used public transport, including man-pulled rickshaws, to move about, and experienced heat, humidity, grime, mosquitoes and officialdom at first hand. Ute Grass shopped, cooked and knitted. Her husband took notes and sketched, and also visited places away from the city such as Tagore's university at Shantiniketan. Later, when commuting fazed them, they moved to a small flat in Lake Town.

While in Calcutta, apart from being taken for Graham Greene, Grass toured a red-light district under covert police protection, visited burnt-out slum dwellers, entered a crumbling Marwari house in Barabazar, and watched the potters of Kumortuli at work. Militant young Muslims mobbed him and his wife at Metiaburz near Garden Reach when they went to visit the place of exile of Wajid Ali Shah, the last nawab of Oudh, who left Lucknow and settled in Calcutta after he was deposed by the British in 1856. At the Victoria Memorial, he was unimpressed by the haphazard displays, and during Durga Puja he was outraged by the lavishness. He was also bored by the famous Bollywood blockbuster *Sholay*, which he saw for an hour at a local picture house.

His play, *The Plebeians Rehearse the Uprising*, was staged but he was disappointed at the lack of response. But when he visited the Calcutta Social Project at Dhapa, which educates the municipal dump's child rag pickers, he was impressed. He dedicated his book on Calcutta, *Show Your Tongue*, to the project and its organizers Mr. and Mrs. Karlekar. (He continues to send donations to this project and keeps in touch through emails with people associated with it.) There was time, on this second visit, and freedom, since he was not a state guest, for Grass to have peeped into the heart of the city and to have talked with some genuinely creative people. But, once again, he strangely avoided Satyajit Ray, despite Ray's having made many trenchant and pessimistic films about Calcutta which might have been expected to interest a political radical like Grass. Films such as *Pratidwandi* (*The Adversary*), *Seemabaddha* (*Company Limited*) and *Jana Aranya* (*The Middle Man*), which, to quote Andrew Robinson's biography of Ray, *The Inner Eye* (1989):

> *depict, through the world of work, the stress of Calcutta living on young educated men at a time when this had never been more intense: the rise of revolutionary terrorism and massive government repression, followed by the Bangladesh war and refugee crisis, corruption and nationwide Emergency, leading eventually to the emergence of the Communist government that ruled Bengal in the 1980s.*

Grass even did his best to avoid the presence of Tagore, despite visiting Shantiniketan. When at a meeting with Bengali poets, somebody opined that Grass might soon receive the Nobel prize, he tetchily responded: "To you the Nobel prize means the climax of literary achievement because your greatest poet Rabindranath Tagore, had won it. To me however it is not all that important." Another time he told a Bengali woman friend: "Your first and last word is Rabindranath. You are unable to go beyond him. By 'literature' you only mean Rabindranath. That is your limitation." Fair enough as a reaction to Bengali provincial vanity about Tagore—but not at all an adequate response from a major writer wishing to know Calcutta. The fact is that both Tagore and Ray are demanding artists (as we shall see in Chapter 9) and Grass was unprepared to take them on. He learned no Bengali—when Bengali authors presented him with their works he would curtly refuse, saying "What shall I do with them? Do I have to learn Bengali now?"—but even without bothering with the language, he made little effort to comprehend the city's finest artistic products.

The outcome was a trite and inconsequential book, packed with his own oppressive scribbled drawings, illustrating a relatively short, incoherent text with significant factual errors. One might have expected that in revisiting a place he disliked first time around, Grass would have cultivated his knowledge and understanding of it. But reading *Show Your Tongue*, Grass' Indian interviews, and the memoirs of people who met him (recently published as *My Broken Love: Günter Grass in India and Bangladesh*), the impression is similar to that given by Lévi-Strauss and Malle: that Grass, too, wanted to gratify his curiosity about human degradation in Calcutta's slums and streets. Sadly, none of these three talented Europeans shows any sustained interest in Bengali "high" culture, apparently regarding it as enfeebled by western influences. All three sought to reinforce the idea of the "otherness" of the East, and did not feel it worth their while to move beyond their immediate sensory experience.

The Rise of the Left

When Lévi-Strauss visited Calcutta in the 1950s, the city was ruled by the Congress Party under B. C. Roy. By the time of the mass demonstrations filmed by Louis Malle in 1968, the Congress was being forced to give way to communist parties. In the 1970s, these parties came to dominate Bengal politically; by the time of Grass' second visit in the 1980s, the Left Front was entrenched in power.

There were two chief reasons for the left's success. First, the Bengali intelligentsia, which dominated the political life of Calcutta to the almost total exclusion of the business communities (Marwaris, Punjabis, Chinese, Armenians and so on), had long favored left-wing ideology of the Soviet variety, with an accompanying distrust of commerce. The businessmen, for their part, had done well out of the city, but had invested little in return (unlike in Bombay). The distrust between the Bengali babus in charge of politics and the people running the city's economy was peculiarly destructive of good civic governance.

Second, of course, there was Calcutta's unique refugee

predicament. The central government failed to grant a budget appropriate for dealing with the enormity of the city's population problem, and so civic conditions deteriorated from bad to worse after 1947. By 1966, there were estimated to be about 400,000 slum dwellings in and around the city with inadequate water supplies and sanitation. Their occupants were naturally inclined to vote for political parties of the radical left.

In spite of the slums, peasants from the surrounding rural areas continued to enter Calcutta to escape the declining agricultural conditions in the rest of West Bengal. Unable to find employment, these unskilled people often fell in with criminals and shady dealers and reinvented themselves as contract henchmen for dishonest businessmen and dubious political groups. As a lumpenproletariat involved in various protection rackets, they could be hired to break strikes, sabotage picket lines or infiltrate a political march and turn it into mayhem. Uprooted and unemployed, they were a destructive force without scruples. Their disaffection was further exacerbated by the new rich of the city and the culture of consumerism that was evolving to satisfy the wealthy minority's growing needs. Smart hotels and fancy houses were being built in expensive areas of the city like Alipur, while most of the population was barely surviving. The gap between the rich and the poor became so blatant in the 1960s that the situation was explosive.

At the beginning of 1967, due to drought, India yet again faced a food shortage of about ten million tons. There were repercussions in Calcutta's industrial sector: high food prices compelled people to refrain from buying consumer goods, which hit production and increased unemployment. Between January and March that year, over 23,000 workers were laid off in 95 industrial establishments. In elections the Congress government was finally toppled in Bengal, and replaced in February by a shaky coalition of breakaway Congress groups allied with two communist factions, one pro-Soviet Union the other pro-China. The communists' priority, as soon as they came to power, was to entrench themselves rather than trying to govern. At the beginning the communists achieved some minor successes by reducing taxes on slums and by rehabilitating some refugees. In rural areas, using politically active volunteers, the pro-China party legalized a land-grab procedure to reduce landlords' large holdings. A procession chanting "Mao Tse Tung Zindabad!" (Long Live Mao Tse Tung!) would arrive at a targeted plot and mark its four corners with red flags, declaring the land to be the property of the citizens' committee. As a result, the party managed to increase its peasant membership by 450,000 in West Bengal.

Against such a background of political and social upheaval, a small peasant uprising in May 1967 at a small place known as Naxalbari created a volcanic impact in Bengal and added a new word to the vocabulary of revolution—Naxalite. Naxalbari is near Darjeeling at the northeastern tip of India, on a strip of land between Nepal and East Pakistan (now Bangladesh). The country is hilly with tea gardens and dense forest and its tribal population has some reputation for insurrection. In Calcutta, the Naxalbari uprising was perceived as the action of desperate peasants taking up bows and arrows to fight the police and oppressive landlords. Although crushed within a few months, it set the educated youth of Calcutta aflame. The students of Presidency College created a poster celebrating Naxalbari, and soon the city was plastered with posters shouting "Naxalbari Zindabad!" Peking Radio immediately reported a great people's revolution in Bengal and predicted that the Indian masses would proceed along the path pointed out by the Great Helmsman Mao.

Like the revolutionaries of the Swadeshi movement half a century before, most of the Calcutta Naxalites were young, clever and idealistic students, from relatively well-off progressive middle-class families. Abandoning the security and comfort of home, metropolis and secure career prospects, many went to the villages for months to work among the peasants as Red Guards. To begin with they found the rural existence trying but they gradually won the trust of the villagers and politicized many in favor of armed revolution. Others went to work among the city's industrial slums, taking new identities to avoid police persecution and remaining out of contact with their families for long periods. Both groups were appalled by the poverty and squalor they encountered in the villages and in the slums, and felt increasingly militant. Working in secret at grass-roots level, they started to build a movement to overthrow the establishment.

Many older Bengalis had a degree of sympathy with the young radicals. Satyajit Ray, for instance, shows us a young revolutionary in

Pratidwandi, which was filmed at the height of the movement in 1970, who is intelligent and decisive but fundamentally one-track minded, unable to understand his elder brother's scruples about violence. When V. S. Naipaul interviewed at length a former Naxalite, who had been a student of physics at Presidency College in the mid-1960s, in *India: A Million Mutinies Now* (1990), the man recalled:

> *Many of the comrades before had succeeded in forming squads and carrying out annihilations, mainly in the area covered by the old uprising... Indians are basically a very violent people. I was doing Red Guard Action in new areas, and in spite of my best efforts I could not persuade the peasants to carry out a single annihilation—which was a cause of great remorse to me, and led to a feeling of inadequacy.*

He had not recanted his belief in violence but added, when pressed by Naipaul, that the "major mistake" of the Naxalites had been to accept the Marxist position that the intellectuals could lead the revolution: "I feel the people must liberate themselves. The intellectuals can only hand them the equipment for doing so."

It took two or three years before the violence in the countryside was unleashed in Calcutta itself. Superficially, in 1967-69, the city remained calm, apart from noisy street demonstrations. In Park Street and Chowringhee life remained as easygoing as before, as remembered by Sumanta Banerjee in his chronicle, *In the Wake of Naxalbari* (1980):

> *Swanky business executives and thriving journalists, film stars and art critics, smugglers and touts, chic society dames and jet-set teenagers thronged the bars and discotheques. All mention of the rural uprising in these crowds was considered distinctly in bad taste, although the term 'Naxalite' had assumed an aura of the exotic and was being used to dramatise all sorts of sensationalism in these circles—ranging from good-natured Bohemianism to Hippy-style pot sessions.*

But in 1970, the city once more became violently disturbed. The economy was collapsing because of trade-union militancy and factory lock-outs, the unwillingness of business to invest in West Bengal, and the reluctance of a "people's government" to use the police to restore

order. As film director Ray commented, with unusual despair, in an
article published in February:

*Here, while a shot is being taken, one holds one's breath for fear the lights
might go down in the middle of the shot, either of their own accord, or
through a drop in the voltage; one holds one's breath while the camera
rolls on the trolley, lest the wheels encounter a pothole on the studio floor
and wobble—thus ruining the shot; one holds one's breath on location
in fear of a crowd emerging out of the blue...*

One of those directing the agitation was Charu Majumdar (1918-
72). The clever son of a landlord from Naxalbari, he joined the
pro-Soviet Communist Party of India in 1938 and worked tirelessly for
it. But in 1969 he split from the party and on Lenin's birth anniversary
formed the Communist Party of India (Marxist-Leninist), which he
launched on May Day at one of the seething public meetings on the
Maidan that were a feature of Calcutta life in those days. Later he
coined the notorious slogan, "China's chairman is our chairman." Soon
Majumdar ordered his Naxalite followers to kill policemen and
informers in broad daylight, along with small businessmen,
government officials, and college teachers, which led to the murder of
a vice-chancellor by a young boy. For the next year or so the city was
an arena for guerrilla warfare. The *goondas* took advantage of the
situation and in the name of political activism started to vandalize and
loot anything that could be interpreted as being part of the
establishment. They also disposed of opposition gang members under
cover of political assassinations. Predictably, the government was soon
blaming all anti-social acts on the Naxalites.

Almost every day there were massive disturbances on the streets.
Bomb blasts were a constant background to ordinary life—in public
places but also in private homes when terrorist experiments went
wrong. Cinema halls and theaters were torched by hooligans, who
wrecked the racecourse and began attacking foreigners: British, West
German and French embassy officials all suffered. As robbery and
mugging reached a peak, many left the city. Incapable of controlling
such unbridled vandalism, and unable to get the political leaders to
cease fighting each other, the governor of West Bengal suspended the

state's Constituent Assembly and asked the central government to send in the army, as had happened under the British during the 1930s.

For a year and more, the military took over parts of Calcutta with orders to shoot to kill. Ordinary citizens were obliged to raise their hands over their heads simply to cross the road. Sumanta Banerjee again:

> *Clumps of heavy, brutish-faced men, whose hips bulged with hidden revolvers or daggers, and whose little eyes looked mingled with ferocity and servility like bulldogs, prowled the street corners. Police informers, scabs, professional assassins, and various other sorts of bodyguard of private property stalked around bullying the citizens. Streets were littered with bodies of young men riddled with bullets.*

During "combing operations" the army would often kill Naxalite suspects on the spot; others were beaten to death in prison. Between March 1970 and August 1971 the official death toll of Communist Party (Marxist-Leninist) members was 1,783, but historians think this figure should be at least doubled. After the movement had died down in Calcutta in late 1971, many of the Naxalites in prison were granted an amnesty and in some cases inducements for rehabilitation; the activist interviewed by Naipaul agreed to go to London to do a Ph.D in physics (he was accompanied right up to the aircraft at Dum Dum by police). Today Naxalbari itself is quiet again, languishing in neglect along with its busts of Lenin, Stalin and Charu Majumdar.

But Calcutta's agony was not yet over. During the second half of 1971, there was a new influx of refugees running from torture, rape and death at the hands of West Pakistani soldiers during the bloody birth of Bangladesh. Once again, as in 1947, refugee colonies had to be established. The civic amenities could not stand the strain; the slums mushroomed, there were constant power shortages, garbage mounted in the streets, and the water supply became seriously polluted. Hundreds of thousands of graduates, many with good degrees, were unable to find work, even as clerks. For a while, during the early 1970s, it seemed as if Calcutta would become completely dysfunctional.

Marxism Calcutta-style

When the Left Front took over in 1977, there were a few improvements in basic services, at least to begin with, but Calcutta's general economic stagnation continued. An ingrained absence of work ethic in government and the public services, combined with a carefully cultivated romantic notion about revolution in the general population, is a poor recipe for progress. By voting in the Left Front throughout the 1980s and 1990s—despite the collapse of the Soviet Union and its satellites—Calcuttans performed their sole political duty. Many voters liked the government's Marxist ideology, others knew that it would be sympathetic to strike action, which meant time off from work; and anyway there were no serious alternative parties in Bengal. But the poor labor relations under the Left Front drove industries and foreign investment away from the city—so much so that the long-running chief minister, Jyoti Basu, had to spend much time abroad in the 1990s trying to make West Bengal attractive to foreign capitalists. (Of course, his all-expenses-paid trips to London, New York and other commercial capitals came from state funds.)

The Left Front claimed to have intellectual and cultural aspirations, but their policies delivered little. Serious academics, especially scientists, have increasingly deserted Calcutta for other parts of India with a more creative and congenial intellectual atmosphere and better facilities. In the 1950s, the state government had supported some good work in the arts, such as funding Satyajit Ray's first film *Pather Panchali* and giving land for the Academy of Fine Arts building in Cathedral Road. But apart from building a major cinematheque, known as Nandan, in central Calcutta, the Rupayan film technology studio at Salt Lake in the 1980s, and the sports complex in Salt Lake in the 1990s, the Left Front government did little else to promote the city's culture other than changing street and place (and city!) names for reasons of political correctness. Now the government is even debating the idea of changing the name of the state from West Bengal to Bangla. Cultural icons like Tagore and (later) Ray have been liberally cited as evidence of Calcutta's international importance, but most Left Front ministers, including Basu himself, have revealed themselves to be embarrassingly ignorant of Tagore's and Ray's actual works. (It took the National Film Theatre in London, not Calcutta's Nandan, to stage the first complete retrospective of Ray's films, in 2002.)

Salt Lake City and the Metro

Yet even as it decays, Calcutta renews itself. The 1970s saw the beginning of an entirely new middle-class housing development to the east of the city. The project was inspired by the chief minister B. C. Roy, who launched it officially just before he stepped down in 1962, whereupon it was named after him: Bidhan Nagar. The concept—which appeared quite radical at the time—was to extend the city by filling up low-lying land in two swampy expanses known as the northern and southern salt lakes, beginning with twenty square miles of the northern part of the lake that lies close to the city. A Yugoslav contractor filled the salt lakes by ingeniously pumping silt dredged from the Hugli River. The pumps worked almost constantly for nine months. In the process, they not only reclaimed the land but also improved the navigability of the river.

This is the place where in the 1970s at a rudimentary rehabilitation center for refugees from Bangladesh, Senator Edward Kennedy spotted one of Mother Teresa's nuns, Sister Agnes, washing the clothes of a cholera patient and wanted to shake her hand. When she said her hands were dirty, he replied: "The dirtier they are the more honored I am."

Salt Lake is a project that has been well planned from the start. The area was divided into five sectors, of which the first three are residential and the last two industrial and commercial. The residential plots were deliberately kept small so that the middle-income group could afford them; and there are height restrictions on the buildings to avoid vertical congestion. Water supply, sewerage, drainage, population density and road space were all conceived together, and the result is a pleasant and clean environment with good amenities for shopping, sports, health and education, and good transport connections to the airport and the city. The biggest sports stadium in India, the 120,000-seater Yuva Bharati Krirangan, is close by, and next to it is the Netaji Subhas National Institute of Sports, a forty-five-acre sports center with modern training facilities and a boating lake. There are good modern hotels, too, because of the airport location, although Calcutta's best hotel, the

Taj Bengal, remains tucked away in Alipur. But all this means that since the 1980s, property prices have rocketed beyond the means of middle-income earners; Salt Lake becomes year by year more like a suburb for the wealthy with designer houses set beside tree-lined spacious roads. Also, the area between it and the city is fast developing with new industries, including electronics and chemical plants. But in spite of creeping urbanization, in the roadside ponds of brackish water along the Eastern Bypass you can still spot birds such as cormorants, little grebes and herons, and animals like otters and jackals and even, if you are lucky, a rare marsh mongoose. In spite of dense urbanization, the suburbs of Calcutta have a thriving bird population.

The Calcutta Metro is a success story too. But when its construction began in the 1970s, there was considerable skepticism from Calcuttans. For a start, the idea of an underground railway in a city built on a swamp is difficult to credit. Then there is the endemic problem of monsoon flooding. And what about the city's hordes of pavement dwellers? Surely they would simply move underground and clog the system. Most people were pessimistic—and became more so as the seemingly endless digging rendered the city's main thoroughfares, such as Ashutosh Mukherjee Road in the south and Chittaranjan Avenue in the north, almost impassable for well over ten years. I recall a wall poster likening the Metro project to the story in *The Ramayana* of King Ravana who conceived the impossible idea of building a staircase from the earth to heaven. The poster designer jokingly asked "Patal rail ki Ravaner sinri?" ("Is the underground rail Ravana's steps?") After twelve long years of disruption—massive holes in the streets, all-day traffic snarls, defunct telephone connections, dirt, dust and noise—the first stretch (only a handful of stations between Bhabanipur and Maidan) opened in 1984. Another eleven years later, in 1995, the line from Dum Dum to Tollygunj was complete. Soon traveling by Metro caught on and people became proud of the Metro.

The system is clean, efficient, cheap and comfortable—worth a joy ride. As you descend, you leave behind the chaos of the streets with dangerously overcrowded buses, taxis, lorries, scooters, rickshaws and many other forms of transport, along with teeming crowds, and suddenly enter an orderly environment. The ten-mile journey from Dum Dum to Tollygunj, which can occupy several sweaty and irritable hours above ground during the rush hour, is done by Metro in 33 cool and clean minutes for under ten rupees; and trains arrive at intervals of less than ten minutes. Neither monsoon flooding nor the homeless nor the graffiti writers have managed to spoil the Metro system. At Rabindra Sadan station you even have the added bonus of some attractive blow-ups of Tagore poetry in his own handwriting.

Calcutta Metro

CHAPTER EIGHT

City of Learning

Although educated Bengalis have always responded to western culture with obvious interest and pleasure, formal education in Calcutta has been regarded mainly as a means of economic advancement. The city is obsessed with getting qualifications; when its biggest English-language newspaper, *The Telegraph*, announces annual awards for the best school in Calcutta, it is an occasion for much competition and publicity. During rush hours, schoolchildren are ferried to school in a strange contraption like a tin box, approximately a cuboid, with two facing benches, a roof and cut-out side-windows, all of which sits on two wheels and is pulled by bicycle. As the box passes by, you may hear its occupants chanting lists of spellings (Bengali and English) and multiplication tables. Academically successful schools are much sought after by parents; with 12,500 pupils, South Point School in Ballygunj was listed in *The Guinness Book of Records* for having the largest number of pupils in the world until recently overtaken by a Filipino school, and is compelled to teach its students in two shifts. Parents of modest income often work long hours to send a child to a reputable school. At arrival and departure times in the respectable primary schools, mothers and fathers can be heard nagging their children about the homework carried in their heavy satchels crammed with books and papers. And as the time comes for a school's annual tests, the entire household suspends its leisure activities so that the student can concentrate. When at last he or she passes the exam, it is customary to share with family and friends a box of milk-white or light-brown *sandesh*, a unique Bengali delicacy made from milk solids and either refined or unrefined sugar (the best *sandesh* is made from the newly harvested sugarcane). In Bengali, the word has a dual meaning, both as the name of the sweet and as the Bengali for "good news". *Sandesh* is a part of all joyous occasions in Bengal. Try to buy it from the old-established confectioners Bhim Nag or Ganguram.

But perhaps the most impressive display of devotion to schooling is at the institutions run by welfare organizations for the children of the coolies who carry travelers' luggage at Haora station. The coolie children come willingly to school but fly from their studies like a flock of pigeons as soon as a long-distance train pulls in. Their haste is a financial reflex, as they run to collect empty bottles from the carriages. Within ten minutes or so, however, they settle again at their interrupted lessons, calm and collected. As a teacher it was a heart-warming experience for me to witness this scene. There is no doubt that average seven-year olds in Calcutta have far better literacy and numeracy skills than their British or North American counterparts, at least those in the state-run system. For education is perceived to be the only way to escape from the harshness of life—as a coolie or as an ill-paid clerk.

Many schools trade on this belief by forcing parents to donate money on top of the official school admission fee, demanding as much as £2,500 per annum. Most English-medium schools ask euphemistically how much potential parents are prepared to pay towards "philanthropy"; the more they offer, the more likely their child is to gain admission. And once admitted, further demands for donations to school funds for computers, furniture, air-conditioners, generators, playground equipment and so on, flow in. If parents are unable to comply, their child suffers. Thus, seeking admission to a good school and educating children have become among the greatest stresses on Calcutta's middle-class parents.

But learning purely for mental development rather than improving career prospects has never been totally absent from the educational picture in Calcutta. Individuals such as Dwarkanath Tagore and Iswarchandra Vidyasagar helped to establish schools and learned societies and foster the spread of education in Bengal for the general betterment of society. In the mid-nineteenth century, Rabindranath Tagore shunned conventional schools and was taught mainly at home in his family's house at Jorasanko, immersed in a demanding, if stimulating environment (apart from his English lessons, which he hated). He went on to found his own school at Shantiniketan, outside Calcutta, in 1901 and later a university there, Visva Bharati, along with a center for village development, which together were the inspiration behind the Dartington Trust and Dartington College of Arts in Devon, back in Britain. In the words of Leonard Elmhirst, who founded Dartington in 1925 after working with Tagore in Shantiniketan:

There was no aspect of human existence which did not exercise some fascination for him and around which he did not allow his mind and fertile imagination to play. Where, as a young man, I had been brought up in a world in which the religious and the secular were separate, he insisted that in poetry, music, art and life they were one, that there should be no dividing line.

Rabindranath despised the conventional, exam-oriented, textbook-based system in Calcutta's schools that allowed no scope for the free play of curiosity, imagination and pleasure—particularly in the arts—in the process of learning. In a satirical fable published in 1918 called *Tota Kahini* (*The Parrot's Training*), he tells of an ignorant but free bird who is put in a cage to receive a "sound schooling" at the whim of a raja and ends up stuffed with paper by the raja's pundits and choked to death. (Copies of the book, amusingly illustrated, were sent to the members of the Calcutta University Commission.)

Today, Tagore's educational ideal finds embodiment in many individual efforts to promote joyful spontaneous learning. One I know personally is north Calcutta's Children's Art Theatre, a non-profit organization which recently celebrated its twenty-fifth anniversary. It was set up by a group of parents who regularly meet at a venue in Bidhan Sarani (Cornwallis Street) at the weekends to encourage local children to develop their talents in arts and crafts, dance and music, drama and games. The children regularly perform at theaters and hold art exhibitions, but receive no payment. Apart from a few professional teachers, no one receives a salary.

Schools and Colleges

Before the British came, the nawabs and zamindars of Bengal encouraged education by making grants, known as *inam*, to learning establishments: Hindu *pathshalas* and Islamic *madrassas*; they also patronized learned men and a few women as court scholars. There is a colored engraving of an old *pathshala* by the artist Solvyns on display in the Victoria Memorial. In Satyajit Ray's *Pather Panchali*, a village *pathshala* is memorably depicted, in which the jovial local grocer supplements his income by teaching basic arithmetic and Bengali, while administering regular doses of corporal punishment with his cane. For higher, Sanskrit-based education, pupils would have to attend a *tol* run by pundits. In 1818 there were 28 such *tols* in the city, mostly situated in the Hatibagan and Simla areas of north Calcutta.

But it was the Christian missionaries of the nineteenth century who worked tirelessly to introduce mass education in Bengal, including the first elementary school for girls, founded in 1820. They taught in both Bengali and other vernacular languages and in English, with their pupils writing on sand, banana leaves, and palm leaves as well as slates and paper. The first local textbooks were produced by the Calcutta School Book Society founded in 1817 (no longer in existence), which had a close link with the missionaries in Serampore discussed in Chapter 3. In the first four years of its existence, the society printed 78,500 books—48,750 of them in Bengali, 3,500 in English and the rest in Hindustani, Persian, Sanskrit and other languages.

Macaulay's controversial minute on education of 1835, mentioned earlier, moved the course of Calcutta's official educational institutions away from traditional learning and Indian languages towards the teaching of western knowledge in English. His motives were as much, if not more, pragmatic as philanthropic. Training natives as civil servants was far more cost effective than importing clerks from London. Nowhere in Calcutta will you see Macaulay's educational ideas more confidently embodied than in the city's oldest existing school, and one of its best, La Martinière in Loudon Street (now U. N. Brahmachari Street). Although founded (in 1835) as a gift from General Claude Martin to the "children of India", for a century, until 1935, no Bengalis were admitted. La Martinière's portico and tall Ionic columns, its Round Chapel, its four houses named after Charnock, Hastings, Martin and Macaulay, its Latin motto "Labor et constantia", and its library of western classics—all bring to mind Macaulay's notorious comment that "a single shelf of a good European library is worth the whole native literature of India and Arabia."

Yet, as we know, the Bengali gentry supported English education. It opened up wider employment prospects for them and, of course, it brought them closer to western literature, science and philosophy. Although education in Calcutta has always remained a domain of conflict between Anglicists and nationalists, after 1854 the British recognized the responsibility of the government for education and established a system in which English would be used for higher studies by the few and vernacular languages for lower-level study by the masses. Three universities, in Calcutta, Madras and Bombay, were founded, with examining and degree-giving powers.

The prestige of Presidency College, located opposite Hare School on the northern side of College Square, dates from this time. It was the best source of western enlightenment for the babus of the nineteenth century, who flocked there in large numbers. Alumni in the early to mid-twentieth century included Subhas Chandra Bose, Satyajit Ray, and the city's latest Nobel laureate, Amartya Sen. In the 1960s the college became a hotbed of Naxalite activity. In *India: A Million Mutinies Now*, Naipaul describes the atmosphere for the young science student then at Presidency who later became a Naxalite:

> *One night [he] was coming back from South Calcutta by bus. He saw a crowd in the grounds of Presidency College. He got off the bus to see what it was about. He didn't find anyone he knew, but the next day, when he went back, he discovered that the leaders of the student movement, and others, were his friends. He began to spend more and more time with those friends, in Presidency College, in the coffee house opposite, and in the college hostel.*
>
> *He began to do political work among the students who were not committed.*

Since then, the standard of Presidency has somewhat declined with the Left Front government's anti-elitist stance on education, and some of the best lecturers have moved to other institutions. But it remains the city's most significant educational institution at college level.

Calcutta Cricket Club: Sport

English education and ideology inevitably brought in their wake English sports like cricket, hockey, rugby, football, tennis and golf, mainly from around the early part of the nineteenth century. Calcutta Cricket Club, founded in 1792, is generally regarded as the oldest cricket club outside the British Isles. The first organized match, watched by the bemused natives, was played on the Maidan in January 1804 between the Old Etonians (who were in Calcutta as East India Company writers) and the non-Etonians, designated as "Calcutta". The Etonians won, with Robert Vansittart scoring a century.

Fifty years later, in 1854, the club managed to secure a permanent playing field at the Eden Gardens (named after the two sisters of Lord Auckland who nurtured the two square miles of park land and gifted it to the citizens of Calcutta for recreation and enjoyment). Apart from the cricket ground, which has a capacity for 85,000 spectators, the Eden Gardens contain an indoor cricket stadium, two sports complexes, a band stand, a Burmese pagoda, and the prominent Akashbani Bhavan—Calcutta's radio station; it also has space for equestrian activities.

The first English cricket team visited the city in 1888-89 and the first MCC tour took place in 1926-27. Sarada Ranjan Ray, a grand-uncle of Satyajit Ray, is reputed to have introduced the game to the Bengalis in the 1870s and was dubbed by the British the "W. G. of India" (after the immortal W.G. Grace). During the twentieth century cricket become wildly popular, and it is played all over the city in the evenings and at the weekends, wherever there is some space—which means in the many quieter side streets, as well as on the Maidan and in the other parks. On the days when the trade unions call for a general strike, people even set up a wicket on the tram tracks and start to play. Now the sport has received a further boost as Calcutta is basking in the reflected glory of another Bengali cricketer. The captain of the Indian team from 2000, Saurav Ganguly, made his test debut at Lords in 1996 at the age of twenty-four with a masterful century. When he scores, Calcuttans beat drums and blow horns. With him as a role model, thousands of Bengali middle-class parents are sending their boys for expensive coaching. Suddenly cricket is perceived as a viable career, alongside the more traditional pursuits of medicine and the civil service. Biographies of Ganguly—there are already several in Bengali—are selling well, partly for lack of any other Bengali heroes but also because Ganguly is the quintessentially Bengali *bhadralok*: charming, cultured, charitable and hospitable, showing none of the aggressive characteristics apparently admired elsewhere in Indian cricket.

Street cricket

After cricket, football (or soccer) is the most popular sport. The first club was formed at Presidency College in 1884. Students of Presidency founded further clubs when they left the college, and in 1893 the Indian Football Association was formed. Bengal's favorite team is Mohon Bagan, founded in 1889. When it won the IFA Shield in 1911, defeating the East Yorkshire team 2-1, Bengalis in Calcutta were ecstatic. After the partition of India in 1947, Mohon Bagan regularly played against the East Bengal Club founded in 1921, which enjoyed the support of the refugees from East Bengal living in the city. The third popular club is the Mohammedan, supported by local Muslims.

Tennis, hockey, wrestling and body-building also attract a lot of enthusiasm; Monotosh Roy became the first Indian Mr. Universe in 1951. Golf, too, appeals to a small number of wealthier Calcuttans because the Tollygunj Club has an excellent course. Women, not surprisingly, are less involved in sport, though they started to play after independence. In the 1952 Helsinki Olympics two Bengali women took part, the athlete Nilima Ghosh and the swimmer Arati Saha, who in 1959 became the first Asian woman to swim the English Channel, while in 1988 Soma Datta competed in rifle-shooting at the Seoul Olympics.

Laboratories and Discoveries: Science in Calcutta

It was Rammohan Roy who first made the case for science education in India. Writing to the governor-general in 1823, he demanded a system of instruction in mathematics, natural philosophy, chemistry, and astronomy "with other useful sciences". Through his initiative and that of Dwarkanath Tagore, the Calcutta Medical College was established in 1835 to train doctors. The following year, when a Bengali instructor, Madhusudan Gupta, dissected the first human corpse, guns were fired at Fort William to celebrate the great event, although Gupta was ostracized by orthodox Hindus. (Prior to this, wax models had been used for teaching dissection, in deference to religion.) Dwarkanath also sent four young Bengali men to England to study medicine in 1839, and paid the entire expenses incurred by two of them.

The other noteworthy institution for science at this time was St. Xavier's College in Park Street founded in 1860 by Belgian Jesuits. It remains a sought-after college today, though not especially for science. St. Xavier's produced India's first modern scientist, Sir Jagadish Chandra Bose (1858-1937), who read physics at the college before going to Cambridge, achieving a brilliant result in the tripos, and eventually returning to Calcutta as the first Indian professor of physics at Presidency College. But since he was offered two-thirds of the salary granted to the European professors, in protest he refused to accept any salary at all, while continuing to teach; eventually the government conceded.

Funds were not easily forthcoming from Bose's countrymen either. Tagore was Bose's greatest Bengali advocate and raised money from the maharaja of a local state to enable Bose to stay in Europe in 1900 and carry on his research. Commenting on the prospect of his future glory and its effect on Bengali society, Rabindranath Tagore wrote wryly to Bose:

> ...when victory is yours, we too—all of us Bengalis—will share in the honour and the glory. We do not need to understand what it is you have done, or to have given you any thought, time or money; but the moment we hear the chorus of praise in The Times from the lips of an English-man we shall lap it up. Some important newspapers in our country will observe that we are not inferior men; and another paper will observe that we are making discovery after discovery in science. ...

Sowing and ploughing you will do alone; reaping we shall do together.

Scientifically, Bose had two distinct careers. Before 1900 he was a physicist, whose pioneering work in the late 1890s on the effects of electromagnetic radiation on metals received invaluable early recognition in the West, and contributed to the development of wireless telegraphy and radio. But, unlike the business-minded Marconi, Bose refused to patent his inventions because he believed that financial gain was inappropriate for a true scientist. After 1900, he extended his study to the effects of radiation on plant and animal tissues. He invented and built some highly ingenious and sensitive apparatus to reveal striking but debatable similarities in the responses to electrical stimulus of living and non-living substances. His instruments can be viewed with special permission at the Bose Research Institute at Lower Circular Road (now Jagadish Chandra Bose Road), which he founded in 1917. Although this later physiological work was greeted with less enthusiasm in the West than his work as a physicist, Bose became a celebrity, was given a knighthood, and in 1920 became the first Indian scientist to become a fellow of the Royal Society (following the first Indian fellow, the mathematician Srinivasa Ramanujan).

The bacteriologist Sir Ronald Ross (1857-1932), a member of the Indian Medical Service, worked in Calcutta for a brief period in the 1890s and discovered the cause of malaria there, for which he was awarded a Nobel prize in 1902. It was in a tiny laboratory in Calcutta's Presidency General Hospital (now with the tongue-twisting name Seth Sukhlal Karnani Memorial Hospital, abbreviated as SSKM Hospital), that Ross established how mosquitoes transmit the malarial parasite in their bite. A commemorative tablet at the entrance to the hospital carries a verse composed by Ross (who fancied himself as a poet):

This day relenting God
Hath placed within my hand
A wondrous thing; and God
Be praised, at his command
Seeking his secret deeds
With tears and toiling breath

I find thy cunning seeds
O million-murdering death.
I know this little thing
A myriad men will save.
O death where is thy sting
And Victory, O grave?

One of the new, post-colonial street names of the city is Ronald Ross Sarani. The city authorities always include Ross in the roster of Calcutta's Nobel laureates.

Although the south Indian physicist Sir Chandrasekhara Venkata Raman (1888-1970), who also won a Nobel prize, is primarily associated with the Indian Institute of Science at Bangalore, the work for which he is best known was done in Calcutta. He arrived in the city from Madras in search of a job in 1907, and in 1917 became professor of physics in Calcutta's new University College of Science at Rajabazar, in the south. During a voyage to Europe in 1921 he became fascinated by the azure hue of the Mediterranean's water. He decided to find out more about the scattering of light by different substances, and his experiments demonstrated a change in the wavelength of light when a light beam is deflected by molecules, best explained by regarding the light beam not as a wave but as a stream of particles: an important piece of evidence for the truth of quantum theory. His discovery of this "Raman effect" won him the Nobel prize in 1930, three years before Raman left Calcutta after a sharp dispute with his Bengali colleagues.

In chemistry, the city's most notable figure is undoubtedly Sir Prafulla Chandra Ray (1861-1944). Like Bose, Ray joined the staff of Presidency College after studying in Calcutta and completing his degree in England. Again like Bose, he was discriminated against over pay, but he set up a good laboratory and turned his attention to both pure and applied science. My father knew Ray personally and told me that as well as being an inspiring teacher, he was a man of immense practical vision who favored a democratic approach to science rather than the hierarchical one typical in India—though he was also a passionate nationalist (and later became a devoted supporter of Gandhi). This led to his almost single-handed founding of Bengal Chemicals in 1892, and the writing of his two monumental volumes, *The History of Hindu Chemistry*. In 1900 the firm became the Bengal Chemical and Pharmaceutical Works and began to manufacture drugs, toiletries and cosmetics of a high standard—both from the western pharmacopoeia and from the ancient Indian Ayurvedic system. From 1904 it operated from 82 Maniktola Main Road under the management of another remarkable man, Rajsekhar Basu, who later become a famous humorous writer in Bengali. Ray was also instrumental in establishing the Bengal Pottery Works, the Calcutta Soap Works, the Bengal Enamel Works, and the Bengal Canning and Condiment Works. His essays on many subjects show a remarkable clarity and power of expression in both English and Bengali.

Among the next generation of scientists, the most remarkable was probably Satyendranath Bose (1894-1974), who unusually among Calcutta scientists never studied abroad. An outstanding student at Presidency College, he left Calcutta in 1921 and went to teach in Dacca (Dhaka). From there he sent a paper to Einstein, who himself translated it into German and published it in the journal *Zeitschrift für Physik*. Their contact led to the development of the Bose-Einstein statistics in 1924-25 regarding the gas-like qualities of electromagnetic radiation, which account for the cohesive streaming of laser light and the frictionless creeping of helium when cooled until it becomes a superfluid—and the behavior of subatomic particles now known as bosons. Bose returned to Calcutta in 1945 to teach at the university where he founded a laboratory for studying X-ray crystallography and thermo-luminescence. Calcutta's latest center for basic science at Salt Lake was named after Satyendranath Bose (not to be confused with the already-mentioned Bose Research Institute named after J. C. Bose). Tagore dedicated his science primer *Biswa Parichay* (*Our Universe*) to Bose, who loved literature and was also a competent player of the *esraj*, the Indian violin. Indeed, according to an Indian physicist, "Bose loved science but he loved literature even more."

Other pioneering scientists of Calcutta include the astrophysicist Meghnad Saha; U. N. Brahmachari, who discovered a treatment for the dread disease kala azar and founded Calcutta's blood bank (the world's second such bank); the applied psychologist Girindrasekhar Bose, who founded the mental home at Lumbini Park; and the statistician

Prasanta Mahalanobis, founder of the Indian Statistical Institute at Baranagore, who became a key figure in Indian national planning in the 1950s.

The study of science remains popular among bright students of the city, but as soon as they pass their first examinations, they are often picked up by universities and institutions abroad, particularly in the United States and Canada. Those who stay tend to seek out opportunities elsewhere in India or spend much time on lecture/study trips abroad in order to keep pace with innovations in their field. Visit the libraries of the United States Information Service or the British Council and you will soon sense the keenness of young Bengalis to study science overseas. Apart from the atom smasher at the Saha Institute of Nuclear Physics at Salt Lake, there is a lack of advanced research facilities in Calcutta, a stifling atmosphere of mediocrity in the educational institutions, and frequent interruptions to work due to strikes. The city's scientific brain drain is endemic, and in the absence of serious initiatives by the state government, it will continue.

To kindle interest in science among the younger generation, a public science park—the first of its kind in India—was recently set up at the crossing of the Eastern Bypass and J. B. S. Haldane Avenue (the biologist Haldane emigrated to India and worked at the Indian Statistical Institute for a while in the late 1950s). The architecture is space age, consisting of solid geometrical shapes set among trees and lawns, and the galleries display interactive exhibits on mechanics, sound, optics, geography, environment, space (there is a planetarium), time machines, biology, information technology and much else; there is also a 2,000-seat conference hall.

A Love Affair with English

Long before Macaulay promoted English as the preferred medium of higher education in India—in the humanities as much as in the sciences—the inhabitants of Calcutta had naturally embraced the language as a means of communication with the Company traders. Individuals such as Raja Nabakrishna Deb, Warren Hastings' Persian tutor and Clive's ally against Siraj-ud-Daula, and Raja Darpa Narayan Tagore, the ancestor of one branch of the Tagore family, had picked up the language while working for the British as commercial middle men.

The washerman Ratan Sarkar was even able to overcome the rigid caste hierarchy and become wealthy by exploiting his self-taught knowledge of English. By the beginning of the nineteenth century, Bengalis like Andiram Das and Ramram Misra had set up schools for teaching elementary English to native employees of the Company. The arrival of the missionaries, with their zeal for print, made English still more accessible to Bengalis.

Gradually, English became the accepted medium of both administration and education in the city. India's first modern journalist, Ramananda Chatterjee (1863-1943), ushered in serious journalism by Indians in English through his monthly journal *The Modern Review*. Daily newspapers such as *The Statesman*, established in 1875, the older *Amrita Bazar Patrika* and *The Telegraph*, established in the early 1980s, all published in Calcutta, have capitalized on the growing need for reporting and analysis in English. Although the circulation figures of the Bengali-language press, notably the daily *Ananda Bazar Patrika*, are still higher than for the English-language press, the trend is towards reading in English. In terms of numbers of English speakers, the Indian subcontinent ranks third in the world, after the US and the UK. If you tune into conversations on the streets of Calcutta, you may be surprised to notice the high incidence of English words, many of which are pronounced in a way that sounds incongruous to western English-speaking ears.

The most significant difference between the way English is spoken in Calcutta and in an English-speaking country lies in the rhythm, composed of stressed pitch, loudness, speed and silence. Words like "university" or "psychology", for instance, sound like "ini-ver-citi" and "sycologi". There is also confusion about the position and manner of articulating certain sounds, for example where to place the tongue when pronouncing English words containing "th", or how to use the soft palate to pronounce initial consonants like "p" or "b". Most Bengalis pronounce "v" as "bh", while words beginning with "qu" are perhaps the hardest, hence "question" comes out as "koschen" and "quote" as "kote". It may take a foreigner a little while to get used to Bengali-English pronunciation, but the sensitive listener cannot fail to notice the originality and richness of expression which are the prerogative of some talkative bilingual Bengalis. And then, of course, there are the words that have entered English from Bengal as a result of the colonial period, such as "bungalow". Here I recommend an enjoyable dip into the famous *Hobson-Jobson*, a glossary of Anglo-Indian words and phrases.

In writing English, the most common mistakes made by Bengalis used to thinking in their own language are in singulars and plurals, prepositions and word order. Tagore captured the grammatical and syntactical situation beautifully in a letter he wrote from England to his Bengali niece a few months before he won the Nobel prize (for his own translations of his poetry into English) in 1913. Of course, the original letter is in Bengali and this is a colloquial translation:

The English language has many pitfalls—think of the definite and indefinite articles, the prepositions, the use of "shall" and "will"—which cannot be grasped by intuition, only by tuition. I have reached the conclusion that these elements are like insects that have burrowed into my subliminal consciousness. When I blindly set sail with my pen, these little creatures creep silently out of their dark holes and perform their appointed tasks—but as soon as I consciously focus upon them they go higgledy-piggledy. And so I never feel confident of controlling them, and even now I say I do not know the English language. In stating this I perhaps exaggerate a little—actually I know English well enough to say that I do not know it. That is the truth.

In fact, Tagore knew English pretty well and he improved through contact with friends like the missionary C. F. Andrews, the littérateur E. J. Thompson (father of E. P. Thompson), and Leonard Elmhirst, the founder of the Dartington Trust. Nevertheless, his power of expression in English was still way below that in his own language Bengali. And since 1947, with the withdrawal of Englishmen and women from India, the general standard of both spoken and written English in Calcutta has undoubtedly become less expressive and more of a mishmash lingo known as Benglish (an admixture of Bengali and English) or Hinglish (Hindi and English), notwithstanding the clarity and vigor of a few writers in English such as Nirad C. Chaudhuri, Satyajit Ray and some others.

Indian English Fiction

If the general standard of English has declined, the quality of a small number of literary writers educated in English has probably increased, and their novels have received international acclaim. Of course, most of these writers, even though they have written about Calcutta and have some roots there, have lived outside the city for long periods and compare themselves with writers of English and American fiction. Among them are Kunal Basu, Amit Chaudhuri, Anita Desai, Amitav Ghosh, Jhumpa Lahiri, Bharati Mukherjee, as well as the Mills and Boon-style writer Chitra Banerjee Divakaruni. Each of them deals with his or her experience of Bengal in a unique way but all have felt a compulsion to grapple with their relationship to the city and have found it a rich source of material. Even Vikram Seth, not a Bengali but who was born in Calcutta, felt compelled to recreate the linguistic complexity of the city in his portrait of the Chatterji family in the novel *A Suitable Boy*. The Chatterji elders are portrayed as almost congenitally reverential to Tagore—so much so that their children predictably turn rebellious.

Without having the space in this book to delve into these writers in depth, I should like to give a flavor of their differing reactions to Calcutta by quoting briefly from their stories and novels. Kunal Basu, for instance, tries in his debut novel *The Opium Clerk* (2001) to make sense of the mysteries of the colonial merchant city through the eyes of a Bengali opium clerk born in 1857. Here he evokes Kidderpore docks where the cargo ships used to moor:

Leadsmen waiting to take charge of incoming and outgoing ships had set up surface nets—large bags tied to spars and held in the water by menials. The catch usually consisted of shrimps, swarming at the water's surface, bumalo, pomfret, and silver fish used as bait. Sometimes a sailor would holler in excitement at a river snake caught in the nets. They would rush down the masts or break away from scrubbing gullies, and chatter over the yellow and black creature, lifting it up by its tail. Captains usually took notice too, especially with rare marine fauna, strange-coloured shells, or sea-spiders. Men were instructed to soak these in spirits and keep them in glass jars till a junior officer found time to take a batch over to the Calcutta Museum.

Anita Desai, born in Mussoorie and brought up in Delhi, prior to first living in Calcutta after her marriage, visualized the place through her Bengali father's nostalgic feelings about his homeland. But when she went there in the late 1950s, her romantic notion of the place "was rapidly and drastically modified." She recalled the experience of being in a "metropolis that made Delhi seem a village by comparison." In her delicately structured story, "Private Tuition by Mr. Bose", she poignantly captures the predicament of a dreamy teacher of poetry condemned to giving mundane Sanskrit tuition to bored and hopeless students. Calcutta abounds in such sad characters full of suppressed emotions. In a few expert strokes she conjures up the sounds, smells and sights of the city:

Pritam, the scabby, oil-slick son of the Brahmin priest, coughed theatri-cally—a cough imitating that of a favourite screen actor, surely, it was so false and over-done and suggestive. Mr. Bose swung around in dismay, crying, 'Why have you stopped? Go on, go on.'

'You weren't listening, Sir'.

Many words, many questions leapt to Mr. Bose's lips, ready to pounce on this miserable boy whom he could hardly bear to see sitting beneath his wife's holy tulsi plant that she tended with prayers, water-can and oil-lamp every evening. Then growing conscious of the way his moustache was agitating upon his upper lip, he said only, 'Read'.

'Ahar va asvam purustan mahima nvajagata…'

Across the road someone turned on a radio and a song filled with a pleasant, lilting Weltschmerz twirled and sank, twirled and rose from that balcony to this. Pritam raised his voice, grinding through the Sanskrit consonants like some dying, diseased tram-car. From the kitchen only a murmur and the soft thumping of the dough in the pan could be heard—sounds as soft and comfortable as sleepy pigeons. Mr. Bose longed passionately to listen to them, catch every faintest nuance of them, but to do this he would have to smash the radio, hurl the Brahmin's son down the iron stairs… He curled up his hands on his knees and drew his feet together under him, horrified at this welling up of violence inside him, under his pale pink bush-shirt, inside his thin, ridiculously heav-ing chest.

Though Amitav Ghosh was educated mainly outside Bengal, according to his own account he developed many of his notions of Bengal from the films of Ray: "Many of my images have come from Satyajit Ray. They are part of my internal landscape, part of the way I now see Bengal in my mind's eye. It is a great fortune for me that Ray has made films about a particular milieu from which I happen to come as well, so that what he says about Bengal and what I feel about it are in so many ways totally intermingled." His portrait of his formidable grandmother from East Bengal in his novel *The Shadow Lines* (1988) and his description of a refugee colony have some of the clarity of Ray's films about the seedier side of Calcutta:

We turned off Southern Avenue at Gole Park, and found, inevitably, that the gates of the railway crossing at Dhakuria were down. We had to stew in the midday heat for half an hour before the gates were lifted again. We sped off past the open fields around the Jodhpur Club and down the tree-lined stretch of road that ran along the campus of Jadavpur University. But immediately afterwards we had to slow down to a crawl as the road grew progressively narrower and more crowded. Rows of shacks appeared on both sides of the road now, small ramshackle structures, some of them built on low stilts, with walls of plaited bamboo, and roofs that had been patched together somehow out of sheets of corrugated iron. A ragged line of concrete houses rose behind the shacks, most of them unfinished.

My grandmother, looking out of her window in amazement exclaimed: 'When I last came here ten years ago, there were rice fields running alongside the road; it was a kind of place where rich Calcutta people built their garden houses. And look at it now—as filthy as a babui'*s nest. It is all because of the refugees, flooding in like that.'*

'Just like we did,' said my father, to provoke her.

'We're not refugees,' snapped my grandmother, on cue. 'We came long before Partition.'

Amit Chaudhuri, like Ghosh, grew up in Bombay, but now lives in Calcutta. His first novel, *A Strange and Sublime Address* (1991), subtly records his childish and adolescent impressions of visits to relatives in Calcutta. He said of the book, "I had no intention of telling a story, or of conveying any political feelings—I wanted to convey what it was to be alive in that place." For his child character, the sprawling and indifferent metropolis is also delightful and magical—as I too recall of my childhood there. During a power-cut (endemic to the city from the 1970s until the 1990s), the whole city would suddenly fall under the cloak of a tropical night sky. With the return of artificial light, suddenly there would come a different kind of magic—something like the magic of Snow White's awakening—exhilarating to everyone:

Each day there would be a power-cut, and each day there would be the unexpected, irrational thrill when the lights returned; it was as if people would never get used to it; day after day, at the precise, privileged moment when the power-cut ended without warning as it had begun, giving off a radiance that was confusing and breathtaking, there was an uncontrollable sensation of delight, as if it were happening for the first time. With what appeared to be an instinct for timing, the rows of fluorescent lamps glittered to life simultaneously. The effect was the opposite of blowing out candles on a birthday cake: it was as if someone had blown on a set of unlit candles, and the magic exhalation had brought a flame to every wick at once.

The last two extracts are about Bengalis living abroad and thinking about Bengal. Both writers live in the United States. Bharati Mukhejee was the first to write about the lives, loves and disappointments of Bengalis living physically in the US but mentally still in Bengal. At her best she sketches them with penetrating irony and wit. Here, in "The Tenant", a liberated single woman at a US university, Maya Sanyal, has unwillingly drifted into having tea with a conventional physics lecturer, Dr. Rab Chatterji, and his wife:

'What are you waiting for, Santana?' Dr. Chatterji becomes imperious, though not unaffectionate. He pulls a dining chair up close to the coffee table. 'Make some tea.' He speaks in Bengali to his wife, in English to Maya. To Maya he says, grandly, 'We are having real Indian Green Label Lipton. A nephew is bringing it just one month back.'

His wife ignores him. 'The kettle's already on,' she says. She wants to know about the Sanyal family. Is it true her great-grandfather was a member of the Star Chamber in England?

Nothing in Calcutta is ever lost. Just as her story is known to Bengalis all over America, so are the scandals of her family, the grandfather hauled up for tax evasion, the aunt who left her husband to act in films. This woman brings up the Star Chamber, the glories of the Sanyal family, her father's philanthropies, but it's a way of saying, I know the dirt.

Jhumpa Lahiri, the youngest of these writers, born in England and brought up in the US and thus only a visitor to Calcutta, writes in a brilliant story, "Mrs Sen's", about her mother's generation, who were almost perpetually homesick and looked for comfort in reinventing a Bengali atmosphere in an alien environment: by listening to Bengali songs on cassette, reminiscing about monsoon flooding in College Street, and waiting expectantly for blue aerograms from home. Mrs. Sen is the thirty-year-old wife of an economic migrant who does not really like living in Boston. She still uses her Bengali *bonti,* a chopper with a curved upright blade, instead of a knife, for chopping vegetables, and craves to cook fresh fish using her authentic and favorite Calcutta recipes. But she cannot get the right fish from the local US supermarket. Having grown up eating fish twice a day, she says proudly: "in Calcutta people ate fish first thing in the morning, last thing before bed, as a snack after school if they were lucky. They ate the tail, the eggs, even the head. It was available in any market, at any hour, from dawn until midnight. All you have to do is leave the house and walk a bit, and there you are." (Most Bengalis love fish and are renowned for interesting recipes such as baked hilsa in mustard (*sorshe-ilish*), carp in yogurt (*doi machh*), prawns in coconut sauce (*malaikari*) and fish heads with vegetables (*murighanto*).)

Ten years ago Anita Desai appropriately asked:

Can the English language convey thoughts, emotions and situations that are alien to English experience? What about those that have grown out of the contact of the two languages, a contact which has infiltrated many English words into Bengali (and a few vice versa, such as bungalow),

> *where they have taken on a connotation and flavour very different from their usage in English?*

The answers remain unclear. The huge success of Indian writers in English in recent years suggests that English can cope with any experience. But when I have translated Tagore and other excellent Bengali writers into English, I have often felt that their excellence cannot be adequately conveyed. Using lots of Bengali words within the English text, as some of the above writers do, is generally unsatisfactory. It may give an appearance of authenticity, but fails to meet the literary challenge of conveying the atmosphere of a different culture. When you look at Satyajit Ray's films about Calcutta through Bengali eyes and ears and then through foreign eyes and English subtitles—or for that matter read the masterly stories of R. K. Narayan, who generally eschews Indian words—you realize that the gap between cultures cannot be erased by using vernacular words within English sentences; the problem is more subtle and difficult.

The issues concerning the growing use of English in Calcutta are fiercely and emotionally debated among the city's writers and intellectuals. Whatever the outcome, the English language will always be an integral part of Calcutta's cosmopolitan ethos. And with the embracing of satellite television, email, chat rooms and the internet in the 1990s, English is fast becoming the pan-Indian language that Macaulay called for nearly two centuries ago. Whether he would have been pleased with what Bengalis are writing in this, their own English, one can only speculate.

CHAPTER NINE

Artistic Calcutta

Behind its grimy exterior and poverty and in spite of its reduced intellectual and artistic stature within India, no other city in the country, and perhaps not many others in the world, displays such public enthusiasm for culture as Calcutta. I have already described the annual book fair on the Maidan, which attracts large crowds, not to speak of the city-wide festivals like Durga Puja. At least once a year, every institution in the city, regardless of whether it is educational or not, likes to stage an event with poetry readings, theater, music and dance—all of which support a large community of artistes and craftspeople who make the costumes, sets and props, and do the stage painting and make-up. In early May, in a salute to individual genius probably without parallel in any other city, Tagore's birth anniversary is celebrated with performances of his songs and plays as well as lectures and seminars on his influence. Almost all this cultural activity occurs in Bengali, not English.

In fact at all times, even in times of trouble, there is a lot happening culturally in Calcutta. The press lists dozens of shows, but there are also numerous unadvertised events in the lanes and alleys of the city, especially at weekends. In literature, new writing is constantly published, both in books and in little magazines and journals (with an upsurge during Durga Puja). The various theaters and halls are often packed for performances, some of which are translations into Bengali of western classics and popular hits. In music, apart from a steady stream of new recordings, concerts of all kinds are well attended, including both Indian classical and western classical music (the latter generally heard at the Max Mueller Bhavan and St. Paul's Cathedral); western orchestras such as the London Philharmonic, the London Symphony, the Berlin Symphony and the New York Philharmonic have all performed in Calcutta. In painting and sculpture, regular exhibitions take place at the established Academy of Fine Arts in Cathedral Road, which also has an auditorium, and at successful commercial galleries like CIMA, Gallerie 88, or Gallery Katayun; a growing body of serious collectors buys the work of the exhibited Bengali and Indian artists. In the cinema, there are the expected song-and-dance imports from Bombay and Madras and some Hollywood films, but there is also a surprisingly strong interest in art films, both Bengali and foreign-made. The still relatively new cinematheque at Nandan—named by Satyajit Ray—and the older cultural complex at Rabindra Sadan with a theater and concert hall, among other venues, show a full program of more demanding international films.

Of course, some of these events are of mediocre quality or worse. But what is remarkable is people's enthusiasm. Most Calcuttans dabble in at least one art form, and no Bengali celebration, however minor, would be complete without someone singing, dancing or reciting a poem. It is quite common to hear ordinary-looking housewives singing Tagore songs with deep feeling and artistry. Young street children in Calcutta can draw a better human face with more interesting features than nursery pupils in England. The walls of the city provide a canvas for graffiti and caricatures that are often of a high standard. As Satyajit Ray honestly observed in 1966, in an article entitled "The Odds against Us", reflecting on the trials and tribulations of the Bengali filmmaker: "It is the bareness of means that forces us to be economical and inventive... And there is something about creating beauty in the circumstances of shoddiness and privation that is truly exciting."

A City Made of Words

For the Bengali, it can sometimes seem as if Calcutta is really a city made of words. People talk incessantly, write obsessively. Almost everyone reads some literature and has an opinion on what is good and bad in contemporary writing. Best-selling authors are mobbed, established poets recite to mass audiences, most people can quote poems by Tagore and others. Many Calcuttans compose their own poems for weddings and festivals, have them printed, and circulate them among friends and relations. They never forget the nonsense poems they grew up with as children written by Sukumar Ray, Satyajit's father. For example here is one in Bengali:

Holdey sabuj orang-otang
Eint patkel chit patang
Muskil asan uray mali
Dharmatolay karmakhali

In Sukanta Chaudhuri's translation:

A green and gold orang-outang,
Rocks and stones that jolt and bang,
A smelly skunk and izzy-tizzy,
No admission, very busy.

Nearly everyone I know in Calcutta would like to write something, be it poetry, a short story or novel, a memoir, or just a letter to the press. As in the *addas*, the talking shops mentioned in Chapter 2, Bengalis relish spinning words into something enjoyable on the page. I was moved, after the deaths of my mother and of my mother-in-law, to discover that both had written memoirs.

In the last chapter, we came across Bengalis writing about Calcutta in English. It is less easy to give a sense of literature in Bengali, especially poetry, though we have already come across the poetry of Michael Madhusudan Dutt and the novels of Bankim Chandra Chatterjee. This is partly because of the difficulty of translation, and partly because Tagore was so vast a creative figure that his works should by rights swamp the other writers, even though he is particularly tough to translate. All I can do is give a taste of how Bengali writers have turned Calcutta into a "city of the imagination". (Which means I shall have to omit several of my own favorite writers who did not write much about Calcutta like the poet Jibanananda Das and the novelist Kamal Kumar Majumdar.)

The Bengali language is richly alliterative and abounds in metaphor because of its oral heritage. It lends itself naturally to religious poetry, so it is not surprising that the earliest Bengali writings, from nearly a millennium ago, are mystical songs. This tradition carried on in poetry down to Tagore, whose mystical songs, translated as prose poetry in *Gitanjali*, won him the Nobel prize in 1913. These naturally make no specific reference to Calcutta, though they are widely known in the city.

But Tagore also wrote some strikingly modern, unrhymed narrative poetry in his later years, some of which does describe the city. Rather than quoting lines from several poems, here are the first two stanzas of a poem titled "Banshi" ("Flute Music") that Tagore wrote in 1932 about an impoverished Calcutta clerk:

> *Kinugoala Lane*
> > *A two-storey house*
> > *Ground-floor room, bars for windows*
> > *Next to the road.*
> > *On the rotting walls patches of peeling plaster,*
> > *The stains of damp and salt.*
> > *A picture label from a bale of cloth*
> > *Stuck on the door shows*
> > *Elephant-headed Ganesh, Bringer of Success.*
> *Apart from me the room has another denizen,*
> > *Living rent-free:*
> > *A lizard.*
> > *The difference between it and me is simple—*
> > *It never lacks food.*

I earn twenty-five rupees a month,
　As a junior clerk in a trading office,
　Eat at the Duttas' house
　Tutor their boy in exchange,
Then it's off to Sealdah Station
　To spend the evening.
　Saves the expense of lighting.
Engines chuffing,
　Whistles screeching,
　　Passengers rushing,
　　　Coolies yelling,
　　　It's half-past ten
When I head for my lonely, silent, gloomy room.

After Tagore came a group of competent poets such as Buddhadeva Basu, Bishnu Dey and Samar Sen. Basu published a poetry magazine with a somewhat high-flown, purist agenda. Dey regarded this attitude as a form of stagnation and responded with a magazine encouraging poets to be socially conscious, to write concretely about the reality around them, more in the manner of Tagore's "Banshi". Samar Sen took up this challenge.

In prose, Bengali was the first Indian language to develop (during the nineteenth century) a secular literature in the form of novels and plays. In the first part of the twentieth century many of the leading writers, such as Bibhuti Bhusan Bandopadhyay and Tarashankar Bandopadhyay wrote mainly about rural life, but some, like Manik Bandopadhyay and the eternally popular Sarat Chandra Chattopadahyay, also dealt with Calcutta. Two registers of language, a more literary style known as *sadhu bhasa* inherited from the nineteenth century and a more colloquial modern style with realistic local dialect known as *chalit bhasa*, existed side by side.

The Second World War, the famine, the communal riots and the partition of 1947 caused these two styles to coalesce into the Bengali used today—as in Tarashankar Bandopadhyay's novel *Manwantar* (Famine) about the famine-stricken city. Calcutta's writers formed an Anti-Fascist Writers' and Artists' Association at 46 Dharmatala Street (now Lenin Sarani), with the poets Bishnu Dey and Subhash

Mukhopadhyay as joint secretaries. A new genre of short stories by writers like Samaresh Basu, Premendra Mitra, Subodh Ghosh and Narendra Mitra began to describe the contemporary city of strife. In Narendra Mitra's "Ek Po Dudh" ("A Drop of Milk"), for instance, the members of a poor but close-knit lower middle-class Calcutta family quarrel bitterly over a precious cup of milk, but are finally reunited in a spontaneous act of kindness, offering the drink to a more deserving neighbor—a gem of a story that conveys well Calcutta's undying humanity. In 1963, Satyajit Ray filmed one of Mitra's novels about Calcutta as *Mahanagar* (*The Big City*), and noted his admiration of the author for his "innate honesty or abundance of invention or both. I like to think it is both."

Ray's first job was as a graphic designer for an advertising agency in the 1940s, which brought him into contact with Signet Press, a small publishing house in Bankim Chatterjee Street (off College Street) founded by Dilip Gupta in 1943. Signet created a small revolution in book publishing and jacket design, with Ray as its chief designer, and published many worthwhile writers and a free bulletin still fondly remembered for its literary news and quizzes.

In the 1960s Ray himself began to write stories, the most popular of which were his novellas for children about his Calcutta-based detective Felu Mitter (known as Feluda). At the same time, a group of young writers who had grown up disillusioned in the aftermath of the freedom movement, called themselves the Hungry Generation. Influenced by American beat writers like Ginsberg and Kerouac, they flouted social taboos and described the city as a place of degradation through sex, drugs and perversion. The most successful of them was Sunil Gangopadhyay, a poet who also wrote novels. Two of these were immortalized on film by Ray as *Aranyer Din Ratri* (*Days and Nights in the Forest*), about four footloose young men from Calcutta on a spree in the jungle, and the already mentioned *Pratidwandi* (*The Adversary*), which describes the pressures that turned some idealistic young men into drifters and others into Naxalite revolutionaries.

Gangopadhyay continues to write, but his later work, though commercially successful, has lacked his earlier serious engagement with his characters. Sadly, the same is true of almost all Bengali writing since the 1980s, except for the work of Mahasweta Devi (which does not really concern Calcutta). Bengali literature seemed to lose its way at this time, just as the English-language fiction about Bengal, described earlier, began to find a new voice—perhaps partly because of the increasing dominance of English in Calcutta life.

Theatrical Calcutta

The modern theater of Calcutta has European origins, but it has become an integral part of the city's artistic life. There was an indigenous style of drama before the arrival of Europeans in Bengal—a type of highly melodramatic folk theater known as *jatra* which continues to be a popular form of entertainment, both in the city and especially in the more rural areas. (A wonderful example can be seen in Ray's *Pather Panchali*.) But in the nineteenth century *jatra* was gradually spurned by the English-educated elite such as Michael Madhusudan Dutt and Bankim Chandra Chatterjee. The proscenium stage with an elaborate set and lavish lighting—not to speak of the plays of Shakespeare—easily won the hearts of the babus.

The city's first theater, built in 1753, was destroyed by Siraj-ud-Daula during the siege in 1756. The second was built during Hastings' time in 1775 and functioned for three decades until mounting debts forced its closure. Its performers were exclusively European and its audiences included hardly any native spectators. But with the active interest and enthusiasm of influential babus, particularly Dwarkanath Tagore, Bengalis became involved in theater during the 1820s and 1830s. Dwarkanath was one of the founder members of the European-run Chowringhee Theatre, which started in 1813 and from which Theatre Road (now Shakespeare Sarani) derived its name.

Curiously enough, it was a Russian visitor to the city, Gerasim Lebedef (1749-1818), and not a Bengali, who produced Calcutta's first play in Bengali. He had learnt Bengali on arrival and used his knowledge to translate two plays, *The Disguise* and Molière's *Love is the Best Doctor*, into Bengali. He built a small theater in Dom Tollah (now Dharmatallah), located Bengali actors, and produced the plays in 1795. They drew a full house of about 200 spectators. But when Lebedef left the city soon after, there was no one to continue with Bengali theater. In 1831 Prasanna Kumar Tagore built a theater in his garden house at Narkeldanga, an eastern suburb, and called it the Hindoo Theatre, but he staged no play in Bengali. Not until 1835, some forty years after Lebedef, was *Vidyasundar*, a traditional Bengali love story, performed at the house of Nabinchandra Basu near Shyambazar in the north of the city. Soon, however, many affluent babus added a theater (*nat mandir*) to their grand houses, and started putting on theatrical performances in Bengali for their friends and extended families. The early plots were either from Sanskrit dramas or improved versions of *jatra* stories.

These held no appeal for the English-educated members of Young Bengal, who started a long Bengali tradition of acting Shakespeare in the original, at the David Hare Academy in College Street and at the Oriental Seminary in Chitpur Road. When, in 1848, a youth called Baishnav Charan Auddy took the lead role in *Othello*, Calcutta was "agog" at the "debut of a real unpainted nigger Othello", according to the *Calcutta Star*. The first social satire on polygamy and the caste system was produced at the house of Ramjay Basak at Tagore Castle Street in 1857. By the 1860s, theater in both English and Bengali was a well-established draw for middle- and upper-class residents of the city. Highlights in the second half of the century included the plays of Michael Madhusudan Dutt, notably his already-mentioned *Sharmistha* (performed on a private stage in the northern outskirts of the city at Belgachhia belonging to the Sinha family of Paikpara), works by Dinabandhu Mitra (author of *Nildarpan*, the attack on the indigo planters mentioned in Chapter 5), and translations of Sanskrit, English and French plays, many of them farces.

Not surprisingly, the Tagore family took a leading role. In 1881 they established their own private performance space at Jorasanko. Jyotirindranath Tagore, the gifted elder brother of Rabindranath, was the most talented in theatricals. Besides acting, he wrote original plays in Bengali, translated fluently from Sanskrit and French, and introduced awards to encourage new playwrights. Rabindranath, for his part, acted, produced and wrote distinctive plays from 1877 right up to the 1930s, containing elements from opera, musicals and Bengali tradition. One of his best-loved dramas, *Valmiki Pratibha* (*The Genius of Valmiki*), even borrowed from the Scottish and Irish songs he had heard on his visit to England in 1879-80. Later, he revolutionized stage decor and costumes with a symbolist and minimalist approach that was relatively unpopular. But when his style was imaginatively adapted by the Bohurupee production company in the 1960s under its innovative actor-producer Shambhu Mitra, some of Tagore's plays proved successful.

While theater flourished both in the Black Town and in the White Town, the audiences were quite different because of the language barrier, not to mention the large cultural differences. Although some more adventurous Bengalis attended European-produced plays in English with real appreciation, there was scarcely any reciprocation by the Europeans.

A process of professionalization took place with the legendary actor Girish Chandra Ghosh (1844-1912), who made a particular impression with his adaptations for the stage of Bankim Chandra Chatterjee's novels. His flamboyant style dominated Calcutta Bengali theater right up to the 1920s. He was also the first producer to cast real women. But he disliked the commercialization involved in charging for attendance. Binodini Dasi (1863-1941), originally a prostitute, was the best of the early actresses. Ghosh coached her, and introduced her to Bengali literature and English theater. Starting at the age of eleven, she acted in some fifty dramas and also built the historic Star Theatre, but was ousted from it because of her association with prostitution. All of which is recorded in her memoirs *Amar Katha* (My Story), one of the key records of early Bengali theater. To get a flavor of those days visit north Calcutta's Minerva Theatre. Built in 1893, though substantially altered in 1922, the Minerva still has the feel of an old Victorian theater with its tiled floor, part-tiled walls and winding staircase adorned with oil paintings of bygone thespians and dramaturges.

The Minerva and the Star not only enjoyed commercial success, but they maintained a high standard of plays. This was partly due to Sisir Bhaduri (1889-1959), an actor-producer who came from an affluent family with a master's degree in English. He was an experimentalist who introduced elements of realism into Bengali theater and was an intelligent actor whose power of delivery, interpretation and psychological understanding of character became an inspiration for the next generation of actors, such as Soumitra Chatterjee (most famous for his many roles in the films of Ray). Although Bhaduri's troupe did not inspire much appreciation when it toured the United States in 1930, Bhaduri himself was much admired.

In Calcutta, the range of his productions proved too much for the audience, but he gave local theater a new depth.

The independence period gave a fillip to Bengali drama and made its language less artificial. The first production in 1944 of the Indian People's Theatre Association (IPTA), *Nabanna* (New Crop), broke new ground by treating the concerns of ordinary people in the language of the streets. IPTA's performances pulled huge crowds in the city. They also started the careers of the music director Salil Chaudhuri, the set designer Khaled Chaudhuri and the lighting designer Tapas Sen. Meanwhile, in 1947, Utpal Dutta (1929-93) founded the Little Theatre Group. He had cut his teeth performing Shakespeare in English with the touring company of Geoffrey Kendal (father of the actresses Jennifer and Felicity), whose story was the basis for the movie *Shakespearewallah* (directed by James Ivory, with music by Satyajit Ray). Switching from English to Bengali in the 1950s, Dutta secured the lease of the Minerva Theatre and produced a series of plays on workers' issues such as *Angar*, about a coal mine disaster, and *Kallol*, about a naval mutiny. In the 1960s he produced plays about political events such as the Vietnam war and became involved in revolutionary politics, ending up in jail at the time of the Naxalite movement.

Of course, much of the best Bengali theatrical activity in Calcutta continues to be based on classics by Ibsen, Brecht and so on. But, for whatever reason, original plays in Bengali have continued to maintain a higher standard in recent years than original Bengali literature.

Music Old and New

Bengal has a long and distinguished vocal musical tradition, both classical (*dhrupad* and *tappa*) and popular (*kirton* and *baul* songs), much of which is highly romantic. The deposed king of Lucknow, Wajid Ali Shah, brought along over a hundred musicians from Lucknow to Metiaburz in the late 1850s, who introduced the city to *thumri*, a light classical genre suffused with emotion. But during the nineteenth century, under the influence of Calcutta's babus, music began to degenerate into cliché and vulgarity. Fortunately, Rabindranath Tagore, equally gifted as a poet and composer, came to its rescue. He successfully combined both strands of the tradition into his own rich form of song, known as *Rabindrasangit* (Tagore Song)—a rare fusion of word, mood and beat. There are more than two and half thousand of his songs, and they mean more to Bengalis than any other part of his vast oeuvre. It is well-nigh impossible to move around Calcutta without hearing a snatch of a Tagore melody.

Needless to say, these songs do not really translate well. One of his popular love songs, *Keno Jamini Na Jete Jagale Na*—literally, "Why Didn't You Wake Me At Night's End?"—describes a woman's embarrassment in the morning at the obvious love marks on her countenance. The lyrics are reminiscent of the erotic poetry of the fifteenth-century Bengali Vaishnava poets Vidyapati and Chandidas, yet the words feel extraordinarily modern. In a mere eight gracefully rhymed lines, Rabindranath manages to include four Sanskrit synonyms for night (*jamini, nisha, rajani* and *bivabari*) without making the lyric sound stilted. Each word signifies a specific part of the night suggestive of a specific mood, while the melody is in the introspective raga *Bhairavi*, a late morning raga with the rhythm *ek taal*—languid in tempo. The alliterative language makes a fine poem in its own right, if untranslatable; but when the melody is added, the combination becomes ineffable.

Yet it has to be admitted that if one does not know Bengali, *Rabindrasangit* may sound plaintive and monotonous. As a Bengali, I know that these deceptively simple songs are wonderfully suited for intimate humming, and that the words and melodies together waft me to a realm of delight. But as someone who has lived in the West for a long time, I also realize that there is no hope of fully sharing these feelings with non-Bengalis. Let me take refuge in *The Music of Hindostan* (1914) by Arthur Fox Strangways, music critic of the London *Observer*, who visited Rabindranath in Bengal and listened to his songs:

> *To hear him sing them is to realise the music in a way that is seldom given to a foreigner to do. The notes of the song are no longer their mere selves, but the vehicle of a personality, and as such they go behind this or that system of music to that beauty of sound which all systems put out their hands to seize. These melodies are such as would have satisfied Plato. 'I do not know the modes,' said Socrates, 'but leave me one that will imitate the tones and accents of a brave man enduring danger or distress, fight-*

> *ing with constancy against fortune; and also one fitted for the work of peace, for prayer heard by the gods, and for the successful persuasion or exhortation of men.'*

It is surely in the fitness of things that Tagore is the only composer to have produced *two* national anthems: those of India and Bangladesh.

Yet with Tagore himself long dead, and his direct disciples also practically gone, the study and practice of authentic *Rabindrasangit* in Calcutta may be in decline. It still, even with the dominance of film songs and pop music, accounts for nearly a fifth of the five million Bengali tapes and CDs sold annually. And there are still a number of good singers and teachers around, with special schools dedicated to *Rabindrasangit* in Calcutta University's music department and at the Rabindra Bharati University at Jorasanko, as well as well-known private music schools like Gitabitan and Dakshini. But so much of the success of its rendition depends on an exquisite balance between intelligence and emotion, restraint and spontaneity—not to speak of sensitive instrumental accompaniment. (The harmonium was not favored by Tagore himself, but is all too common in today's performances.) Sadly, very few singers are prepared to take up such a formidable challenge for the sake of being appreciated only by the few. So what one generally hears now is an over-orchestrated version of *Rabindrasangit* with the vocal nuances suffocated and the feeling coarsened by lack of sophistication.

Fortunately for posterity, there are recordings by many great singers, such as Kanika Bandopadhyay, Rajeshwari Dutta, Suchitra Mitra and Subinoy Ray—and fine renditions by them in films, such as Ray's *Rabindranath Tagore, Monihara, Kanchenjungha* and *Agantuk*, Ritwik Ghatak's *Meghe Dhaka Tara*, Aparna Sen's *Paromitar Ek Din* and Rituparno Ghosh's *Utsav*, to name only the most satisfying examples. Ray also creatively adapted *Rabindrasangit* for the soundtracks of some of his films based on Tagore, notably *Charulata* and *Ghare Baire*. The moment that sophisticated Bengali viewers detect a few bars of such film music, they connect directly with the psychological mood of the action on the screen.

Many of Tagore's popular tunes—though not the lyrics—have even appeared in Hindi films made in Bombay, particularly in the compositions of the phenomenally successful S. D. Burman, and it is likely that more will be lifted now that Tagore is no longer in copyright (from 2002 onwards). They are virtually certain to become part of the contemporary fusion music scene in Calcutta, as has already happened with bands like Bhumi and Chandrabindu.

It is always difficult to write about music, especially music that is unfamiliar to the reader. So I shall leave Tagore songs by quoting from two highly gifted artists. Ravi Shankar remarked in 1991: "Tagore had the genius of composing ten different tunes from whatever he heard… I don't think his creativity ever knew any bounds." While Satyajit Ray, a composer steeped in western and eastern music, commented in 1982: "As a Bengali I know that as a composer of songs, Tagore has no equal, not even in the West—and I know Schubert and Hugo Wolf."

Sitar recital

Unique though *Rabindrasangit* is, Calcutta is full of other kinds of home-grown music and song. There is a diluted version of north Indian classical *kheyal* and *thumri* known as *ragpradhan gan*, in which Kazi Nazrul Islam and Atul Prasad Sen composed some good songs. The older forms of music like *kirton* have achieved new popularity through their use in period films. A number of composers, such as S. D. Burman, Jaganmoy Mitra, Hemanta Mukhopadhyay, Sandhya Mukhopadhyay and Pankaj Mullick created a post-Tagore movement of *adhunik gan* (modern songs), many of which have remained popular. And with the founding of the IPTA theater movement in the 1940s, "people's music" was born. Folk music began to be broadcast over Calcutta radio, along with rustic forms of musical entertainment in which village singers compose extempore songs competing with each other in musical duels. The oral culture of Bengal, once despised by Calcutta's babus, is now regarded as part of the Bengali heritage.

With the arrival of the singer-songwriter Suman Chattopadhyay (b.1950) in the 1990s, this demotic musical trend has intensified. Born in the city, he left Calcutta and lived in Germany and the United States for fourteen years working as a radio journalist. He returned with an ability to handle a classical guitar and keyboard and some resonant and melodious songs that cull their inspiration from every kind of popular music from around the world. Some critics have compared his music to the Latin American *nueva canción*. Standing on stage strumming the guitar strapped over his shoulder like a US country singer, he encapsulates urban anxieties, frustrations and hopes in lyrics that are deeply rooted in Bengali imagery and literary allusions. He cracks jokes on the paradoxes of the city, fearlessly condemns inefficient and corrupt politicians, and celebrates the indomitable vitality of Calcuttans. His is a rare example of a talent that can fuse a western tradition of satire and protest songs with purely Bengali content that gets through to today's hybrid generation of MTV-loving youth as well as to their parents. Suman has inspired a whole generation of new musicians to compose and sing about life in Calcutta—warts and all. He is assuredly the best chronicler of contemporary Calcutta.

Painting and Sculpture

One of the effects of the nationalist Swadeshi movement of a century ago was to create a Bengal School of art, led by a nephew of Rabindranath Tagore, Abanindranath (1871-1951). In an attempt to break away from western academic art of the kind admired by the babus of nineteenth-century Calcutta, Abanindranath Tagore and later his students took the miniature painting of the princely courts of western India along with classical Indian myths and legends as their chief sources of inspiration. In the same spirit, as a professor of fine arts at Calcutta University from 1921, Abanindranath attempted to revive the classical Indian *shastras* (prescriptions) on aesthetics in his teaching of the theory of art, and he also introduced Chinese and Japanese art techniques in an effort to create an art that was pan-Asian. Okakura Kakuzo, the nationalist Japanese artist who visited Calcutta at the turn of the century (see Chapter 6), collaborated with Abanindranath and helped him to master the use of wash in a far-eastern style. But the result of all this searching for new, non-western inspiration and techniques was mainly insipid imitation (especially among the students of Abanindranath), wispy, sentimental, "ethnic" and above all unfelt painting. This is not to say that Bengal School works are not sought after in today's Calcutta—but then so are the works of even the lesser pre-Raphaelite painters in Britain.

Uncle Rabindranath clearly perceived his nephew's failure. Writing from Japan in 1916 he told him:

> *The more I travel and see Japan, the more it has struck me that you people should have come with me. How vital it is to get into close contact with the living art of this country in order to infuse life into our own art—this you will never realise if you remain ensconced on your south verandah [at Jorasanko]. Our country has no artistic atmosphere, there is no arterial link between our social life and our art—for us art is a superficial thing, neither here nor there; which is why you people can never derive your full nourishment from indigenous sources.*

Yet Abanindranath's brother, Gaganendranath Tagore (1867-1938), painted work in the same period, which is more dynamic, stimulating and engaged with the social reality around him than the Bengal School artists led by Abanindranath. The skillful and original caricatures he painted around 1917 in *Adbhut Lok* (*The Realm of the Absurd*) satirizing Bengali social hypocrisy and the aping of western manners by the babus are sometimes as scathing as Grosz—and worthy successors of the Kalighat *pat* paintings of the nineteenth century. A bloated babu is shown squandering money on dancing girls and sycophants while raising his stick to drive away poor beggars; a monstrously obese priest is seen indulging in prohibited food, wine and women, on the sly.

Dhanyeshwari (The Imperishable Sacredness of a Brahmin)
by Gaganendranath Tagore, 1917

When Rabindranath himself finally took to painting, in the late 1920s, he was nearly seventy years old. In his last decade or so, in an extraordinary outpouring unprecedented for a novice painter of his age, he produced more than 2,000 paintings and drawings. Despite his total lack of training, many of them are remarkable and are now international collector's items, selling for tens of thousands of dollars in western auction houses. The main collection is at Shantiniketan, but there are a number to be seen in the Tagore museum at Jorasanko, and some are also in private hands in Calcutta. For a long time, the Bengali public largely ignored or decried them as the scribblings of an amateur (as had been predicted by Tagore himself during his lifetime), but today they adorn dozens of book covers in Bengal. From near-pariah status, they have become favorites of the art market.

As an instinctive and spontaneous painter, Tagore's brush strokes are not refined but earthy and vigorous with a profound sense of rhythm, color and composition; he often did not use a brush at all, but applied the ink with some unorthodox object like a rag or stick. The subject matter is mainly Indian, but not transparently so (very few of the paintings have titles) and is absolutely free of "literary" references to Indian myths and legends. He painted landscapes, including buildings—some of which might be Calcutta scenes—and many portraits, but he also portrayed fantastical beasts, birds, fish, flora and fauna belonging to the realm of his imagination, dissimilar to any known species but still half recognizable. There is more conflict in Tagore's painting than in his songs: he seems to be groping for the inner connections between form and deformity, beauty and ugliness, light and darkness, with restless vigor. His paintings of women interest me most. The faces and postures are recognizably Bengali, yet their moods and expressions are mysteriously universal. There is nothing pretty, unlike the Bengal School, in Rabindranath's depiction of women: the dominant mood is not one of desire but of contemplation, soulful and haunting. Rabindranath Tagore's painting is essentially detached from the rest of Bengali art, especially the Bengal School. As Satyajit Ray (who trained in fine art at Tagore's university) remarked in his foreword to *The Art of Rabindranath Tagore* (1989): "It is important to stress that he was uninfluenced by any painter, eastern or western. His work does not stem from any tradition but is truly original. Whether one likes it or not, one has to admit its uniqueness."

Self-portrait by Rabindranath Tagore, 1936

As the search for an Indian identity took hold among artists, they continued to study and teach western art in Calcutta's official art institutions, especially the Government Art School. Pupils from here went on to teach all over India, at art institutions in Bombay, Delhi, Lahore and Madras, as well as other smaller centers like Baroda, though a few, in particular Abanindranath Tagore and his student Nandalal Bose (the first Indian artist to appreciate Rabindranath's paintings) settled at the new art school in Shantiniketan. Among the graduates who stayed in Calcutta, and who eventually became one of the city's favorite artists, was Jamini Roy (1887-1972).

Roy's first works were in the western academic tradition, including Victorian-style nudes. But then he totally changed and began to adapt wholly Indian motifs taken from the Kalighat tradition and the tribal art of the Santhals of Shantiniketan. He used confident curves reminiscent of Modigliani with small folk-style brush strokes, jewel-like dots and a highly colored palette, to create a style as distinctive as Australian aboriginal art. The boldness and simplicity of line combined with the bright colors have made Jamini Roy as widely reproduced in Calcutta as Matisse's paintings are in the West. And not only among Bengalis: the foreign soldiers posted to Calcutta during the Second

World War fell for Jamini Roy's too, as did some British collectors of Indian art during the last days of the Raj. (There is a collection at the Victoria and Albert Museum in London, deposited by one such collector, W. G. Archer.)

As in literature and the theater, the 1940s were a productive period for Bengali painting. There were artists of the famine such as Chittaprasad and Zainul Abedin, and a significant Calcutta Group of modern artists, of whom the most significant names are Gopal Ghosh, Nirode Mazumdar, Paritosh Sen and the sculptor Ramkinkar Baij. They were the first to break away from the western academic tradition and to be strongly influenced by contemporary western artists and the western movement towards abstract art. They held group shows at 15 Park Street from 1945 until 1953, and a joint exhibition in 1950 with the Bombay Progressive Group, which included M. F. Husain, who had begun his career as a painter of Bombay cinema hoardings. (Husain has remained attached to Calcutta, and is particularly well known for his series of works on Mother Teresa.)

While Ghosh produced some good landscapes, Nirode Mazumdar mostly followed the Tantric tradition in which a painting evolves from a central point. I like his powerful swift sketches of Kali. Sen, who is the only surviving member of the Calcutta Group, created a memorable series of what he called "pavement" paintings depicting the lower strata of society. One shows a group of coolies and rickshaw pullers singing folk songs with tremendous gusto—a scene familiar to most Calcutta dwellers. When I look at this painting, I hear the drumbeats and the lusty singing. Most of the energetic and rugged sculptures of Baij are kept at Shantiniketan, except one at Bidyut Bhavan in Bidhan Nagar.

The sculptor Somnath Hore, though not a member of the Calcutta Group, empathized deeply with the famine victims and refugees in the 1940s and continues to draw inspiration from that experience. His "wounds" series of white molded print on pulp, sculpted in 1971, exude a sense of repressed anger. His textured and burnt-wax strip sculptures cast in bronze are my own favorites, combining as they do anguish and delight.

Among Calcutta's current artists, Ganesh Pyne's paintings reveal a love of the crepuscular, the play of light and shadow in a twilight zone with a fairy-tale-like atmosphere. Like Rabindranath, Pyne draws anthropomorphic masks, strange animals and deformed humans inhabiting a realm of fantasy. But unlike Tagore, he is happy to draw on childhood memories of the Hindu religious rituals; his Durga paintings are particularly popular. Jogen Chaudhuri, who trained and worked in Paris but now lives in Calcutta, is noted for his sense of the grotesque in the Indian scene, somewhat reminiscent of Gaganendranath's caricatures (but without much use of color). A favorite Chaudhuri subject might be a pot-bellied politician seated next to a woman, in which the loose clothing of both is almost an extension of the sitters' sagging anatomy; his Ganesha series, concerning the elephant-headed god generally found as a luck-bringer in the shops and houses of merchants, evokes corrupt Marwari businessmen. Bikash Bhattacharjee is best at portraits, in which he gets at the essence of the subject through selected details and the juxtaposition of objects representative of the overcrowded city. His "photomorphic" portrait of Angurbala, an early actress and recording artist on gramophone records, tells the poignant story of yesterday's diva through the awkwardness of her expression and the exaggerated freshness of the flower garland round her neck lying on the sagging flesh of her arm.

Other modern artists with a relationship to the city include the painters Binode Bihari Mukherjee, K. G. Subramanyan and Meera Mukherjee. But since they have not depicted Calcutta much, I mention them only briefly, although they are influential figures in Bengali art and undoubtedly among the most talented of twentieth-century Indian artists.

Cinema and Satyajit Ray

Cinema caught on very early in Calcutta, and film-making soon after. Bioscope pictures were shown as far back as 1898, and the Star and Minerva Theatres ran shows of imported silent films with live musical accompaniment along with dancing and theatrical performances in triple bills. J. F. Madan, an enterprising Parsi merchant based in Calcutta, bought equipment from Pathe and launched a Bioscope show in a tent on the Maidan and at Shyampukur in 1902. This grew into Madan Theatres Ltd., with a chain of theaters in India, Burma, and Ceylon. In 1919 Madan distributed his first full-length Bengali film.

Hiralal Sen, perhaps Calcutta's earliest movie buff, shot a documentary film on the Delhi Durbar of 1911 besides supplying imported short films to wealthy patrons like Raja Jatindra Mohan Tagore for screening at the Tagore Castle in north Calcutta.

Madan's Bengali film had been directed by his non-Bengali manager. But soon Bengali financiers were showing interest in producing films. Four Bengalis founded the Indo-British Film Company, produced a zestful comedy, *Bilat Pherot* (England Returned), and released it in 1921 at the Russa Theatre (now Purna Theatre) in Bhabanipur. The movie poked fun at Bengali pretentiousness—both among the conservatives and the English-educated—and went down very well. It set the norm for the gentle, humorous and above all *theatrical* style of Bengali films later developed by directors like Debaki Bose and Madhu Bose. They worked with stars such as Pramatesh Barua and Kanan Devi in the studios of Tollygunj not far from the Tollygunj Club—an area soon almost inevitably dubbed Tollywood. Drawing-room repartee, doomed melodrama and cloying romance, supported by traditional music like *kirton*, ruled Bengali cinema from the beginning—and still have a powerful hold, even today. In the 1950s and 1960s, the ruling hero and heroine were Uttam Kumar and Suchitra Sen, playing in sentimental and deeply moral stories with melodious songs by Salil Chaudhuri and Hemanta Mukhopadhyay, against the backdrop of both big city and village.

Satyajit Ray never felt remotely a part of this cinema, except for using some of its gifted actors (notably Uttam Kumar in his 1966 film, *Nayak*, which depicts the real inner conflicts of a film hero). Of course, nothing in Bengali cinema beats the range, depth and subtlety of Ray's Calcutta films made between 1959 and 1991: *Apur Sansar* (*The World of Apu*), *Paras Pathar* (*The Philosopher's Stone*), *Mahanagar* (*The Big City*), *Charulata* (*The Lonely Wife*), *Pratidwandi* (*The Adversary*), *Seemabaddha* (*Company Limited*), *Jana Aranya* (*The Middle Man*), *Shakha Prasakha* (*Branches of the Tree*), and *Agantuk* (*The Stranger*). In spite of offers to work elsewhere in India and abroad, including Hollywood, Ray remained loyal to the city of his birth and upbringing. He said: "I don't feel very creative when I'm abroad somehow. I need to be in my chair in Calcutta!" As he explained in an article, "Calm without, fire within", written in 1963:

I cannot even begin to elucidate, through films or in writing, the complexity of the people that inhabit my films. I concentrate on one— the Bengalis, of which I am one—out of a possible score or so, each with a different topography, dress, habits, tongue, physiognomy and even philosophy. Asia may be one, but India is by no means so.

Take a single province: Bengal. Or, better still, take the city of Calcutta, where I live and work. Accents here vary between one neighbourhood and another. Every educated Bengali peppers his native speech with a sprinkling of English words and phrases. Dress is not standardised. Although women generally prefer the sari, men wear clothes which reflect the style of the thirteenth century or conform to the directives of the latest Esquire. The contrast between the rich and the poor is proverbial. Teenagers do the Twist and drink Coke, while the devout Brahmin takes his daily dip in the Ganges and chants his mantras to the rising sun....

What should you put into your films? What can you leave out? Would you leave the city behind and go to the village where cows graze in the endless fields and the shepherd plays his flute? You could make a film here that would be pure and fresh and have the flowing rhythms of a boatman's song.

Or would you rather go back in time—way back to the Epics, when the gods and the demons took sides in the great battle where brother killed brother and Lord Krishna revivified a disconsolate prince with the words of the Gita? One could do exciting things here, using the great mimetic tradition of the Kathakali, as the Japanese use their Noh and Kabuki.

Or would you rather stay where you are, right in the present, in the heart of this monstrous, teeming, bewildering city, and try to orchestrate its dizzying contrasts of sight and sound and milieu?

I have mentioned Ray frequently in this book, because he is such a great artist and so close to Calcutta. His intimate knowledge of the place and people, its history and their culture, comes through in his films without a trace of chauvinism or propaganda. He captures a young man's awakening to love, the loneliness of a wealthy wife, the frustrations and dreams of an ordinary clerk, the anguish and dilemmas of young idealists trapped by unemployment or consumerism, the insidious spread of bribery and corruption, the passionate desire for change, the love of words and word play of ordinary people—in other words, the gamut of middle-class Bengali preoccupations. Yet he does not moralize or pontificate, and he is never sentimental. He does not make a film to make the blood rush to your head, but to provoke you to think and feel, to sharpen your mind and expand your sensibility. Though he was deeply affected by the Bangladesh war of 1971, the torture of East Bengalis and the exodus of the refugees, and considered making a film on the subject, on reflection he realized that what really interested him as a filmmaker was not so much their plight as the process of their assimilation into the life of Calcutta, "the way the normal rhythm of life is slowly but surely being restored. But I doubt if a film on this would make the right kind of propaganda impact", as he wrote to a British friend. So he abandoned the idea.

Ray, like Tagore, harbored a faith in humanity that gives his art a resilient quality—the quintessence of his native city.

Still from Mahanagar (The Big City) by Satyajit Ray, 1963

Other significant Bengali filmmakers have measured themselves against him or alluded to his work. Ritwik Ghatak (1925-76), though chiefly moved by the 1947 partition and the life of the refugees, made some powerful films about Calcutta mores. But they were largely ignored in his lifetime and only began to attract something of a cult following after his death. Unlike Ray, Ghatak deliberately seeks to elicit strongly emotional responses with his depiction of the extremes of human behavior, and the effect is often melodramatic. But, at his best, Ghatak is earthy, gripping, violent and impassioned. His films remind us of the volcanic forces beneath the city's placid surface.

Mrinal Sen (b.1923) is more of a propagandist, certainly than Ray, but also than Ghatak. "I strongly feel that I, as a social being, am committed to my own times. And since poverty, drought, famine and social injustice are dominant facts of my own times, my business as a filmmaker is to understand them. I try to understand my own period. I try to put it across". Sen has made many films about Calcutta, most of them overtly political. The four films he made in the early to mid-1970s—*Interview, Calcutta '71, Padatik* and *Chorus* are almost documentaries on the city; and they are interesting largely as period pieces. His more enduring films are probably the ones that have least to do with Calcutta.

Among the present generation of Calcutta-based filmmakers, Aparna Sen, Gautam Ghosh and Rituparno Ghosh have all made worthwhile films about the city. Aparna's *36 Chowringhee Lane* and *Paromitar Ek Din*, Gautam's *Dekha*, and Rituparno's *Utsav* and *Bariwali* are linked by an unconscious common theme: they all show a city living in its past, with gently decaying surroundings and inhabitants resistant to change.

Calcutta Spirit

Of course, there is a lot to regret. Calcutta is most unlikely ever again to produce anyone as extraordinary as Tagore or Ray, because that period of intimate East-West intellectual interaction is gone. But a different kind of exchange is occurring today through the invasive channels of satellite television and the internet. Calcuttans now communicate with the world through chat rooms and websites. They discuss politics, religion, art, money and even marriage prospects. This change is probably more influential than overt colonialism, at any rate for the MTV-watching younger generation. As a result social taboos (particularly in sexual matters) have become far less strict.

There is also rampant consumerism and hedonism among the large numbers of Calcuttans who can afford such a lifestyle. Most of Calcutta's middle class is now much better off economically than before, although poverty is still the lot of the majority and will remain so in the foreseeable future. But the current sense of stability and even hope has promoted a positive outlook among many residents. PUBLIC (People United for Better Living in Calcutta), a citizen's organization, has been campaigning successfully through posters and hoardings. Schools and colleges are also becoming increasingly involved in local environmental projects. Instead of just moaning about lost heritage, citizens are now organizing themselves to restore Calcutta's historical buildings and monuments. Over a thousand buildings have been listed for preservation. Calcuttans should be proud of their colonial architecture and advertise it as a fascinating fusion of styles. V. S. Naipaul rightly observed:

> All the four main cities in India were developed by the British, but none has so British a stamp as Calcutta's... and what has resulted in Calcutta is a grandeur more rooted than that of New Delhi: "the city of palaces" they called Calcutta, the palaces, Indian or British, built in a style which might best be described as Calcutta Corinthian.

If the West Bengal Government can shake off its stubborn attitude of political correctness and take an active interest in collaborative restoration (as in the case of the Victoria Memorial and the South Park Cemetery), Calcutta may once more become an architecturally exciting city for visitors.

Calcutta has endured a great deal and survived. If for me, much of what was unique about the city no longer exists, I am nevertheless optimistic about its idealistic core. The violence, fanaticism, and blatant vulgarity that have disfigured much of India in recent years have not deeply affected Calcutta. Indeed, during the terrible riots in Gujarat in 2002, Calcuttans came out in their thousands to march peacefully along the same route taken by Tagore in 1905 in protest against the partition of Bengal.

Calcutta may lag behind much of the world economically, but it is still a city where the pursuit of knowledge, beauty and justice for their own sake are admired and cherished. It is still a relatively safe city for travelers. People here are cooperative, hospitable, resilient and refreshingly witty. I once heard the following Bengali conversation in a jam-packed Calcutta bus when a skinny young man was trying to get aboard and squeeze himself past three large and pot-bellied men: "Please, kindly move a little and let me get a foothold." "Can't you see there is no room even for a fly!" "Please brothers, shuffle yourselves a bit. You can always slip a thin card between three volumes of fat dictionaries!" Of course this disarming argument won the desperate commuter room on the bus and lightened the stifling atmosphere of the rush hour a little. The incident seems somehow typical of Calcutta's true spirit.

Further Reading

Most of the books are in English or English translation, though a few books in Bengali are included that are referred to in the text.

Banerjee, Sumanta, *In the Wake of Naxalbari*. Subarnarekha: Calcutta, 1980.

— *The Parlour and the Streets: Elite and Popular Culture in Nineteenth Century Calcutta*. Calcutta: Seagull, 1989.

Banerji, Chitrita, *Life and Food in Bengal*. London: Weidenfeld and Nicolson, 1991.

Baron, Archie, *An Indian Affair: From Riches to Raj*. London: Channel 4 Books, 2001.

Benodini Dasi, *Amar Katha*. Calcutta: Subarnarekha, 1973.

Bose, Buddhadeva, *An Acre of Green Grass: A Review of Modern Bengali Literature*. Calcutta: Orient Longman, 1948.

Busteed, H. E., *Echoes from Old Calcutta*. Calcutta: Thacker, Spink, 1888.

Chatterjee, Bankim Chandra, *Sampurna Rachanabali*. Calcutta: Sahitya Samsad, 1957.

Chaudhuri, Nirad C., *The Autobiography of an Unknown Indian*. London: Macmillan, 1951.

— *Thy Hand, Great Anarch!* London: Chatto and Windus, 1987.

Chaudhuri, Sukanta, ed., *Calcutta: The Living City* (two volumes). Calcutta: Oxford University Press, 1990.

Cotton, H. E. A., *Calcutta Old and New*. Calcutta: W. Newman, 1907.

Dalrymple, William, *White Mughals*. London: Harper Collins, 2002.

Das, Suranjan, *Communal Riots in Bengal 1905-1947*. New Delhi: Oxford University Press, 1991.

Dutt, Michael Madhusudan, *Rachanabali*. Calcutta: Haraf, 1977.

Dutta, Krishna and Andrew Robinson, *Rabindranath Tagore: The Myriad-Minded Man*. London: Bloomsbury, 1995.

French, Patrick, *Liberty or Death: India's Journey to Independence and Division*. London: HarperCollins, 1997.

Ghosh, Benoy, *Vidyasagar o Bangali Samaj*. Calcutta: Orient Longman, 1973.

Ghosh, J. C., *Bengali Literature*. London: Oxford University Press, 1948.

Gilmour, David, *Curzon*. London: John Murray, 1994.

Gordon, Leonard A., *Bengal: The Nationalist Movement 1876-1940*. New York: Columbia University Press, 1974.

— *Brothers against the Raj: A Biography of Sarat and Subhas Chandra Bose*. New York: Columbia University Press, 1990.

Grass, Günter, *The Flounder*. London: Pan, 1977.

— *Show Your Tongue*. London: Secker and Warburg, 1989.

Gupta, R. P., *Kolkatar Firiwalar Dak ar Rastar Awaj*. Calcutta: Ananda Publishers, 1984.

— *Mach ar Bangali*. Calcutta: Ananda Publishers, 1989.

Heehs, Peter, *The Bomb in Bengal: The Rise of Revolutionary Terrorism in India 1900-1910*. New Delhi: Oxford University Press, 1993.

Hutnyk, John, *The Rumour of Calcutta*. London: Zed Books, 1996.

Isherwood, Christopher, *Ramakrishna and his Disciples*. London: Methuen, 1965.

Jain, Jyotindra, *Kalighat Painting: Images from a Changing World*. Ahmedabad: Mapin, 1999.

Kämpchen, Martin, ed., *My Broken Love: Günter Grass in India and Bangladesh*. New Delhi: Viking, 2001.

Killingley, Dermot, *Rammohun Roy in Hindu and Christian Tradition*. Newcastle upon Tyne: Grevatt and Grevatt, 1993.

Kling, Blair B., *Partner in Empire: Dwarkanath Tagore and the Age of Enterprise in Eastern India*. Berkeley: University of California Press, 1976.

Lapierre, Dominique, *The City of Joy*. New York: Doubleday, 1985.

Lévi-Strauss, Claude, *Tristes Tropiques*. London: Jonathan Cape, 1973.

Losty, J. P., *Calcutta: The City of Palaces*. London: British Library, 1990.

Macfarlane, Iris, *The Black Hole or The Making of a Legend*. London: George, Allen and Unwin, 1975.

Malle, Louis, (Philip French ed.), *Malle on Malle*. London: Faber and Faber, 1993.

Mitra, Radharaman, *Kalikata Darpan*. Calcutta: Subarnarekha, 1988.

Moorhouse, Geoffrey, *Calcutta: The City Revealed*. London: Penguin, 1983.

Murray, Alexander, ed., *Sir William Jones 1746-94: A Commemoration*. Oxford: Oxford University Press, 1998.

Murshid, Tazeen M., *The Sacred and the Secular: Bengal Muslim*

Discourses 1871-1977. Calcutta: Oxford University Press, 1995.

Naipaul, V. S., *An Area of Darkness.* London: Andre Deutsch, 1964.

— *India: A Million Mutinies Now.* London: Heinemann, 1990.

— *The Writer and the World.* London: Picador, 2002.

Nair, Thankappan P., *Calcutta: Origin of the Name.* Calcutta: Subarnarekha, 1985.

Oddie, Geoffrey, *Missionaries, Rebellion and Proto-Nationalism: James Long of Bengal 1814-87.* London: Curzon Press, 1999.

Pal, Ashit, ed., *Woodcut Prints of Nineteenth Century Calcutta.* Calcutta: Seagull, 1983.

Pal, Pratapaditya, ed., *Calcutta through 300 Years.* Bombay: Marg, 1990.

Ray, Rajat Kanta, *Social Conflict and Political Unrest in Bengal 1875-1927.* New Delhi: Oxford University Press, 1984.

Ray, Satyajit, *Childhood Days.* New Delhi: Penguin, 1998.

— *Our Films Their Films.* New Delhi: Orient Longman, 1976.

Raychaudhuri, Tapan, *Europe Reconsidered.* New Delhi: Oxford University Press, 2002.

Roberts, Joe, *Abdul's Taxi to Kalighat.* London: Profile, 2000.

Robinson, Andrew, *The Art of Rabindranath Tagore.* London: Andre Deutsch, 1989.

— *Satyajit Ray: The Inner Eye.* London: I. B. Tauris, 2003.

Rushby, Kevin, *Children of Kali: Through India in Search of Bandits, the Thug Cult and the British Raj.* London: Constable Robinson, 2002.

Sarkar, Sumit, *The Swadeshi Movement in Bengal 1903-1908.* Calcutta: People's Publishing House, 1973.

Sebba, Anne, *Mother Teresa: Beyond the Image.* London: Weidenfeld and Nicolson, 1997.

Sinha, Kaliprasanna, *Hutom Pyanchar Naksha.* Calcutta: Subarnarekha, 1994.

Sykes, Laura, *Calcutta: Through British Eyes.* Delhi: Oxford University Press, 1992.

Tagore, Rabindranath, *Glimpses of Bengal,* 2nd edition. London: Macmillan, 1991.

— *My Reminiscences,* 2nd edition. London: Macmillan, 1991.

— (Krishna Dutta and Andrew Robinson eds.), *Rabindranath Tagore: An Anthology.* London: Picador, 1997.

— (Krishna Dutta and Andrew Robinson eds.), *Selected Letters of Rabindranath Tagore*. Cambridge: Cambridge University Press, 1997.

Thakur, Tekchand, *Alaler Gharer Dulal*. Calcutta: Bat-tala edition, 1858.

Vaughan, Philippa, ed., *The Victoria Memorial Hall: Conception, Collections, Conservation*. Bombay: Marg, 1997.

Fiction about Calcutta

Basu, Kunal, *The Opium Clerk*. London: Phoenix House, 2001.

Chaudhuri, Amit, *A Strange and Sublime Address*. London: Heinemann, 1991.

Desai, Anita, *Games at Twilight*. London: Heinemann, 1978.

Divakaruni, Chitra Banerjee, *Sister of My Heart*. London: Doubleday, 1999.

Dutta, Krishna and Andrew Robinson, eds., *Noon in Calcutta: Short Stories from Bengal*. London: Bloomsbury, 1992.

Ghosh, Amitav, *The Shadow Lines*. London: Bloomsbury, 1988.

Lahiri, Jhumpa, *Interpreter of Maladies*. London: Flamingo, 1999.

Mukherjee, Bharati, *The Middleman and Other Stories*. New York: Grove Press, 1988.

Seth, Vikram, *A Suitable Boy*. London: Viking, 1993.

Appendix: Select Calcutta street names old and new

Lower Circular Road	Acharya Jagadish Chandra Bose Road
Upper Circular Road	Acharya Prafulla Chandra Roy Road
Grey Street	Arabinda Sarani
Chowringhee Road (south)	Asutosh Mukherjee Road
College Street	Bankim Chatterjee Street
Cornwallis Street	Bidhan Sarani
Central Avenue	Chittaranjan Avenue
Beadon Street (west)	Dani Ghosh Sarani
Mayo Road	Guru Nanak Sarani
Old Court House Street	Hemanta Bose Sarani
Red Road	Indira Gandhi Sarani
Central Avenue (north)	Jatindra Mohon Avenue
Chowringhee Road (central)	Jawaharlal Nehru Road
Garden Reach Road (central)	Karl Marx Sarani
Hastings Street	Kiran Shankar Roy Street
Elgin Road	Lala Lajpat Rai Sarani
Dharmatalla Street	Lenin Sarani
Harrison Road	Mahatma Gandhi Street
Lindsay Street	Nellie Sengupta Sarani
Clive Street	Netaji Subhas Road
Chitpur Road	Rabindra Sarani
Amherst Street	Raja Rammohan Sarani
Wellesley Street	Rafi Ahmed Kidwai Road
Corporation Street	S. N. Banerjee Road
Lansdowne Road	Sarat Bose Road
Theatre Road	Shakespeare Sarani
Loudon Street	U. N. Brahmachari Street

The babu's wives, Kalighat pat

Index of People

Index of Places